MARTYRDOM AND
NOBLE DEATH

Today's society is uncomfortable with death, and willingly submitting to a violent and ostentatious death in public is seen as particularly shocking and unusual. Yet classical sources give a different view, with public self-sacrifice often being applauded – the Romans admired a heroic end in the battlefield or the arena, suicide in the tradition of Socrates was something laudable, and Christians and Jews alike faithfully commemorated their heroes who died during religious persecutions.

Martyrdom and Noble Death explores the fascinating phenomenon of noble death through pagan, Jewish and Christian sources. The authors look at Jewish and Christian articulations of noble death as martyrdom, asking how we construct the figure of a martyr, and what makes a passage a 'martyr text'. The book combines accessible introductions with a wide range of relevant translated texts, dating from the eighth century BCE to the rabbinic period (up to the fifth century CE).

The cross-cultural approach and wide chronological range of this study make it valuable for students and scholars of ancient history, religion and literature.

Jan Willem van Henten holds the chair in New Testament and Hellenistic Jewish literature at the University of Amsterdam. He is director of the Netherlands School for Advanced Studies in Theology and Religion (NOSTER). His publications include *Studies in Early Jewish Epigraphy* (edited with P.W. van der Horst, 1994) and *The Maccabean Martyrs as Saviours of the Jewish People* (1997).

Friedrich Avemarie is a research and teaching assistant at the Institut für antikes Judentum und hellenistische Religionsgeschichte, Evangelisch-theologische Fakultät, University of Tübingen. His most recent publication is *Die Taufberichte der Apostelgeschichte: Theologie und Geschichte* (1999, 2001).

MARTYRDOM AND NOBLE DEATH

Selected texts from Graeco-Roman,

Jewish and Christian Antiquity

*Jan Willem van Henten and
Friedrich Avemarie*

London and New York

First published 2002
by Routledge
11 New Fetter Lane, London EC4P 4EE

Simultaneously published in the USA and Canada
by Routledge
29 West 35th Street, New York, NY 10001

Routledge is an imprint of the Taylor & Francis Group

Typeset in Garamond by
M Rules
Printed and bound in Great Britain by
TJ International Ltd, Padstow, Cornwall

British Library Cataloguing in Publication Data
A catalogue record for this book is available from the British Library

Library of Congress Cataloging in Publication Data
Henten, J. W. van
Martyrdom and noble death: selected texts from Graeco-Roman, Jewish, and
Christian antiquity / Jan Willem van Henten & Friedrich Avemarie.
p. cm. – (The context of early Christianity)
Includes bibliographical references and index.
(pbk.: alk. paper)
1. Martyrdom – Comparative studies. 2. Death – Religious aspects –
Comparative studies. I. Avemarie, Friedrich. II. Title. III. Series.

BL626.5 .H44 2002
306.9 – dc21   2001045715

ISBN 0 415 13890 6 (hbk)
ISBN 0 415 13891 4 (pbk)

FOR DANNY, DAVID
AND HERMANN

CONTENTS

CONTENTS

PREFACE

This book primarily aims at offering undergraduate students in various disciplines (Religion, Classics, Jewish Studies, etc.) a survey of ancient sources about those kinds of noble death that can be called martyrdom or are rather similar to martyrdom. It is designed as a sourcebook, but has fuller introductions to the texts than most sourcebooks.

The Introduction discusses the phenomenon of noble death as represented by pagan, Christian and Jewish sources and the Jewish and Christian articulation of noble death as martyrdom. Each of the following four chapters is devoted to one body of literature: Chapter 1 to pagan forms of noble death dating from the eighth century BCE to the third century CE; Chapter 2 to Jewish passages from the Second Temple period; Chapter 3 to the earliest Christian documents of martyrdom up to the Constantine era; and Chapter 4 contains introductions and translations of the most important early rabbinic stories about martyrdom. Thus, the reader is offered a representative survey of passages about noble death in a wide range of socio-cultural ancient contexts: Graeco-Roman, early Jewish and Christian, as well as rabbinic-Jewish. The broad horizon of the book enables the reader to make cross-cultural comparisons. The general introductions to Chapters 1–4 offer accessible syntheses of the relevant textual material, which have not been available for the pagan and rabbinic documents. Readers who intend to use this book just as a sourcebook can easily skip these introductions, as all information strictly necessary for understanding the texts is given in the introductions to the individual passages and the notes to the translations. The translations of the selected passages are our own except in the case of the *Ascension of Isaiah*. We warmly thank Professors Michael A. Knibb (London) and James H. Charlesworth (Princeton) for allowing us to use the translation of *Asc. Is.* from *The Old Testament Pseudepigrapha*.

The Introduction and Chapters 1–3 were written by Jan Willem van Henten and Chapter 4 was written by Friedrich Avemarie, but we have commented upon each other's chapters extensively. In the translated passages square brackets indicate lacunae in the manuscripts filled by the editor or by us; sometimes round brackets indicate words that have been added for reason of clarity.

ACKNOWLEDGEMENTS

We warmly thank David Aune and Richard Stoneman for suggesting that we write this book for Routledge. We also thank Professor Alex Levitzki, Mrs Liba Maimon and Mrs Pnina Feldman, director and vice-directors of the Institute for Advanced Studies at the Hebrew University in Jerusalem, and their staff, for the wonderful facilities offered to one of us during the academic year 2000–2001. The fellows of the 'From Hellenistic Judaism to Christian Hellenism' group, Danny R. Schwartz, David Satran, Tessa Rajak, Adele Reinhartz, John Gager, Hermann Lichtenberger and Greg Sterling have commented upon sections of this book and made many helpful suggestions. Omert Schrier (Amsterdam) checked the translations in Chapter 1 meticulously and proposed many alternative translations. Leigh Gibson (Oberlin) read Chapters 1 and 2 with her usual methodological rigour and quest for a frugal style. Wayne Coppins (Durham) checked the English of Chapter 4. We thank all three warmly for their generous help. We also thank Professors Michael A. Knibb (London) and James H. Charlesworth (Princeton) for allowing us to use the translations of *Asc. Is.* from *The Old Testament Pseudepigrapha*. And finally we thank Susan Dunsmore, Mike Hauser and the team at M Rules and Kate Rogers for a wonderful job with the editing, typesetting and indexing.

Jan Willem van Henten and Friedrich Avemarie

ABBREVIATIONS

Ancient Sources

1 Clem.	Clement of Rome, *Letter to the Corinthians*
2 Macc.	2 Maccabees
4 Macc.	4 Maccabees
1QS	*Manual of Discipline* (Qumran document from cave 1)
1QpHab	*Habakkuk Commentary* (Qumran document from cave 1)
4Q 45	a specific Qumran document from cave 4
4Q 286	a specific Qumran document from cave 4
Act. Just.	*Acts of Justin*
Act. Scil.	*Acts of the Scillitan Martyrs*
Aelianus, *Var. hist.*	*Varia historia* (= *Historical Miscellany*)
Anth. Gr.	*Anthologia Graeca* (= *The Greek Anthology*)
Aristotle, *Eth. Nic.*	*Nicomachean Ethics*
Aristotle, *Rhet.*	*Rhetorica*
As. Mos.	*Assumption of Moses*
Asc. Is.	*Ascension of Isaiah*
Cicero, *De div.*	*On Divination*
Cicero, *De fin.*	*De finibus bonorum et malorum* (= *On Good and Evil*)
Cicero, *De nat. deor.*	*The Nature of the Gods*
Cicero, *Tusc. disp.*	*Tusculan Disputations*
Clement of Alexandria, *Strom.*	*Stromateis* (= *Miscellanies*)
Didymus, *Com. in Eccl.*	*Commentary on Ecclesiastes*
Diogn.	*Writing to Diognetus*
Ennius, *Ann.*	*Annals*
Ep. Arist.	*Epistle of Aristeas*

Euripides, *Hec.*	*Hecuba*
Euripides, *Her.*	*Heraclidae* (= *Children of Heracles*)
Euripides, *Phoen.*	*Phoenissae* (= *Phoenician Women*)
Eusebius, *Chron.*	*Chronology*
Eusebius, *De mart. Palaest.*	*On the Palestinian Martyrs*
Eusebius, *Hist. eccl.*	*Historia ecclesiastica* (= *History of the Church*)
Eusebius, *Praep. ev.*	*Praeparatio evangelica* (= *Preparation for the Gospel*)
Ignatius, *Eph.*	*Letter to the Ephesians*
Ignatius, *Mag.*	*Letter to the Magnesians*
Ignatius, *Phil.*	*Letter to the Philippians*
Ignatius, *Pol.*	*Letter to Polycarp*
Ignatius, *Rom.*	*Letter to the Romans*
Ignatius, *Smyr.*	*Letter to the Smyrnaeans*
Ignatius, *Tral.*	*Letter to the Trallians*
Isocrates, *Areop.*	*Areopagiticus*
Isocrates, *Pan.*	*Panegyricus*
Jerome, *Com. Is.*	*Commentary on Isaiah*
Josephus, *Ant.*	*Jewish Antiquities*
Josephus, *Ap.*	*Against Apion*
Josephus, *War*	*Jewish War*
Jub.	*Jubilees*
Justin, *1 Apol.*	*First Apology*
Justin, *2 Apol.*	*Second Apology*
Justin, *Dial.*	*Dialogue with Tryphon*
Lactantius, *Div. inst.*	*Divine Institutions*
Lucanus, *Phars.*	*Pharsalia* (= *The Civil War*)
Lycurgus, *Contra Leocr.*	*Contra Leocratem* (= *Against Leocrates*)
M.	*Mishnah* (followed by the name of a tractate)
Macrobius, *Sat.*	*Saturnalia* (= *Festival for Saturnus*)
Mart. Agap.	*Martyrdom of Agape*
Mart. Apol.	*Martyrdom of Apollonius*
Mart. Carp.	*Martyrdom of Carpus*
Mart. Fruct.	*Martyrdom of Fructuosus*
Mart. Lugd.	*Martyrdom of the Martyrs from Lyon and Vienne*
Mart. Max.	*Martyrdom of Maximilian*
Mart. Pauli	*Martyrdom of Paul*
Mart. Pion.	*Martyrdom of Pionius*
Mart. Pol.	*Martyrdom of Polycarp*

Mart. Ptol.	Martyrdom of Ptolemy
NT	New Testament
Or.	Oration
Origen, Ep. ad Afric.	Letter to Africanus
Origen, Com. Mat.	Commentary on Matthew
Orosius, Hist.	Histories
Ovid, Metam.	Metamorphoses
Par. Jer.	Paraleipomena Jeremiou (= Remaining Things about Jeremiah)
Pas. Perp.	Passion of Perpetua
Philo, All.	Allegorical Interpretation of the Laws
Philo, Ebr.	De ebrietate (= On Drunkenness)
Philo, Hyp.	Hypothetica
Philo, Jos.	On Joseph
Philo, Op.	De opificio mundi (= On the Creation of the World)
Philo, Prob.	Quod omnis probus liber sit (= Every Good Person is Free)
Philo, Prov.	On Providence
Philo, Spec. leg.	On the Special Laws
Philo, Vit. Mos.	On the Life of Moses
Philostratus, Vita Apol.	Life of Apollonius
Plato, Apol.	Apology
Plato, Tim.	Timaeus
Plato, Men.	Menexenus
Pliny, Ep.	Epistulae (= Letters)
Plutarch, Adv. Col.	Adversus Colotem (= Against Colotes)
Plutarch, Alex.	Life of Alexander
Plutarch, De garrul.	De garrulitate (= On Chattering)
Plutarch, De Isid.	On Isis and Osiris
Plutarch, De stoic. repugn.	On Stoic Self-Contradictions
Plutarch, De tranq. animi	On Tranquillity of the Mind
Plutarch, De virt. mor.	De virtute morali (= On Moral Virtue)
Plutarch, Mor.	Moralia
Polycarp, Phil.	Letter to the Philippians
Ps. Kallisthenes, Vit. Alex.	Life of Alexander
Ps. Sol.	Psalms of Solomon
Sib. Or.	Sibylline Oracles

Spartianus, *Hadr.*	*Hadrian*
Statius, *Theb.*	*Thebais*
Suetonius, *Hist. aug. Cal.*	*Historia Augusta Concerning Caligula*
Tacitus, *Ann.*	*Annals*
Tacitus, *Hist.*	*Histories*
Tatian, *Or.*	*Oration to the Greeks*
T.B.	*Talmud Bavli/Babylonian Talmud* (followed by the name of a tractate)
Tertullian, *Apol.*	*Apology*
Tertullian, *De pat.*	*On Patience*
Tertullian, *Scorp.*	*Scorpiace*
Tob.	Tobias/Tobit
Tos.	*Tosefta* (followed by the name of a tractate)
T.Y.	*Talmud Yerushalmi/Palestinian Talmud* (followed by the name of a tractate)
Vit. Isa.	*Life of Isaiah*
Vit. Proph.	*Vitae prophetarum* (= *Lives of the prophets*)

Modern Editions or Resources

CIL	*Corpus Inscriptionum Latinarum*
CSEL	*Corpus Scriptorum Ecclesiasticorum Latinorum*
GCS	*Die griechischen christlichen Schriftsteller der ersten drei Jahrhunderte*
ILS	*Inscriptiones Latinae Selectae*
KBL[3]	L. Koehler, W. Baumgartner *et al.*, *Hebräisches und Aramäisches Lexikon zum Alten Testament*, 3rd edition
LSJ	H.G. Liddell, R. Scott, and H.S. Jones, *A Greek–English Lexicon*
PL	*Patrologia Latina*
PSI	*Papyri greci e latini*

INTRODUCTION

Ostentatious forms of violent death hardly fit in with modern views of life. Most people must have felt highly uncomfortable watching the news about the self-cremations by members of the Falong in Beijing, that of Jan Palach in Prague during the Russian repression of the peaceful revolution in Czechoslovakia or that of the Buddhist monks during the Vietnam War. Likewise, hunger strikes as the last means of protest against an unwilling government may evoke some sympathy, but many consider them an extreme act of self-destruction. These observations match the trend described by Philippe Ariès in his comprehensive history of death.[1] Our urbane and technocratic society has banished death from private as well as public life. The normal way of dying is to pass away in a hospital under the supervision of medical professionals who concentrate on preventing their patients from suffering and dying consciously. A quiet, quick and lonely death through cardiac arrest is considered a blessing by many. If there is a public and ceremonial dimension of death, it usually concerns the post-mortem phase of cremation, burial or memorial ceremony.

Ancient sources show a very different perception of death, especially of death as self-sacrifice in a public setting. The Roman mob lived by 'bread and games' and was thrilled by the bloody deaths of gladiators. Roman intellectuals admired not only a glorious death on the battlefield or in the arena, but also a suicide in the tradition of Socrates' famous death.[2] Even the sophisticated work *Crowns of Martyrdom* by the Christian Spanish poet Prudentius (late fourth century CE) shows this admiration for spectacular ways of dying. Prudentius composed

---

1 Ariès (1978).
2 See Chapter 1, pp. 12–14.

the second hymn of his *Crowns* in honour of the Roman deacon Laurentius, who was executed during Decius' persecution (249–251 CE). After half his body had been burned on the gridiron the martyr said to the judge: 'This part of my body has been burned long enough; turn it round and try what your hot god of fire has done.' After Laurentius had been turned around, he said: 'It is done . . . eat it up, try whether it is nicer raw or roasted' (2.401–8). Just before dying Laurentius said an intercessory prayer for Rome with the wish that the city might become Christian. There is no doubt that Laurentius, like other Christian or Jewish martyrs, was considered a hero by his own group.

This book will offer translations of pagan, Christian and Jewish passages about noble death. Each chapter will have a general introduction to the sources translated as well as brief introductions to the individual passages. Readers who would like to concentrate on the texts themselves and do not need much information about their context and purpose can dispense with the general introductions. Many but not all passages concern martyrs, because we aim to present Jewish and Christian martyrdom in the broader cultural context of noble death in antiquity.

'Martyr' has become an established expression for persons who die a specific heroic death, especially in Christian, Jewish, or Muslim sources. Scholarly definitions of martyrdom often mention the aspect of witness or confession as a central characteristic of the martyr's action, taking a semantic development of the Greek noun *martys* ('witness') and the related verb *martyrein* into the early Christian title 'martyr' and 'die a martyr's death' as the point of departure.[3] Presently there is considerable consensus that the meaning 'martyr' of *martys* occurs only in Christian literature from 150 CE or later.[4] The meaning 'martyr' referring to people who were executed because they remained obedient to their Christian faith and identity and refused to make concessions to the Roman authorities occurs for the first time in the *Martyrdom of Polycarp* (155–160 CE). This document reports the arrest and execution of Polycarp, bishop of Smyrna, and begins as follows:

---

3 At the beginning of the twentieth century scholars tended to derive this 'martyrological' meaning from New Testament occurrences of the Greek *martys*, see Holl (1914). Further references in Dehandschutter and van Henten (1989), 5–8; Schwemer (1999).
4 Strathmann (1942); Baumeister (1980), 239–45; Buschmann (1994), 136–41; Buschmann (1998), 98–107.

'We write you, brothers, an account of those who died a martyr's death (*tous martyrēsantas*) and especially about the blessed Polycarp . . .' (1.1; cf. 2.1; 14.2).[5] In a similar way, the specific rabbinic terminology referring to martyrdom, such as *qiddush ha-Shem* (the sanctification of God's Name) and *Asarah Haruge Malkhut* (the Ten Slain by the [Roman] Kingdom), is not yet found in the oldest references to martyrdom in rabbinic literature. Statements by rabbinic sages living in the first two centuries CE still contain a considerable variation of references to martyrdom, with phrases like 'give one's life for the commandments' and 'offer oneself to be slaughtered for the Torah', which echo Greek terminology.[6] In passages from the third century onwards, however, one frequently finds *qiddush ha-Shem* as the shorthand expression referring to the experiences, acts and statements of Jewish martyrs.[7]

In short, the phenomenon of martyrdom is older than the Christian or Jewish terminology that indicates it. Therefore, we propose a functional definition of martyrdom that has its basis in Jewish as well as Christian sources: a martyr is a person who in an extremely hostile situation prefers a violent death to compliance with a demand of the (usually pagan) authorities. This definition implies that the death of such a person is a structural element in the writing about this martyr. The execution should at least be mentioned. The *Acts of Justin*, for example, include at least an announcement of the verdict and conclude with the note that the martyrs went to the place of execution while glorifying God (Chapter 6; see Chapter 3, pp. 96–8; 116–20).

In antiquity early Christian writings about martyrdom were called *martyrium*, report of a martyr's death, *passio*, passion narrative, or *acta*, martyr acts. The fairly fixed form of the third type shows affinity with official Roman records of trial and scholars have argued that the form of the Christian *Acts* derives from such protocols.[8] In fact, there is a lot of variation in form as well as content of the early Christian martyr texts. Several documents look like trial or eyewitness reports, but have been considerably reworked by Christian redactors. Moreover,

---

5 About two decades later, the Latin equivalent of *martys* occurs for the first time as a self-designation and a reference to the martyrs' vindication in the North African *Acts of the Scillitan Martyrs* (*Act. Scil.* 15).

6 Safrai (1983), 146 with references.

7 *Sifra Ahare-mot*, *pereq* 13.14, on Lev. 18:5; *T.B. Zevahim* 115b; *Targum Neofiti* Gen. 38:25–6; *Shir ha-Shirim Rabbah* 2.7 (16b).

8 Lanata (1973); Berger (1984), 1248–9; Bisbee (1988).

some of the most famous Christian texts show striking similarities with Jewish martyr texts or New Testament passages about the death of Jesus, which supports our view that writings about martyrdom should primarily be considered literary texts.

Several Jewish and Christian narratives not only match our definition of the martyr, but show also a common pattern of narrative elements in the same sequence:

1   An enactment issued by the (pagan) authorities is the point of departure for the narrative.[9] Transgression of this enactment results in the death penalty.
2   The enforcement of the law brings Jews or Christians into a conflict of loyalty, since Jews cannot stay faithful to their God, the Law and their Jewish way of life and Christians have to make concessions to their religious convictions.
3   When Christians or Jews are forced – for instance, after their arrest – to decide between complying with the law of the government or remaining faithful to their religion and practices, they choose to die rather than obey the authorities.
4   This decision becomes obvious during the examination by the ruler or other officials, which is sometimes accompanied by tortures.
5   The execution is described, or at least indicated.[10]

This pattern also occurs in Dan. 3 and 6 (see Chapter 2), although the execution is followed by a miraculous deliverance in those stories.

If one is willing to look at Christian and Jewish martyrdoms as literary phenomena and compares them to related pagan traditions, striking correspondences as well as great differences become apparent. Jewish and Christian authors have, for example, used the famous image of the philosopher Socrates in creative ways in their descriptions of the behaviour and statements of their martyrs (see Chapter 1, p. 14). Christian and Jewish authors build on the patriotic motives for

9   Christian writings of martyrdom frequently refer to a demand to sacrifice or swear allegiance to the emperors and the gods: *Mart. Pol.* 9.2; *Mart. Carp.* 2 (Latin recension); *Acts of Justin* (rec. B 2.1; C 1.4); *Acts Scil.* 3; *Mart. Perp.* 6.3; *Mart. Pion.* 3.2–3; or the question 'Are you a Christian?', *Acts of Justin* 4; *Mart. Ptol.* 10; *Mart. Lugd.* 10; *Mart. Apol.* 1. Bisbee (1988), 103–4.
10 Apart from most Christian and rabbinic descriptive passages about martyrdom, this pattern already occurs in 2 Macc. 6:18–31 and 7, the oldest Jewish martyr texts, if the context of these stories is taken into account.

self-sacrifice highlighted in multiple pagan writings: the Athenian funeral orations, the tragedies of Euripides, the Roman descriptions of *devotio* and the *Alexandrian Acts* (see Chapter 1). The decision to die violently rather than give up one's conviction, or to die for the benefit of others are motifs elaborated in pagan as well as Jewish and Christian writings. On the other hand, pagans rarely have been willing to sacrifice their life for religious motives, as Christian and Jewish martyrs did.

Our definition of 'martyr' is problematic in connection with most of the pagan sources. Nevertheless, the analogies between the Jewish, Christian and pagan traditions are considerable as well as complex. Therefore, we have decided to devote one chapter fully to various kinds of glorious death in pagan sources. This allows the reader to read the Jewish and Christian passages in the broader context of various cultures in the ancient world. We also include passages on suicide in this book, since unlike modern people the ancients did not distinguish between glorious ways of suicide and other violent deaths.[11] In fact, the ancient Greeks put several kinds of glorious death in one category of *biaiothanasia* ('violent death'): death on the battlefield by falling victim or forcing one's own death, execution, as well as other forms of self-sacrifice and suicide. These deaths are described in passages that belong to very different genres and literary forms: elegies, tragedies, apologies, funeral orations, histories, biographical narratives (*teleute, exitus illustrium virorum*), diatribes, letters and so-called acts of pagan martyrs (see further the general introduction to Chapter 1). The various writings that are incorporated in this book can be displayed in a pyramid figure (Figure 1). The lowest level of the pyramid indicates various forms of noble death in pagan documents. The middle level indicates Jewish and Christian passages that are closely related to martyrdom, but differ in one respect from it. The wisdom stories focus on righteous individuals who remain faithful to God in a situation that threatens their life and who are saved in the end. A second group of related passages concerns heroic suicides, sometimes in a military context (e.g. 1 Macc. 6:43–6). The violent death of prophets, the third group, differs from martyr texts because the prophet is not executed by a foreign government but by his own king or people.

The passages included in this book date from the eighth century

---

11 This is well argued by Droge and Tabor (1992).

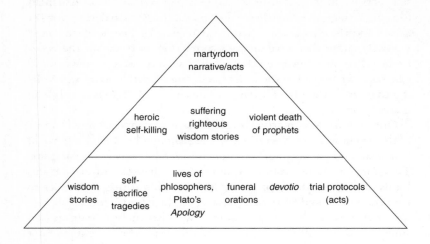

Figure 1 Noble death in antiquity.

BCE to about the fifth century CE. The rabbinic passages (Chapter 4) partly derive from the *Babylonian Talmud*, a work that was set out in its present shape to a great extent in the fifth century CE but was revised later. We have decided to include this material for two reasons. First, the Jewish martyrs that are the key figures in these rabbinic passages are mostly situated in the second century CE, a period when important Christian writings about martyrdom were composed. By incorporating rabbinic passages the reader is able to compare these with the Christian texts. Second, the rabbinic stories demonstrate that the phenomenon of martyrdom did not end with the Christian martyrs, as one might conclude when reading a Christian document like the *Writing to Diognetus* (see Chapter 3, pp. 102–4; 129–31). In late antiquity Christians as well as Jews reinterpreted traditions regarding the violent deaths of famous people belonging to their communities.

The structure of this book is as follows. Chapter 1 is devoted to pagan traditions about various forms of heroic death dating from the eighth century BCE to the third century CE. Chapter 2 deals with the early Jewish texts about martyrdom and related ways of dying, from the second century BCE to the second century CE. Chapter 3 presents selections of Christian writings about martyrdom from the late first to the third century CE. Chapter 4 concludes the book with the rabbinic stories of martyrdom, which mostly date in their present version from the third to the fifth century CE.

By way of conclusion we would like to point to an important aspect of writings about martyrdom. People only become martyrs because others make them so. The Vatican's complicated and time-consuming process involved in declaring persons to be a saint is just one example of this.[12] The martyrs are model figures for the groups who transmit and read the writings devoted to them. Martyr figures play an important role in the process of the formation of self-identity. A very early Christian document that focuses on Christian martyrs already demonstrates this social function, despite the brevity of its section about martyrdom. *1 Clement* 5–6 (end of the first century CE) constructs an image of the Christians with the help of martyrs as exemplary figures, who not only exemplify the ideal way of life, but also demonstrate the uniqueness of the new group of Christians. Later Christian martyr texts explore this further. Origen's *Exhortation to Martyrdom* from 235 CE is just one of the Christian documents that presents martyrs as exemplary figures. In fact, 2 and 4 Maccabees attribute a similar meaning to the Maccabaean martyrs in Jewish contexts.[13] The author of 4 Maccabees emphasises time and again that the martyrs stand in a continuous tradition of famous ideal figures of the Jewish people. The ethnic-patriotic dimension of the self-image in 4 Maccabees is highlighted in the mother's encouragement to her sons to die. The mother parallels the faith of her children with that of Abraham, Isaac, Daniel, Hananiah, Azariah and Mishael during their ordeals (4 Macc. 16:20–2). Thus, the martyrs become part of a chain of heroic events including the Binding of Isaac and the stories of deliverance of Daniel and his companions (Gen. 22; Dan. 3 and 6). The ethnic dimension in 4 Maccabees is stressed by the references to Abraham as 'our forefather' and to Isaac as 'father of the people' (4 Macc. 16:20). Thus the martyrs are the successors of a long series of heroes of the Jewish people. It is fascinating to see that the Christians, who never have been a people in the modern sense of the word, also considered such 'ethnic' traditions important for their self-identity.[14] Christian apologists not only drew on the Maccabaean martyrs but also on the

12 Woodward (1997).
13 Van Henten (1997).
14 Among others, the *Martyrdom of Polycarp* and the *Writing to Diognetus* describe the exemplary function of martyrs as part of the Christian 'people', see Chapter 3.

biblical heroes when they articulated their own traditions. The advantage was obvious: it showed that the Christians, who were widely perceived as newcomers in the religious arena, had, in fact, a glorious pre-history. The rabbinic stories of martyrdom may have been partly the response of the Rabbis to this early Christian glorification of the martyrs.

1

PAGAN TRADITIONS OF NOBLE DEATH

This chapter offers brief introductions to and translations of a selection of passages on the theme of noble death, coming from the non-Jewish and non-Christian ancient world. The oldest tradition incorporated, about Ahiqar the sage, dates from the eighth or seventh century BCE and is of Aramaean origin. The other passages concern Greeks and Romans and date from the fifth century BCE to the third century CE. The general introduction at the beginning of the chapter discusses the various images of noble death presented in these texts as well as their contexts.

General Introduction

The story of Ahiqar

Ahiqar the sage was falsely accused before the Assyrian king, convicted, sentenced to death, rescued in a wonderful way, and finally rehabilitated. Ahiqar did not really die a noble death, but his story has been enormously influential. The many versions of Ahiqar in the languages of ancient and medieval Christianity, like Armenian and Old Slavonic, as well as the references in rabbinic and Muslim literature show the popularity of the traditions about this sage in Late Antiquity. Ahiqar's story and sayings have been copied as an appendix to *A Thousand and One Nights*.

Ahiqar's story runs as follows. Ahiqar acts as councillor and keeper of the royal signet ring during the reigns of the Assyrian kings Sennacherib (704–681 BCE) and Esarhaddon (680–669). As prophesied by an astrologer he could not have children, despite his sixty wives. He therefore adopts his nephew Nadin (Nadan in later versions) and prepares him to succeed him as a courtier. After being installed as councillor at the court, Nadin conspires against his uncle and benefactor and convinces King Esarhaddon that Ahiqar was committing treason. Esarhaddon orders the officer Nabusumiskun to execute Ahiqar. Two other men have to control and report his execution. Ahiqar persuades Nabusumiskun, whom he had rescued earlier, to hide him in his house and to execute somebody else instead of him. The two men back Nabusumiskun up and report Ahiqar's death to the king. Here, the Aramaic story breaks off. Later versions tell, however, that the Egyptian king heard about Ahiqar's death and sent a letter to Esarhaddon in which he offered three years of Egypt's revenues to a sage who could solve difficult riddles and build a castle between earth and heaven, something only Ahiqar would be able to do. King Esarhaddon starts to regret having Ahiqar executed and the officer decides that the time has come to reveal the truth to the king. Ahiqar is, of course, welcomed back and sent off to Egypt. After his successful trip he refuses a reward and instead asks permission to discipline Nadin. He tortures his nephew and addresses a long series of reproaches to him in most versions, after which Nadin swells up like a bag and dies.

The story's pattern of a downfall and later vindication of a sage reoccurs in several biblical tales (Gen. 37–50, Esther, Susannah, Dan. 3 and 6) and is also found in Jewish and Christian passages about noble death. The Ahiqar story is basically a legend about a court *intrigue*. The stories about Daniel and his companions (Dan. 3 and 6) correspond in interesting ways to Ahiqar's story. In both cases it concerns a sage holding a high position at a foreign court as well as a king, who, despite his absolute power, lets himself be influenced by the false accusation by another sage – in Ahiqar's case his own nephew.[1] The sage is supposed to be executed on the basis of the false accusation, but is miraculously saved at the end. In the martyr stories this rescue is transposed after death, for example as a resurrection (see Chapters 2–4).

---

1 Another combination of sayings and narrative setting, the Demotic *Wisdom Instruction of Onchsheshonqy*, starts with a narrative section telling how the protagonist sage unfortunately got involved in a conspiracy against Pharaoh and was thrown into prison on an unjust accusation. Bereft of everything, Onchsheshonqy manages to write down instructions for his son on potsherds. Lichtheim (1980) offers an English translation of this text.

Noble death of philosophers

An important tradition in ancient culture, this time closely linked to the theme of noble death from the beginning onward, concerns the death of philosophers. Ancient philosophers valued sacrifice on behalf of others or for important causes. Some of them put this ideal into practice themselves. They functioned as model figures, because they showed how important goals could be reached even under extremely difficult circumstances. Indeed, Aristotle characterises a virtuous person as somebody who is prepared to sacrifice himself for one's friends and one's homeland and, if necessary, to die for it. He also holds that it would be better to live one year nobly than many years in an ordinary way (Aristotle, *Eth. Nic.* 1169a). Many other philosophers from the classical period into the imperial age expressed a similar view.

Philosophers articulated this choice in various ways. Philostratus' *Life of Apollonius* (second or third century CE) describes a discussion between Apollonius of Tyana, a philosopher and miracle worker from the first century CE, and his pupils Demetrius and Damis. The question that triggers the discussion is whether Apollonius should submit to the Emperor Domitian's accusation of instigating a conspiracy and go to Rome for his trial. One of the pupils, Demetrius, considers death for the liberation of a *polis* or for the benefit of family members or friends appropriate but nevertheless advises Apollonius to flee. Damis, on the other hand, thinks that one ought to die for the sake of philosophy, as one had to do for one's temples, one's city walls and one's sepulchres. Nevertheless, he hesitated when faced with the terrible consequences. Apollonius' death would bring about the ruin of philosophy. Apollonius decisively states that any person should choose to sacrifice himself for freedom, kinsfolk, or friends and his loved ones, since the law prescribes this. Further, wise persons should even be willing to die for interests that were not laid upon them by law and not planted by nature (*Vita Apol.* 7.12–14). Thus, Apollonius decides to travel to Rome.

The figure of the famous conqueror and king Alexander the Great was the source of many traditions about conversations between philosophers and himself that also show this theme. According to several sources, Alexander asked nine of the Gymnosophists ('The Naked Philosophers') tough questions about nature, humankind and the divine. An incorrect answer would bring execution; the tenth evaluated the answers.[2] Sources tell us that the Indian philosopher Kalanus

---

2 Plutarch, *Alex.* 64; Ps. Kallisthenes, *Vit. Alex.* 3.5–7, see Stoneman (1995).

accompanied Alexander during his campaign against the Persians.[3] He forced Onesicritus to listen to him while he was sitting naked upon stones, in line with the tradition of the Gymnosophists. Kalanus' ostentatious suicide in order to show his self-determination has become famous in antiquity. After becoming ill, he decided to organise his own ceremonial self-cremation in Alexander's presence.[4]

The various traditions about philosophers' deaths belong to the 'cultural baggage' of intellectuals in the Hellenistic and Roman periods. A special case of these traditions not discussed so far concerns a dialogue scene between philosopher and tyrant leading to the philosopher's execution. The frequently cited deaths of two philosophers, Zeno of Elea and Anaxarchus of Abdera, are very interesting in this connection. Both philosophers are said to have openly opposed a tyrant, at the cost of their own life. Both deaths show not only ultimate contempt for the tyrant, but also a heroic attitude towards physical suffering. Diogenes Laertius reports both deaths in his collection of the *Lives of the Philosophers* (third century CE). This is the only extant ancient work about the lives and famous statements of philosophers from the beginning of Greek philosophy. Sometimes Diogenes concludes his reports of philosophers' lives with a description of their noble death. His *Lives* show that contempt of suffering or death is commonplace in traditions about famous philosophers like Socrates, Zeno of Elea and Anaxarchus of Abdera. Severe suffering or execution did not shake their convictions.

Socrates

Socrates' death was a special case for Greeks and Romans. The Romans collected and spread Greek traditions about famous persons who exemplified the most important virtues, and expanded this corpus with their own Roman heroes. Among the various philosophical models of virtue (*exempla virtutis*), Socrates clearly had the prime position. His calm but unyielding attitude during his speech of defence and the response to his conviction in Plato's *Apology* compelled the admiration of many.[5]

---

3 Kalanus taught Onesicritus, a pupil of the Cynic philosopher Diogenes, another conversation partner of Alexander, about his theory of a Golden Age, Dio Chrysostom, *Or.* 4.
4 Strabo 15.1.68; Diodorus Siculus 17.107.
5 For a detailed discussion, see Döring (1979).

Socrates was accused of impiety (*asebeia*) and corruption of Athens' youth. Meletus acts in Plato's *Apology* as the main accuser. He may have represented the poets who apparently were angry with Socrates. Anytus, a former military commander, was one of those who supported the charge. The court of 501 citizens convicted Socrates in the spring of 399 BCE. He died by drinking a cup of poison. Many in the ancient world returned to Plato's writings that concern Socrates' trial, especially the *Apology* and *Phaedo*.[6] An especially famous passage in the *Apology* developed into a compact formula and has been frequently quoted by pagan as well as Christian authors.[7] The saying is typical of Socrates' attitude towards his death. It reads as follows:

> For know well, that if you kill me, I being such a person as I say I am, you will not harm me more than yourselves. Since neither Meletus nor Anytus could ever harm me. That would be impossible. For I believe that it is contrary to divine law that a better person is harmed by somebody worse. He may kill him, yes, or ban him or deprive him of his civil rights, and, perhaps, he and others believe that these things are major evils, but I for one do not believe that. On the contrary, in my view, it is a major evil to do what he is doing now, attempting to kill a man unjustly. (*Apol.* 30cd).

Arrian reports that Epictetus has quoted it three times in a way that reminds one of the epigrams on Zeno and Anaxarchus: 'Anytus and Meletus can kill me, but they cannot hurt me.'[8]

Socrates' death has served as a source of inspiration and consolation for several illustrious Romans who decided to end their lives by their own hand after they had fallen into disgrace. Sometimes the emperor more or less forced them to do so. The emperor, in this way, fulfils a role not unlike the tyrants who opposed Greek philosophers like Zeno or Anaxarchus. The depiction of the dramatic death scenes of these Romans, mostly philosophers with a Stoic orientation, clearly shows correspondences with the end of Socrates' life. The

---

6 See also Plato's *Eutyphro* and *Crito*. Cf. Xenophon, *Apology*; also *Memorabilia*, 1.1.1–1.2.64 (fifth/fourth century BCE).

7 Baumeister (1983).

8 Plutarch, *De tranq. animi* 475de; Epictetus 1.29.18; 2.2.15; 3.23.21; cf. *Encheiridion* 53.4, 38. Baumeister (1983) offers a survey.

Roman historian Tacitus, for example, presents Seneca's and Thrasea Paetus' suicides as imitations of Socrates' death. Like Socrates, they received the message that they had to die in the evening. They too admonished and comforted their shocked spouses and friends. They poured out a libation to Jupiter Liberator, while Socrates asked his friends to offer a cock to Asclepius (*Ann.* 15.60–64; 16.34–35). Seneca even drank hemlock as Socrates did in order to speed up his death.[9]

In the Roman period philosophers believed that Socrates also provided an example of how to live. Paradoxically, his death exemplified this way of life. The Stoic philosopher Epictetus, for example, refers to Socrates in his presentation of the ideal philosopher as a witness for the truth who refuses to make any concession that would lead to betraying one's conviction.[10] Socrates' acceptance of death formed the ultimate proof of his steadfastness and ability to maintain his freedom of thinking under any circumstances. Epictetus greatly admires his resolute decision to prefer a noble death to living on dishonourably: 'He saves himself by dying, not by flight.'[11] Socrates figures in Epictetus' argument as the steadfast philosopher who does not shrink away from the threats of a tyrant, who says what he has to say with full frankness and independence, and accepts torture or even execution if these are the consequences of his attitude. Jewish and Christian martyrs also shared Socrates' attitude towards death, which was ideal in the eyes of many in the imperial age.[12]

Euripides' tragedies

The famous Athenian dramatist, Euripides (fifth century BCE), depicts the theme of noble death in several of his tragedies.[13] These

---

9 Seneca himself may have triggered Tacitus' analogy, since he refers more than once to Socrates as *exemplum*. In his work about the happy life, he quotes the following statement of Socrates with great approval: 'Leap upon me, make your assault; I shall conquer you by enduring. Whatever attacks that which is firm and unsurmountable employs its power to its own harm' (*De vita beata* 27.3).

10 Delatte (1953); Döring (1979), 43–79.

11 Epictetus 4.1.165; cf. 1.9.25; 4.1.70; 4.1.161; 4.1.168–9.

12 Gutman (1949), 25–37; Hadas (1953), 101; 116–17; Kellermann (1979), 46–53; Döring (1979), 143–61; Goldstein (1983), 285 and 304; MacDonald (1994), 250–5; Rajak (1997), 39–67.

13 For discussions and references, see Vellacott (1975), 178–205; O'Connor-Visser (1987).

tragedies are often situated in a mythic past. They may, however, have fulfilled an exemplary function for the audience with an eye upon the contemporary political situation. Several tragedies highlight the theme of an atoning or substitute death. The reasons for these deaths may seem futile to us, and cruel as well, but they are bitter realities in the tragedies. Before life could continue, the wishes of an Olympic or anonymous god had to be fulfilled, or the spirit of a deceased person had to be satisfied.[14] Euripides' penchant for the theme of self-sacrifice may be closely connected with the social and political developments in Athens during the difficult period of the Peloponnesian war (431–404 BCE).[15] Euripides composed his *Phoenissae* and *Iphigeneia in Aulis* during the last phase of this war that culminated in Sparta's triumph over Athens.

In his *Phoenissae*, dating from about 410 BCE, Euripides describes how the young Menoeceus saved his home town of Thebes by killing himself. The seer Teiresias had informed Menoeceus' father Creon, the uncle of the Theban king, that it was necessary that 'one from the lineage of the Dragon's tooth' (the royal family of the dragon slayer and founder of Thebes Cadmus) had to be sacrificed and die in order to appease the earth (*Phoen.* 930–59). Only after this destined death would the Thebans be able to defeat their attackers from Argos (*Phoen.* 913–14). Menoeceus accepts his fate, but he fails in his first attempt to kill himself by the sword. In a dramatic action he then jumps from Thebes' walls and succeeds in saving his home town by his death. In the *Hecuba*, Euripides depicts how the death of Polyxena, the daughter of Troy's royal couple Priam and Hecuba, appeases Achilles' spirit after Troy's fall. She was sacrificed at the grave of her father. Her courageous attitude at the moment of dying made her famous.[16] She requested to be released so that she could die as a free woman: 'Out of free will I die. Let nobody touch my flesh, I will offer my neck with stout heart' (*Hec.* 448–9). The tragedy devoted to Heracles' children recounts how one of them, Macaria, saved the life of the others by her own death.[17] The idea of vicarious death is elaborated in Euripides'

14 For a survey of self-sacrifice and the motives for it, see Versnel (1981), 135–94.
15 Cf. de Romilly (1965); O'Connor-Visser (1981), 208–10. Euripides may also have been influenced by contacts between Athens and the Phoenicians in Carthage, see Rebuffat (1972).
16 *Hec.* 38–41; 367–78; 484–582. Cf. Seneca's 'remake' *Troades* lines 190–202; 286–370; 871–87; 1118–64, as well as Ovid, *Metam.* 13.439–532.
17 See especially Macaria's speech with the motivation for her decision to sacrifice herself for her sisters and brothers in *Her.* 500–34.

Alcestis, a tragedy with many echoes up to Lars von Trier's dramatic movie *Breaking the Waves*. Alcestis is prepared to die instead of her sick husband Admetus in order to save his life.

Noble death clearly has a patriotic significance in Euripides' tragedies. The *Phoenissae* repeats time and again that Menoeceus' almost ceremonial self-sacrifice benefited the land of Thebes (*Phoen.* 913–14; 997–8; 1090–92). Likewise, Iphigeneia's sacrifice was absolutely necessary for Hellas to defeat Troy (see below). The patriotic-political motive for self-sacrifice was undoubtedly important in Euripides' lost tragedy *Erechtheus* as well. We are lucky that the Athenian orator Lycurgus quoted extensively from this play about the sacrifice of another maiden, the daughter of the mythic Athenian king Erechtheus.[18] The mother of the girl, Queen Praxithea, agrees to her daughter's sacrifice, because she thinks that it is better that one dies instead of all. Such a depiction of the death of an individual as the substitute for the death of many or all can be found in several later texts, including Christian ones. Famous, of course, is the high priest Caiaphas' statement about Jesus' death in the Gospel of John, which anticipates and comments upon John's passion narrative: 'You do not understand that it is better for you to have one man die for the people than to have the whole nation destroyed' (John 11:50).[19] Praxithea explains the effective meaning of her daughter's death and states that she dies as one for all and for the benefit of the city.[20] Lycurgus concludes his extensive quotation of Euripides' tragedy with the remark that this girl's unsurpassable dedication to the fatherland had elevated the ancestors of his audience (*Contra Leocr.* 101).

Funeral orations

Another body of Athenian literature highlighting the virtue of dying for the homeland concerns soldiers. From the fifth century onwards, funeral orations (*epitaphioi logoi*) were composed in Athens in

---

18 Lycurgus, *Contra Leocratem* 98–101. Lycurgus passionately tried to defend Athens against Philip of Macedonia before it lost its independence to the Macedonians in 338 BCE (see p. 33). He accuses the rich Athenian citizen Leocrates of high treason in his speech and counters his behaviour with many examples of people who were willing to sacrifice themselves for their fatherland.

19 See John 11:47–53 and the reference to this passage in 18:14. Van Henten (1997), 187–269, offers a survey of ancient passages about dying for one's people.

20 Austin (1968), 25–8, fragment 50 lines 18 and 34–5; cf. also lines 51–2.

wartime.[21] An orator appointed by the city–state council would deliver such a speech during the annual state funeral. We have evidence of six classical funeral orations being transmitted, one of these only partially:[22]

1   Pericles' funeral speech at the end of the first year of the Peleponnesian War of Athens against Sparta (431–04 BCE), as rendered by Thucydides 2.34–46.
2   Fragments of a funeral oration by Gorgias (480–380 BCE).[23]
3   Lysias' second discourse, concerning those fallen during the Corinthian War (395–86 BCE).
4   Plato's *Menexenus*; also in praise of the heroes of the Corinthian War.
5   Demosthenes' *Speech* 60, in praise of the victims of the Battle of Chaeronaea (338 BCE).
6   Hyperides, *Speech* 6, having the Battle of Lamia (323–2 BCE) as its setting.[24]

Although the *epitaphios logos* originated as a memorial speech organised by the city–state (*polis*) of Athens for its citizens who had died for it,[25] the funeral speech became a literary genre as well. It is not certain whether Lysias' funeral oration, written in honour of the Athenians who had fallen in the Corinthian War against Sparta (395–86 BCE), was actually delivered. The style of this speech is rather literary. In any case, Lysias cannot have delivered it himself, since being a resident alien (*metoikos*) he did not have the right to address the Athenian assembly. Plato's *Menexenus* was likewise not delivered at

---

21   According to Greek and Roman theories about rhetoric these orations belong to a category which encompasses epideictic speech, to which eulogies (*enkomia*) of deceased who did not necessarily die a noble death also belong. For ancient theories about the *epitaphios logos*, see Ps. Dionysius of Halicarnassus, *Ars rhet.* 6, and Menander, see L. Spengel (ed.), *Rhetores Graeci* 3.418–22, edited again by Soffel (1974), 54–78.
22   For information and references, see Loraux (1986).
23   See Diels (1951–56), 2.284–6.
24   The last funeral speech is exceptional, since it focuses on one person, the Athenian commander Leosthenes. The Battle of Lamia was a last and unsuccessful attempt by the Athenians and other Greeks to free themselves from the yoke of the successors of the Macedonian Alexander the Great. Isocrates, *Pan.* 74–81, and Lycurgus, *Contra Leocr.* 46–51, show correspondences with the funeral orations.
25   Thucydides 2.42–3; Lysias, *Or.* 2.68, 70; Hyperides, *Or.* 6.10, 16, 24, 37.

the grave of the Athenian soldiers who died during the Corinthian War and may even be considered a satire on funeral orations. The framework of this dialogue is clearly fictitious,[26] since it presupposes that Socrates presented the dialogue, written by Pericles' wife Aspasia, to Menexenus. Socrates had already died in 399 BCE, long before the Corinthian War. In the Hellenistic and Roman periods, the *epitaphios logos* became more or less identical to the *enkomion* ('eulogy'). It was usually composed for individuals who had died a natural death, or it functioned simply as an exercise in declamation.[27]

The content of the earlier funeral orations and ancient rhetorical theory both indicate that the glorious deeds of the deceased Athenian soldiers were taken to be common knowledge. They are not referred to in detail and only mentioned in connection with the extensive laudatory passages. The authors focus upon the significance of these noble deaths and their amplification.[28] The praise contains traditional motifs, such as the noble birth (*eugeneia*), good education (*paideia*) and great courage (*andreia*) of the heroes who remained faithful to their ancestral city unto death. Praise of the deceased soldiers is carefully linked to Athens' glorious tradition as established by the ancestors.[29] As in Euripides' tragedies, the funeral orations enhance the praise of Athens through references to heroic acts during its prehistory.[30]

The funeral orations connect the noble death of Athens' soldiers with the fate of the whole of Greece. Some of the orations emphasise, like Euripides' *Iphigeneia at Aulis*, that the Athenian heroes died to preserve Hellas from the tyranny of a foreign king – either Persian or Macedonian.[31] This emphasis indicates again the political-ideological function of the funeral orations. The funeral orations served to legitimise political goals such as the Athenian hegemony over Greece or the promotion of Athens' democracy to other states. The noble death

---

26 Von Loewenclau (1961).
27 Cf. Soffel (1974), 19.
28 Buchheit (1960), 124–5; 221–2. Cf. the short references to the deeds of the heroes in Thucydides 2.42–3; *Men.* 244d–246a; Lysias *Or.* 2.61–70. Demosthenes, *Or.* 60.15–27, pays more attention to these deeds, but does so in a clichéd way without giving much real information.
29 Thucydides 2.36, 41; Plato, *Men.* 237ab; Lysias, *Or.* 2.17; 2.23–4; Demosthenes, *Or.* 60.4, 27; Hyperides, *Or.* 6.7; Loraux (1986), 150–2; 195; 342.
30 Plato, *Men.* 239a–c; Lysias, *Or.* 2.3–16; Demosthenes, *Or.* 60.8.
31 Hyperides, *Or.* 6.38–40. See also Lysias, *Or.* 2.21, 41, 57, 59; Plato, *Men.* 239d–240a.

of the Athenian soldiers was not only considered an instructive example to Athens' citizens, but also proof of the glorious Athenian performance against enemies like the Spartans, the Macedonians and foremost the tyrannical Persians.[32] The audience had to understand that it was Athens that had thrown itself into the breach for the freedom of Hellas time and again, not just once during the famous battle at Marathon (490 BCE), where the Spartans arrived one day late, as Plato sarcastically recalls (*Men.* 240d).[33] In short, the authors of the Athenian funeral orations seize the noble death of Athenian soldiers as an opportunity to praise the special qualities of their native city–state and its people and infuse their speeches with patriotism.

Devotio

The Romans had their own traditions of noble death. Latin sources report a specific form of self-sacrifice on duty. It concerns the so-called *devotio*, the 'dedication' by military persons of themselves, the enemy's army, or both to the gods of the underworld or other, often anonymous, deities. This ceremonial death was apparently the ultimate means to bring about victory.[34] In particular, the two or three successive military heroes with the same name P. Decius Mus who sacrificed themselves in this way were considered famous examples and are mentioned frequently in Roman sources.

In a general sense, *devotio* 'dedication, devotion' means the willingness to sacrifice oneself for the well-being of a group or a major cause. Suicide committed out of loyalty to other people or the city is a common motif in Latin writings.[35] Yet, the phrase *devotio* has a specific technical meaning as well.[36] Macrobius (fifth century CE) describes in his *Festival for Saturnus* (*Saturnalia*), a work written for entertainment, how cities of Roman enemies were consecrated to the gods of the underworld. He uses the verb *devovere* 'to dedicate, devote' for this practice. He also mentions 'a prayer of dedication' in connection with Carthage, one of Rome's arch-enemies. The prayer indicates

---

32 Plato, *Men.* 239c–246a; Lysias, *Or.* 2.20–68; Demosthenes, *Or.* 60.10; Hyperides, *Or.* 6.37.
33 Loraux (1986), 155–71.
34 For a survey, see Versnel (1981), 171–9.
35 Van Hooff (1990), 126–8.
36 For discussions and references, see Deubner (1905); Winkler and Stuiber (1957); Versnel (1976, 1977, 1980).

that the enemy would serve as substitute for the Roman commander and his army, so that both could stay alive (*Sat.* 3.9.9–13). This practice seems to be connected with the ritual death of soldiers, sometimes the commander himself, as a kind of guarantee of victory. The Roman historian Livy (59 BCE–17 CE) describes this ritual in detail in his history of Rome. In preparation for a *devotio* death the army commander would wear his official *toga* and cover his head, stand on a spear and hold his hand against his chin. Then the public priest would dictate a formula of *devotio*. Hereafter, the commander would seek death in the lines of the enemy (8.9.4–9). Livy's report of such a *devotio* in book 8 further mentions a few special arrangements. A soldier from the legion could fulfil the ritual instead of his commander, because the commander had the right to select anyone for this unfortunate job. If such a substitute death failed because the enemy did not kill the soldier, a statue of him of at least seven feet high had to be buried in the ground and a sin-offering sacrificed in addition (8.10.11–14).

The first Publius Decius Mus sacrificed himself to prevent a Roman military defeat against the Latins in 340 BCE in a battle near the volcano at Vesuvius. A generation later, his son followed his example and sought his own death in a battle against the Gauls at Sentinum in 295 BCE, at the place where the enemy lines were the strongest (Livy 10.28.18).[37] A *devotio* of P. Decius Mus' grandson at Ausculum in 279 BCE is hinted at in some sources, but is probably not historical.[38] In the formula dictated by the priest the first Decius Mus dedicated himself and the enemy's legions and auxiliary troops to the Gods of the Underworld and the Goddess of the Earth, for the benefit of the Roman republic, the army, the legions and the auxiliary troops (Livy 8.9.8, see below). Other references also mention the Roman people and the army as motives for such a *devotio* (8.6.13; 8.9.9 and 10.28.14). It is apparent from Livy's description of P. Decius Mus' self-sacrifice in 340 BCE and from texts related to it that it functioned as a kind of atonement to the gods. Livy even uses the technical word *piaculum* ('offer of expiation') to indicate this.[39] The *devotio*, therefore, seems to have a twofold altruistic significance: it was a self-sacrifice

---

37 Decius' son's *devotio* is depicted in Livy 10.28–9.

38 Cicero, *De fin.* 2.61; *Tusc. disp.* 1.89; Ennius, *Ann.* 6.191–4. See about this third Decius, Skutsch (1985), 353–7. Other traditions about the *devotio* of the Decii offer Cicero, *De div.* 1.51; *De nat. deor.* 3.15; cf. 2.10; *Tusc. disp.* 1.89; *Cato* 20.75; Florus 1.17; Lucanus, *Phars.* 2.308; Juvenal 8.254–8, and Orosius, *Hist.* 3.9.3.

39 Livy 8.9.9–10; 10.28.18; Statius, *Theb.* 10.799. About the atoning effect of such deaths, see Versnel (1981).

that brought atonement in the form of compensation to the gods, and a substitute death at the same time, since one died instead of many.

In the Roman imperial age *devotio* could extend to acts of self-sacrifice for the benefit of the emperor. Since the emperor personally guaranteed the order of society, his well-being was crucial. As a result, people vowed that they were willing to die for the emperor if he were in serious trouble. Two persons, Publius Afranius Potitus and Atanius Secundus, offered such a vow when Caligula (37–41 CE) was seriously ill. The emperor recovered, but, showing his cruelty, forced both men to put their oath into practice.[40] Another example of such a substitute death, which corresponds more closely to the *devotio*, is Otho's suicide in 69 CE. After Nero's death in 68 Otho was one of the four candidates to become emperor. He lost the decisive battle against Vitellius and killed himself after settling his affairs in order to save his soldiers. Dio Cassius' summary of events interprets his suicide as a noble end to a most disgraceful life. Dio also reports a statement by Otho that it was far better for one to perish for all instead of all for one (63.13.10–15).[41]

Acts of the Alexandrians

Since the end of the nineteenth century fragments of documents on papyrus have been found that concern the fate of delegates from Alexandria sent to the Roman emperor. These texts, dating from the first century CE or later, have been called 'Acts of the Alexandrians' (*Acta Alexandrinorum*), 'the Pagan Martyr Acts' or 'the Alexandrian Martyr Acts'.[42] Scholars have increasingly dismissed the assumption that the *Alexandrian Acts* were copies of trial protocols or rewritten and expanded versions of these, like the Christian Martyr Acts. They are probably extremely patriotic fictitious writings about confrontations of Alexandrian representatives with the emperor.

Alexandria had remained an independent Greek city (*polis*) since its foundation in the late fourth century BCE. It did not belong to Egypt properly in the Greek era, although it functioned as one of the capitals of Ptolemaic Egypt. Its location in the Nile delta made it

---

40 Dio Cassius 59.8.3; Suetonius, *Hist. aug. Cal.* 27.2.
41 The drowning in the Nile of Antinoos, Hadrian's boy lover, is sometimes interpreted as a *devotio* for Hadrian. Spartianus, *Hadr.* 14. See Versnel (1980).
42 Bauer (1901) argued that these intriguing documents concern martyrs, but this suggestion, followed by several other scholars, is misleading. The writings have little in common with Christian Martyr Acts.

into a very important harbour city, from which enormous quantities of grain were transported to imperial Rome. After Rome itself, it was the most important city of the empire. In addition, Alexandria was a prominent centre of arts and scholarship from the Hellenistic period onwards. Like many present-day large cities it was a multi-ethnic metropolis, with Greek, Macedonian, Egyptian, Jewish and Syrian inhabitants. Under Roman rule the original Greek elite lost much of its independence. The Romans did not allow them, for example, to maintain their own city council (*boule*). As well as this loss of independence, actual confrontations between Greeks and Romans, with the Jews sometimes involved as a third party, may explain the virulent hatred of the Greeks towards the Romans expressed in these writings. Shocking confrontations did occur. We know, for example, of a blood bath ordered by the Emperor Caracalla (211–217 CE) in the fall of 215 or the winter of 215/216 CE, during which Alexandrian youths fell victim. Caracalla associated himself with the Macedonian conqueror Alexander the Great and wanted to establish a corps of elite soldiers, the 'Macedonian phalanx'. Having been lavishly received by the Alexandrian citizens, he ordered all boys to assemble on an open piece of ground. He explained this by saying that he intended to enrol an army unit in honour of Alexander the Great. Next, his armed soldiers surrounded the boys, slaughtered them and dumped them in huge pits. Herodian suggests that Caracalla committed this unbelievable deed because the caricatures and jokes the Alexandrians made at his expense had severely irritated him.[43]

Herbert A. Musurillo's edition of the *Alexandrian Acts* of 1954 contains eleven writings as well as some fragments.[44] New fragments continue to be found. The documents concern a variety of incidents, including the pre-history of a diplomatic mission to Rome, a dialogue between an Alexandrian delegate and the emperor that in certain respects looks like a trial scene, a speech by a delegate, and a few references to the execution of a delegate. The *Alexandrian Acts* share the element of the dialogue between 'victim' and ruler with traditions about the noble death of philosophers as well as Christian and Jewish martyrs. In the *Acts of Isidorus*, for example, the eldest example of the *Alexandrian Acts*, one finds the main character in dialogue with the Emperor Claudius. Some of the documents clearly have an anti-Jewish

---

43 Herodianus Syrus 4.8–9 describes the entire episode.
44 Musurillo (1954). See also his second edition (1961).

bias, which again should be connected with historical events in Alexandria, which include severe clashes between Jews and non-Jews. Two writings by the Jewish philosopher Philo show the counterpart of this picture. The *Acts of Isidorus*, therefore, should be read in combination with Philo's *Embassy to Gaius* and *Against Flaccus*. All three of these documents deal with the same events in 38 CE, which resulted in a pogrom among Alexandrian Jews.[45] The *Acts of Hermaiskos* describe how nearly a century later competing embassies of Greeks and Jews from Alexandria presented themselves at Trajan's court. The Greek Alexandrians bluntly accuse the emperor of having many Jews in his council and playing the advocate of the impious Jews (col. iii, lines 42–3, 47–50).

The *Alexandrian Acts* are probably not official documents. They may not be completely fictitious, but are in their present state definitely not protocols of Roman trials (*commentarii*), as scholars have previously argued. They are literary writings that go back, ultimately, to tensions in Alexandria between the various ethnic groups in the city.[46] A recent comparison of the *Acts of Isidorus* with the official protocols in the *commentarii* leads to the conclusion that the *commentarius*-form has been imitated in these acts.[47] The tone of most acts and some of their motifs recall Greek novels like Chariton's *Kallirhoe*. The Alexandrians' pride of their birth, their piety towards the gods, including Graeco-Egyptian ones like Serapis, the love of their city and the melodramatic emphasis on death and suffering sound familiar to readers of ancient Greek novels. Some acts do, however, resemble trial protocols to a certain extent.[48]

---

45 Isidorus and his fellow-agitator Lampo were executed on the orders of Claudius as a result of their accusation of the Judaean king Agrippa I. This accusation was probably connected with Agrippa's defence of the Alexandrian Jews in 38. Isidorus had apparently acted as delator for the Emperor Gaius (37–41 CE) and brought about the death of some of Claudius' friends. Some scholars argue that Agrippa II is meant in these *Acts* (with 53 CE as date), but a reference to Agrippa I is more probable, see Smallwood (1981), 250–5; Schwartz (1990), 96–8.

46 Hennig (1974), 436.

47 Bisbee (1988), 65–79 states that the possibility cannot be ruled out that they ultimately go back to an edited version of a protocol.

48 See the second version of the *Acts of Maximus*, the *Acts of Hermias*, the *Acts of Paulus*, and, to a lesser extent, the *Acts of Isidorus*, the *Acts of Athenodorus*, the *Acts of Hermaiskos* and finally the *Acts of Appianus*, Musurillo (1954), 251. Musurillo offers an English translation of all acts.

1 Fragment of the Story of Ahiqar
(col. II 22–31), eighth–seventh century BCE

Ahiqar's writing consists of a story of deliverance and a collection of wisdom sayings. It dates from the eighth or seventh century BCE.[49] The story and the sayings have been transmitted in various translations. The original Aramaic version was found in 1907 on a badly damaged papyrus by German archaeologists on the island of Elephantine in the south of Egypt, where an important Jewish military colony was based at the time this papyrus was copied (late fifth century BCE).[50] Although the story clearly has an Assyrian setting and the names of the protagonists have circulated in Mesopotamia, the story and sayings probably originally derive from an Aramaean court in Syria.[51] In any case, by the third century BCE Jews knew them, as is apparent from references in the Jewish wisdom story of Tobit (Tob. 1:21–2).

The translated section concerns the betrayal of the Aramaean wise scribe Ahiqar by his nephew Nadin, as reported by Ahiqar. The ruler Esarhaddon mentioned in the fragment was king of Assyria from 680–669 BCE and Ahiqar and Nadin were his courtiers. See for a summary of the entire story the general introduction to this chapter.

Translation[52]

(22) . . . And this son of mine, (23) whom I had rais]ed and installed in the palace gate[53] [before Esarhaddon, King of Assyria, (24) among

---

49 Lindenberger (1985) offers an introduction to the story and sayings as well as an English translation. Recent research has focused on the sayings: Lindenberger (1983); Kottsieper (1990). Most of the later versions of story and sayings can be found in Conybeare *et al.* (1913).

50 Most of the papyrus is still kept in the library of the Staatliche Museen zu Berlin (catalogued as P 13446), but the sixth column has been sent back to Egypt and remains in the library of the Egypt Museum in Cairo.

51 Kottsieper (1990), 241–7, offers a survey of the discussion and argues for a South Syrian provenance.

52 Many lacunae have to be filled in because of the bad state of the papyrus, but the general content of the text is quite certain, because of the story's repetitive character and its full preservation in later versions. The translation basically follows the edition by Cowley (1923). The new edition by Porten and Yardeni (1993) uses C1.1 as *siglum* for this text, leaves more lacunae open and differs only in one place significantly from Cowley's text (reading 'in the midst of his chiefs' in l. 24 instead of 'among his courtiers').

53 The palace gate is apparently the place where advice was given to the king.

his courtiers], I thought 'He especially will seek [to do me] well, [as I had done to him'. Then (25) the son of my sis]ter, whom I raised, planned something [bad against me. He even thought to himself]: (26) 'I could spe[ak words like these (to King Esarhaddon)]: ["Ahiqar, this old man, who was the keeper of the signet ring for] (27) King Sennacherib, your father, [is bringing damage to your land, since he is councillor, scribe[54] and] (28) sage, and [all Assyria is dependent] on his advice and words [of counsel". Then Esarhaddon] (29) will be highly enraged[55] hearing words [like these, which I will say to him, and he will have Ahiqar killed'. Then] (30) after my son who is not my son had fabricated [this lie against me . . . (31) . . .

2 Diogenes Laertius, *Lives of the Philosophers* 9.26–8 (Zeno)

Diogenes Laertius (third century CE) reports the deaths of the philosophers Zeno of Elea and Anaxarchus of Abdera after giving some biographical data and statements about their philosophical ideas. In doing so he often draws on traditions from several sources. He rounds off both lives with an epigram of his own.[56]

Zeno of Elea was a pupil of Parmenides. His dates are not exactly known, but he probably lived in the first half of the fifth century BCE in his hometown of Elea in Lucania (Italy). Diogenes Laertius tells us that he 'flourished' in the 69th Olympiad (464–61 BCE). His philosophical views concern arguments that observations of movements may be misleading. His statement about the running match between Achilles and the tortoise has become famous. Its point is that Achilles could never make good the tortoise's lead, since at the moment when he reached the point where the tortoise was in front, the tortoise was a little further, and this process would go on endlessly.

Translation[57]

(9.26) He (Zeno) was a most noble man as a philosopher and as a citizen. At all events, people say that his books are full of sagacity. He

---

54 A scribe at a court or a temple was not only a copyist, but also a learned scholar, who often acted as adviser to the king, cf. 1 Chron. 27:32 and Ezra 7:6.
55 Cf. the motif of the anger of the king in Dan. 3 and 6, 2 Macc. 7, and 4 Macc.
56 These epigrams have been gathered also in a huge collection of epigrams from antiquity called *The Greek Anthology* (*Anth. Gr.* 7.129 and 7.133).
57 Translation based on Long (1964).

wanted to kill the tyrant Nearchus – some say Diomedon –[58] but he was arrested, as Heraclides says in his summary of Satyrus.[59] When he (Zeno) was questioned about people who knew of the conspiracy and about the weapons he was bringing to Lipara, he denounced all the tyrant's friends, wishing to isolate him. Next, indicating that he was able to tell something about certain people in his (the tyrant's) ear, he bit it and did not let go until he was pierced through, suffering a similar fate as Aristogeiton,[60] the tyrant slayer. (9.27) Demetrius says, however, in his *Homonyms*,[61] that he bit off his nose. But Antisthenes tells in his *Diadochai*,[62] that when he had denounced the friends of the tyrant and the latter had asked him whether there was somebody else, Zeno said: 'Yes, you are, the plague of the city'; and to those who were standing by he said: 'I marvel at your cowardice, if you serve the tyrant because of what I now endure.' And finally he bit off his tongue and spat it at the tyrant.[63] Impressed by this, the citizens immediately stoned the tyrant to death. Most sources offer these facts more or less. But Hermippus[64] says that he was thrown into a mortar and beaten to death.[65] (9.28) And I have celebrated him as follows:

58 Zeno's confrontation with a tyrant is clearly legendary. The name of the tyrant changes in the various traditions. Even Dionysius, the famous tyrant of Syracuse, is mentioned sometimes. See for references von Fritz (1972), 54–5.

59 Heraclides Lembus (second century BCE) popularised and summarised biographies of famous persons, including the work of Satyrus of Kallatis (3rd century BCE).

60 Aristogeiton and Harmodius tried to murder the Athenian tyrants Hippias and Hipparchus (514 BCE). They managed to kill only Hipparchus and were caught. Harmodius was executed immediately, but Aristogeiton was arrested, tortured and executed afterwards.

61 Demetrius of Magnesia (first century BCE) was a learned compiler. His work referred to as *Homonyms* here was about poets and other writers with the same name.

62 The *Diadochai* ('The Successions of the Philosophers') by Antisthenes of Rhodes (end of the third/beginning of the second century BCE) was one of Diogenes Laertius' sources.

63 The passages about Zeno and Anaxarchus share the theme that they bit off their own tongue and spat it to the tyrant out of contempt for him or as proof of their determination, Diogenes Laertius 9.27; 9.59; Plutarch, *De garrul.* 8 (*Mor.* 505D); *Adv. Col.* 32 (*Mor.* 1126D).

64 In the late third century BCE in Alexandria Hermippus has written 'Lives' of famous persons with a special interest in their death, using Alexandria's wonderful library and building on the work of his teacher Kallimachus.

65 On Zeno's death, see also Valerius Maximus 3.3.2–3; Plutarch, *De garrul.* 8 (*Mor.* 505D); *De stoic. repugn.* 37 (*Mor.* 1051CD); *Adv. Col.* 32 (*Mor.* 1126D); Clement of Alexandria, *Strom.* 4.57; Ammianus Marcellinus 14.9.6.

You wished, O Zeno, you nobly wished, to kill the tyrant and free Elea from slavery. You were subdued. The tyrant seized you and crushed you in a mortar – no, not you, your body.

3 Diogenes Laertius, *Lives of the Philosophers* 9.58–9 (Anaxarchus)

The second passage from Diogenes Laertius concerns Anaxarchus of Abdera (fourth century BCE) who belonged to the philosophical school of Democritus.[66] He developed an ancient 'atoms-theory' arguing that a vacuum (non-being) must exist in order to separate beings ('atoms') from each other. He accompanied Alexander the Great on his trip to the East, and this is the starting-point for Diogenes' report of Anaxarchus' death.

Translation[67]

(9.58) So this Anaxarchus accompanied Alexander and flourished in the 110th Olympiad (340–337 BCE). He considered Nicocreon, the tyrant of Cyprus, his enemy. Once, when they were at a banquet, Alexander asked him what he thought of the meal. He, as is said, responded: 'O king, everything is very costly. We only would need the head of some satrap being served as well', hinting at Nicocreon. (9.59) Once, after the death of the king, Anaxarchus made a trip by sea. Unfortunately, the ship was taken to Cyprus. Resentful, Nicocreon had him arrested. He threw him into a mortar and ordered him to be beaten with iron pestles.[68] Anaxarchus thought little of the punishment and said, in fact, the following famous statement: 'Just pound the bag of Anaxarchus, you do not pound himself.' When Nicocreon also ordered him to cut out his tongue, he bit it off and spat it at him.[69] And this is what I have written upon him:

---

66 His work *About Kingship* is lost, apart from two fragments, and he is sometimes associated with other philosophical schools like the Cynics.
67 Translation based on Long (1964).
68 The traditions about Zeno and Anaxarchus have apparently influenced each other, since apart from the spitting of their tongues at the tyrant also a violent death in a mortar is told of both.
69 Other passages about Anaxarchus' death are Valerius Maximus 3.3. ext. 4; Plutarch, *De virt. mor.* 10 (*Mor.* 449E).

Have them pound, Nicocreon, harder and harder. It is a bag. Anaxarchus is already with Zeus. In a while Persephone will pull you apart with her carding-combs[70] and say: 'Begone, evil miller'.[71]

4 Plato, *Apology* 28a–30b (Socrates)

The passage translated comes from Plato's *Apology* (fourth century BCE). It is part of Socrates' long speech of defence just before the voting that led to his conviction. It is unknown to what extent Plato's writing represents Socrates' actual speech of defence, but the style and arguments of the speech conform to what is considered characteristic of Socrates.

In addition to Socrates' argument in this passage one should note several other reasons for Socrates' refusal of a milder punishment or acquittal mentioned elsewhere in the *Apology*. Socrates presents a religious motive for his perseverance considering his death in accordance with the will of the deity (*Apol.* 29d; cf. *Crito* 43b; 54e). He even considers his death blissful, since it either brings a condition of unconsciousness or a migration of the soul to another world (*Apol.* 40b–41c). Finally, Plato refers to Socrates' exemplary obedience to the laws even against the opinion of all others. He lets Socrates remind his judges in a painstaking way of his refusal as temporary president of Athens' council to collaborate in the unlawful condemnation of ten military commanders after Athens' successful naval battle against Sparta in 406 BCE during the so-called Arginusai trial (*Apol.* 32bc).

Translation[72]

(28a) Men of Athens, that I am not a wrong-doer as written in Meletus' indictment does not really seem to need much of a defence; but enough of this. What I have said to you before, that I was confronted with much hatred from many people, is true, as you know well. And this will lead to my conviction, if there will be a conviction: not Meletus or Anytus,[73] but the prejudice and jealousy of the many.

---

70 Persephone is the spouse of Hades-Pluto, the god of the underworld. The carding-combs were also an instrument of torture (cf. p. 156, n. 128).

71 The reference to Nicocreon as a miller points to the way Anaxarchus was executed.

72 Translation based on Duke *et al.* (1995).

73 Meletus and Anytus are Socrates' main accusers, see above.

This has led to the conviction of many other good men, and, I think, it will do so again. There is no (28b) danger that it will stop with me. Perhaps somebody will say: 'Are you then not ashamed, Socrates, that you have pursued such a practice, because of which you are now in danger of dying?' But I could say a just defence against this person: 'You don't speak well, sir, if you think that a man who is of at least some use must take into account the risk of losing his life and not consider just this when he acts: whether the things he does are just or unjust, or the works of a good or a bad man.' For, according to your statement all the (28c) demi-gods who died at Troy would have been stupid, especially the son of Thetis,[74] who so despised danger in comparison with enduring something shameful, that, when his mother, being a goddess, said to him, as he was eager to kill Hector, something like this: 'Child, if you revenge the murder of your companion Patroclus and kill Hector, you will be killed yourself' – 'for immediately', she said, 'after Hector your fate is at hand.'[75] When he heard this, he thought lightly of death and danger, and fearing much (28d) more to live on being as a coward and leaving his friends unrevenged he said: 'May I die immediately',[76] he said, 'making the one pay who did me wrong. I do not want to stay here, being laughed at beside the curved ships, a burden to the ground.'[77] Do you think he gave much heed to death and danger? This is, men of Athens, how things are in truth: wherever one stations oneself, thinking that position is best, or wherever one is stationed by one's commander, there he must stay, I think, and run the risks, taking neither death nor any other thing more into account than dishonour.

(28e) When the commanders whom you have chosen to command me stationed me, at Potidaea, Amphipolis and Delium,[78] I stayed there where they commanded me, like anybody else, and ran the risk of dying. Thus, I would have done something terrible, O men of Athens, when, after the deity stationed me, as I believed and

---

74 Socrates means Achilles, the champion of the Greeks at Troy. The passage constructs an analogy between Socrates and the Greek heroes of Homer's *Iliad*, who fought their famous battle with the Trojan fighters led by Hector. Homer glorifies the death of the fighters on the battlefield in many lines, which were often quoted.

75 Quotation of Homer, *Iliad* 18.96.

76 *Iliad* 18.98.

77 *Iliad* 18.104.

78 Socrates participated in military campaigns at the locations mentioned in 432–29, 424 and 422 BCE respectively.

understood, to live the life of a philosopher and examine myself as well as others, I would have left my post for fear of death or anything else. (29a) It would be terrible, and in that case somebody could justifiably take me to court on the charge that I do not believe that there are gods, since I would disobey the oracle for fear of death and thinking that I am wise while I am not.[79] For fearing death, gentlemen, is nothing else than thinking one is wise while one is not. For it is thinking one knows what one does not know. For nobody knows death, not even if it does not happen to be for humans the greatest of all gifts. But people fear it, as if they knew (29b) that it is the greatest evil. And yet, is this not the shameful kind of ignorance, to think to know what one does not know? Perhaps, gentlemen, in this case too, I differ from most people in this respect: if I were to say that I was wiser in something than someone else, it would be in this, namely that I do not *think* I know, because I do not know enough about the realm of Hades.[80] What I do know is that acting unjustly and disobeying one's superior, whether a god or a human being, is bad and shameful. I will never fear and flee the things I don't know whether they happen to be good rather than the bad things which I know to be bad . . .

(30a) . . . You must know that the deity commands me this. I believe that nothing better ever has happened in this city than my service to the deity. For I do nothing other than trying to persuade both young and old of you (30b) to care, first and above all, not for your bodies and your money, but for the perfection of your soul, telling you that virtue does not result from money, but money and all other good things for humans, both privately and in public, result from virtue. If I corrupt the youth by saying this, it is this that must be harmful. If, however, someone asserts that I say something different, he would be talking nonsense. This being the case, O men of Athens, I would say, whether you listen to Anytus or not, whether you acquit me or not, I shall not act differently, not even if I were to die many times.[81]

---

79 This refers to Meletus' accusation that Socrates would not believe in the gods and had introduced new superhuman beings (*daimonia*), see *Apol*. 24b. The latter may be connected with Socrates' belief that he was personally guided by a superhuman being that he called *daimonion*.

80 Hades refers to the realm of the dead, where the god Hades was ruler.

81 Socrates also emphasises that he accepts the death penalty as the consequence of his attitude in *Apol*. 28e-29a and 38e-39b.

5 Euripides, *Iphigeneia at Aulis* 1368–401

The first performance of Euripides' tragedy *Iphigeneia at Aulis* in Athens took place some time in the years 405–400 BCE, after Euripides' death. Its setting is the mythic battle of the Greeks against Troy. Iphigeneia is the daughter of the Greek commander Agamemnon, who makes her come from Argos to Aulis, the location of the Greek fleet, pretending that she was to marry the Greek champion Achilles. In fact, Agamemnon had decided to sacrifice his own daughter. Her sacrifice to the goddess Artemis ends a windless period and enables the fleet to put out to sea and overcome the Trojans. Iphigeneia accepts her tragic fate and dies of her own free will, as her speech to her mother Clytemnestra dramatically demonstrates (see below). This passage is the most elaborate political motivation for self-sacrifice in the work of Euripides.[82]

In the tragedy Iphigeneia's role changes from that of a childish girl who begs her father to save her life into an independent woman who realises that Hellas' future depends on her decision alone. The entire tragedy subordinates personal feelings and family bonds to, supposedly, higher values: honour, triumph and freedom for Hellas. Iphigeneia's father shows this double-edged attitude as Iphigeneia herself does, since he decides to overrule his earlier letter with the set-up of the fake marriage to Achilles by another letter. From the beginning to the end there is a tension in the play as to whether Iphigeneia will be saved or not. What kind of father would allow his child to be sacrificed and what military victory would justify such a brutal act? Agamemnon's second letter is intercepted and Iphigeneia arrives at Aulis. Her mother's plea fails to persuade Agamemnon now. Agamemnon's response to his wife and daughter is telling. Iphigeneia has to be sacrificed for the deliverance of Greece (1255–75). Iphigeneia's miraculous deliverance from Artemis' altar in the final part may have comforted the audience. The goddess put a deer on the altar just before Iphigeneia was slaughtered.

Translation[83]

(1368) Mother, listen to my words. There is no reason for you to be angry with your husband.[84] (1370) To endure the impossible is not

---

82 For an introduction and a translation with explanatory notes, see Cavander (1973).
83 Translation based on Diggle (1994).
84 King Agamemnon deceived his wife and their daughter and did not let himself be persuaded by them (1098–275).

easy. It is right to praise the stranger[85] for his willingness to help. But you too have to see that he should not be set against the army. We would win nothing, while he meets misfortune. Listen, mother, to what I have been thinking. (1375) I have decided to die. I want to do this gloriously, by yielding and doing away with my low-mindedness.[86] Come, mother, look at it with my eyes and see how nobly I speak. All of majestic Hellas looks upon me now. It is through me that the ships will be able to sail and the Phrygians[87] will find their grave. (1380) And if barbarians do something to women in the future, it is through me that they will be prevented from seizing them from happy Hellas, since they will have paid the price for Helena's ruin, whom Paris seized.[88] All this I will secure by dying, and mine will be the blissful glory that I brought Hellas freedom. (1385) It does not befit me to cling too much to life. You (mother) brought me forth not for yourself alone, but for all Greeks. Yet, countless men armed with their shields, myriads of them holding their oars, have the courage to act upon the enemies and die for Hellas, because their homeland was wronged. (1390) And should one life, mine, be reason to prevent all this? Would that be just? Could I say a word in my defence? There are other reasons as well. It is not right that this man should go to war against all Greeks and die because of a woman.[89] It is better that one man sees the daylight than ten thousand women. (1395) And if Artemis wants to receive my body, should I, a mortal, try to hinder the goddess? That is impossible. I offer my body for Hellas. Sacrifice me and destroy Troy. That will be my monument for ages to come.[90] That will be my children, my husband, my glory. (1400) It is proper, mother, that Greeks rule over barbarians and not barbarians over Greeks. Because the ones are slaves, the others free.

---

85 Iphigeneia's fiancé Achilles, who was willing to fight alone against the entire army that came to fetch Iphigeneia.
86 This may refer to Iphigeneia's earlier attitude in trying to be saved.
87 I.e. the Trojans.
88 With the help of the goddess of love, Aphrodite, the Trojan Paris was able to seduce Helena, the wife of Agamemnon's brother. The irony is that for a war originally about one Greek woman, another Greek woman, Iphigeneia, has to be sacrificed.
89 Achilles' death for Iphigeneia would be too much honour for a woman.
90 Cf. 2 Macc. 6:31.

6 Demosthenes, *Funeral Oration* (*Or.* 60) 1–2, 23–7

Demosthenes' speech follows the pattern of the other funeral orations (see the General Introduction to this chapter), but he adds a section of praise of the ten Athenian tribes. In fact, Demosthenes praises defeated soldiers. With the victory of Philip II, Alexander the Great's father, at the Battle of Chaeronaea (338 BCE), the era of Macedonian supremacy over Greece began. Demosthenes blames the Thebans for the defeat (60.22). The first section translated below comes from the beginning of the speech and reveals its setting and purpose. The second fragment is part of the central section of the praise of the soldiers (15–27). This passage is much more concerned with the unique features of Athenian society than with the actual performance of the heroes and corresponds in this respect again to the genre. Paragraph 27 rounds the first section of praise off with a summary and forms the transition to the praise of the ten tribes' heroes in the old times.

Thus, Demosthenes praises the victims of Chaeronaea in two sections. After a general section, first of all, he then offers examples of glorious self-sacrifice from all ten Athenian tribes. These examples include the descendants of Erechtheus[91] and those of Leos with reference to the sacrifice of the daughters of Erechtheus and Leos (60.27–30). The daughters of Erechtheus and Leos, all of them mythical characters, function as evidence of Athens' long-standing tradition of heroic death (*Or.* 60.27, 29).[92]

Translation[93]

(1) After the City[94] decided that those who lie in this grave, who proved to be brave in the war, had to be honoured with City funeral rites and ordered me to deliver the customary speech in praise of them, I immediately tried to find out how they could receive the appropriate praise. While I was searching and considering things, I found that saying what would be worthy of those who fell is one of those things impossible to realise.[95] They did not take notice of their

---

91 See p. 35, n. 104.
92 Cf. Aelianus, *Var. hist.* 12.28.
93 Translation based on Blass (1927).
94 The city–state (*polis*) of Athens.
95 This as well as the foregoing sentence is conventional at the beginning of a speech.

33

desire to live, natural to all people, and chose to die nobly rather than live on and see Hellas in misfortune.[96] How could any speech fully express the fame they left behind? Yet, it seems right to me to speak along the lines of those who have spoken here earlier.[97] (2) That the City pays serious attention to those who die in wars can especially be seen from this law that deals with the choice of the person who will speak at the public funeral. Knowing that among noble people the earning of money and the enjoyment of the good things in life are being despised,[98] because their desire fully goes out to fame and praise, the City thought it appropriate to honour them with speeches that will fulfil these wishes, so that the honour they won during their life will also be rendered to them after their death . . .

(23) Everyone can interpret the other matters concerning this war in line with one's opinion of it, but what has become evident to all living alike is that the freedom of all of Hellas was dependent upon the lives of these men. At all events, when Fate took away those people,[99] nobody else withstood the enemy. I hope that nobody will take offence at what I am going to say, but it does seem to me that if someone should say that the virtue of these men is Hellas' soul,[100] he would speak the truth. (24) For the moment their souls were released from the bodies to which they belonged, Hellas' dignity too was taken away. In the eyes of some we may, perhaps, exaggerate, but it has to be said. If somebody took away the light from the existing world, all remaining life would be harsh and difficult. Likewise, now that these men have been taken away, all the former splendour of the Greeks has fallen into darkness and obscurity.

(25) It is clear that many things contributed to make them what they were, but the constitution was not the least reason that they were

---

96 Hellas refers to the Greek mainland, the Peloponnesus as well as the Greek islands and cities around the Aegaean Sea.

97 This is a reference to the orators who had delivered a funeral speech in earlier times, see above.

98 This is a common motif in funeral speeches, see Thucydides 2.42.4.

99 The Greeks thought that the gods determined the life of the mortals by giving all of them a certain portion in life. Fate even was personified in the Moirai, the three Goddesses of Fate.

100 Demosthenes plays with the various meanings of the Greek word *psyche*. A few lines above he uses it in the original meaning 'life'. Here, the idea is that the behaviour of these heroes forms the soul of Greece. Isocrates, *Areop.* 138, calls the constitution the soul of the government. Centuries later, the author of the Writing to Diognetus makes a comparison of the Christians in the world with the soul in the body (Diogn. 6.7–10), see p. 130.

excellent. For oligarchies cause fear among the citizens, but they do not arouse a sense of shame. When the struggle of war appears, everybody will save himself quickly, knowing that if one wins over the rulers by presents or whatever kind of behaviour, even if somebody disgraces himself in the most terrible way, only a slight reproach will attach to him thereafter.[101] (26) Democracies, however, have many good and just features, to which sensible people should cling,[102] the most prominent being the freedom of speech, which, depending on truth cannot be prevented from exposing the truth. Neither is it possible for those who have committed a shameful act to win over all, nor does a person who is alone in uttering a justified reproach give offence.[103] Since even those who would not say a defamatory word themselves derive pleasure from hearing such a word said by somebody else. Fearing this as well as the disgrace of later reproaches, all these men stoutly resisted the danger that was approaching from the enemy. They preferred a noble death to a life in disgrace.

(27) The motives that all these men had in common for willing to die nobly have been indicated now: birth, education, being accustomed to noble behaviour, and the basis of the entire constitution. I will now highlight the motives the members of each separate tribe had for their brave conduct. All Erechthidae[104] knew Erechtheus, who has given his name to their tribe. They were well aware that he, in order to save this land, had offered his own daughters, who are called Hyacinthides,[105] to be killed publicly. They thought it a

---

101 Demosthenes is clearly very critical of oligarchy. The point of this passage seems to be that in oligarchy, contrary to democracy (see § 26), people do not need to take responsibility for their deeds in public. They manage as long as they are friendly with the rulers.

102 Cf. Thucydides 2.37; Lysias, *Or.* 2.18–19.

103 Thus, Demosthenes argues that democracies make it impossible for people who have done something shameful to get away with it. Cf. Thucydides 2.37 and Hyperides, *Or.* 6.25.

104 The Erechthidae were the members of the tribe that derived its name from the mythic Athenian king Erechtheus. Demosthenes' references to self-sacrifice of the early members of the ten tribes are not very reliable. Erechtheus, for example, had only one daughter according to earlier sources (see p. 16). Nevertheless, Euripides, *Ion* 277–8, and Cicero, *Tusc. disp.* 1.116, also refer to two daughters.

105 The second name of Erechtheus' daughters derives from a Spartan hero named Hyacinthus, who had moved to Attica. His daughters were sacrificed by Erechtheus in order to protect Athens against a foreign attack. Apparently, Demosthenes has conflated this tradition with another one about sacrificial death in Athens' mythic past, that of Erechtheus' youngest daughter.

disgrace that while the one begotten by the immortals sacrificed everything to liberate his fatherland,[106] they should appear to consider their mortal body more important than immortal glory.

7 Livy 8.9.1–14[107]

The selected passage is part of Book 8 of Livy's *Roman History*, which covers the period 341–321 BCE and begins with a conflict between Rome and its neighbours and former allies, the Latins. The war broke out because the Romans refused to let the Latins have a share in the government of Rome. The battle of 440 BCE forms the setting of P. Decius Mus' *devotio*. Before the battle P. Decius Mus and the other Roman consul see a nightly vision of a superhuman being. It tells them that a commander – either a Roman or a Latin – had to be sacrificed to the gods of death and the Goddess Earth and that the army of that commander would be victorious (8.6.9–10). The Roman consuls, both commanders, tell each other of the vision and decide that the one whose soldiers would get into trouble would sacrifice himself. The inspection of the organs by the one who had to do this, the *haruspex*, indicates that P. Decius Mus was the consul who had to perform the *devotio*. During the battle he accepts his divinely destined fate without hesitation and devotes himself with the legions and auxiliaries of the enemy to the anonymous gods of the underworld (*Manes*) and to the Goddess Earth (*Tellus*) for the benefit of the Roman legions (8.9.4) and the Roman state. Hereafter, he seeks death in the midst of the enemy's soldiers.

Translation[108]

(9.1) Before the Roman consuls marched out for battle, they brought a sacrifice. It is said that the inspector of the entrails[109] explained to Decius that the lobe of the liver on his part was incised,[110] but that in other respects his sacrifice was accepted by the gods. Manlius'[111]

---

106 The passage hints at Erechtheus, who was considered to be of divine origin.
107 For an elaborate commentary on the passage, see Oakley (1997–98), 2.477–505.
108 Translation based on Walters and Conway (1969).
109 Inspecting of the liver was a common Roman practice to predict the future.
110 Such an incision of the liver meant evil.
111 Titus Manlius was the other Roman consul of this year. He had had his own son executed before the battle, because he disobeyed his commands (Livy 8.7).

omens, he said, had been extremely favourable. 'It is well,' Decius said, 'if my colleague has received favourable omens.' (9.2) With the battle formation as told before,[112] they marched into battle, Manlius commanding the right wing, and Decius the left. (9.3) In the beginning both sides fought with equal strength and the same ardour. Next, the first rank of the Roman left wing could not counter the attack of the Latins and retreated to the experienced soldiers of the second rank. (9.4) In the following confusion, consul Decius shouted loudly to M. Valerius:[113] 'We need to call upon the gods; come on, you public priest of the Roman people, order me to devote myself for the sake of the legions.' (9.5) The priest ordered him to put on his *toga praetexta*,[114] cover his head with it, stretch out his hand to his chin under the *toga*, standing with his feet upon a spear, and say the following words: (9.6) 'Janus, Jupiter, Father Mars, Quirinus, Bellona, Deities of the House, New Deities, Indigenous Deities, Deities who have the power over us and our enemies (9.7), Deities of the Underworld,[115] I beg and implore you, I ask your permission and pray to you to grant the Roman people of the *Quirites*[116] power and victory, and to bestow upon the enemies of the Roman people of the *Quirites* panic, fear and death. (9.8) In accordance with this formal pronouncement, I devote the enemy's legions and auxiliary troops together with myself to the Deities of the Underworld and the Goddess Earth for the benefit of the state and the army, the legions and the auxiliary troops of the Roman people of the *Quirites*.'

(9.9) After this prayer he ordered the *lictors*[117] to go to T. Manlius and report to his colleague quickly that he had dedicated himself for

---

112 Livy describes the new Roman battle array in 8.8.

113 It is not certain whether this M. Valerius actually existed.

114 This outer garment bordered with purple was worn in public by Rome's higher magistrates.

115 The 'double-faced' Janus is the god of doors and beginnings, Jupiter is the supreme Roman god, and Mars is the god of war. Quirinus is the name of the deified Romulus, one of Rome's founders, Bellona is a war goddess, the 'Deities of the House' (*Lares*) are the deities that protect the household, supposedly being the spirits of deceased ancestors, whose statues were standing near the hearth. The 'Deities of the Underworld' (*Manes*) are the gods of the underworld and the spirits of the dead. Most of the deities are anonymous (cf. Acts 17) and some of them seem to overlap. In this formula none of the deities concerned should be missed.

116 The *Quirites* is an honorary name for the Roman citizens.

117 The *lictors* would accompany magistrates in public, make space for them, acknowledge verdicts, etc.

the sake of the army, girded his *toga* in the Gabinian way,[118] jumped on his horse, fully armed, and dashed into the middle of the enemy. (9.10) Clearly visible to both armies, he appeared far more august than humans,[119] like someone sent from heaven as a sin-offering expiating all the anger of the gods and averting the plague from his own people by transferring it to the enemy. (9.11) Thus, all the fear and anxiety caused by him first threw the front lines of the Latins into confusion and subsequently spread deep into their entire army. (9.12) It was clear to all that, wherever he drove his horse, the ene-mies panicked as if struck by a death-bringing star.[120] Where he fell down, however, his body full with javelins, the perplexed cohorts of the Latins surely fled, leaving a huge space open. (9.13) At the same time the Romans, freed from their fear of the divine wrath, came forth as if the signal was given for the first time, and attacked with full force. (9.14) Even the light-armed troops frequently rushed forward between the first and second ranks and had added their force to that of the soldiers of these ranks, while the reservists waited, kneeling on their right knees, for a signal from the consul to stand up.

8 The *Acts of Appianus* as given in P. Oxy. 33

The translated passage comprises the greatest part of the *Acts of Appianus*, one of the so-called *Acts of the Alexandrians*. It dates from the late second century CE.[121] Appianus was a *gymnasiarch* of Alexandria. This implies that he was the supervisor and probably also a large sponsor of the Alexandrian *gymnasium*.[122] In the imperial period *gymnasia* developed from elite educational institutions devoted to sports and arts into baths with a function not unlike cafés and bars in our culture. However, one should take into account two important differences from present meeting places. The gymnasium was open only to males, Greek citizens and those males of the indige-

---

118 This way of wearing a *toga* derived from the inhabitants of Gabii and was practised especially during Roman religious ceremonies.

119 Decius has become a sacred person, belonging to the realm of the gods and that of the dead, although he still has to complete his mission.

120 Ancient people believed that misfortune like illness was caused by certain movements of the planets.

121 Two papyri together preserve the entire text, P. Yale Inv. 1536 and P. Oxy. 33.

122 Jones (1940), 220–2.

nous population who had acquired Greek citizenship. Appianus was no doubt a very prominent member of the Alexandrian citizenship. The text breaks off before the description of his execution. Apparently, Appianus had accused the emperor, probably Commodus (180–192 CE), of making enormous profits at the expense of Alexandrian ship-owners or merchants, to whom the grain supply of Rome had been farmed out. We know nothing about the events that led to Appianus' arrest. The dialogue between him and Commodus, who was a cruel emperor, especially in his last years before his assassination in 192 CE, is both lively and nicely phrased. With pathos Appianus makes it clear that he does not recognise the emperor's authority, since Commodus' deeds do not justify his position. Instead, Appianus advocates his own political function and noble birth. Being an eminent Alexandrian citizen apparently is worth more than being emperor of the Roman world!

Translation[123]

(col. i 35) And while he was saying this, he turned around, and, seeing Heliodorus, he said: 'Heliodorus, do you have nothing to say while I am being carried away for execution?'[124] Heliodorus said: 'To whom can we talk if we don't have (40) somebody to listen to us? Go to your death quickly, son. The glory of dying for your dearest native city will be yours. Be not distressed.'[125] (col. ii) . . . the emperor called him in. The emperor said: 'Now, don't you know to whom you are speaking?' Appianus: 'I know, Appianus speaks to a tyrant.' The emperor: 'No, to a king.' Appianus: (50) 'Don't say that, since it fitted your father, the divine Antoninus, to be an emperor.[126] Listen,

---

123 This papyrus contains five columns of text and has first been published in Grenfell and Hunt (1898). The text is also given in Musurillo's editions of 1954 and 1961. We follow the numbering of Musurillo's edition of 1954 and leave out those lines of text that offer too little information to make sense of.

124 Helidodorus does not seem to be an Alexandrian. Apparently he was an elderly man whom Appianus got to know in prison.

125 The patriotic motif is very important in the *Acts of the Alexandrians*, see, for example, *Acts of Paulus*, col. vi, *PSI* 1160, lines 5–6, *Acts of Hermaiskos*, col. iii lines 44–5, *Acts of Athenodorus*, col. i, lines 12–18.

126 This name could refer to Antoninus Pius (138–161 CE), or to Marcus Aurelius (161–180 CE). The latter emperor is much more probable, being known as the philosopher-emperor and having a good reputation in Egypt, contrary to his son Commodus.

firstly, he was a philosopher, secondly, he was not greedy for money, and thirdly, he loved goodness. With you it's exactly the opposite: tyranny, (55) hatred of goodness and lack of education.'[127] The emperor ordered him to be taken away.

While he was taken away, Appianus said: (col. iii) 'Grant me just this favour, Lord emperor.' (60) The emperor: 'What?' Appianus: 'Order that I be carried away with the signs of my noble birth.'[128] The emperor: 'All right.' Appianus took his head-band and put it on his head, (65) put his white sandals on and shouted, in the middle of Rome: 'Assemble, Romans. See the spectacle of the age, a *gymnasiarch* and delegate of the Alexandrians being carried away for execution.'[129] The *evo*[*catus*][130] (70) immediately ran to report this to the emperor, saying: 'Lord, are you just sitting at this moment? The Romans are muttering.' The emperor: 'About what?' The consul: 'About the arrest of (col. iv) the Alexandrian.' The emperor: (75) 'Let him be called in.'

Appianus came and said: 'Who has called me in for the second time, one who is welcoming *Hades* as well as those who died before me, Theon, Isidorus and Lampon?[131] (80) Is it the Senate now, or you, chief of robbers?' The emperor: 'Appianus, I am accustomed to chasten people who are morally corrupt or have lost their senses. (85) You speak as long as I want you to speak.' Appian: 'By your *Tyche*,[132] I am neither corrupt nor have I lost my senses. I only tell you about my own noble birth (col. v) and [the things I am entitled to].' (90) The emp[eror: 'How?'] Appianus: 'How I am of noble [birth and a *gymnasi*]arch.' The emperor: ['Are you saying that I] am of low birth?' Appianus: 'That I don't know. I am telling you [about my own] (95) noble birth and [the things I am entit]led to.' [The

127 The emperor is characterized as a tyrant, as in 4 Maccabees the Greek king is. See also *Mart. Pol.* 2.4 according to some MSS.
128 The head-band and white sandals belong to Appianus' *insignia* as a *gymnasiarch*.
129 With Musurillo (1954), 216–17. An alternative translation would be: 'See a *gymnasiarch* and delegate of the Alexandrians being carried away from life.'
130 *Evocatus* is the name for elite veteran soldiers who were re-enlisted after their original service and acted, among other things, as secretaries, guards and executioners.
131 *Hades* is the god of the underworld. Theon, Isidorus and Lampon are earlier Alexandrians, their death or execution is referred to in the *Acts of Isidorus*.
132 *Tyche* refers to the Fortune of the emperor. Christian martyrs refused to swear to this Fortune, see, for example, *Mart. Pol.* 4; 9.2–10.1.

emperor]: 'Now don't you know that . . .'. Appianus: '[If you really don't] know that, I will instruct you.'[133] [First Caesar] (100) has saved Cleopatra . . . He/she got the king[dom] in his/her power, [and, as so]me say, borro[wed money . . .'.[134]

---

133 Appianus shares his eagerness to instruct his opponent with Christian martyrs, see, for example, *Mart. Pol.* 10.1.
134 The text does not offer enough information to give a probable interpretation. Musurillo (1954), 220, follows U. Wilcken and others in assuming that the passage refers to the famous queen Cleopatra VII and Julius Caesar. One would expect that Appianus did refer to an important deed of the Alexandrian citizens, but we can only speculate about this.

2

NOBLE DEATH IN EARLY
JEWISH SOURCES

This chapter concerns martyrdom and related deaths in Jewish literature from the second century BCE to the beginning of the second
century CE. The selected passages come from the Hebrew Bible/Old
Testament (Dan. 3 and 6) and various post-biblical sources. The
General Introduction offers a brief sketch of the presentations of noble
death in most of the selected sources.

General Introduction

Daniel 3 and 6

The oldest Jewish stories of martyrdom are part of Second Maccabees
(about 125 BCE), one of the four books named after the Maccabaean
brothers who rebelled against the Greek king Antiochus IV (see
below). Fourth Maccabees elaborates the martyr stories of the second
book. The First Book of Maccabees focuses on heroes as well, but in a
very different way. It highlights other Maccabees, the five sons of
Mattathias the priest, who become freedom fighters and offer resistance to the Greek authorities that is very different from that of the
martyrs. First Maccabees is primarily interested in the Maccabees'
military and diplomatic results, but offers nevertheless one brief story
of noble death (1 Macc. 6:43–6). The biblical Book of Daniel, which
is about forty years older than 1 and 2 Maccabees, already includes
two stories about the execution of sages from Judaea that closely correspond to the Maccabaean martyr stories. Only the last narrative
element, the death of the hero, is missing in these chapters from
Daniel (Dan. 3 and 6).

  The Book of Daniel is probably the result of a lengthy process of
expansion and reworking. It dates in its present form from about 165
CE. Chapters 1–6 concern wisdom tales with the court of the foreign

king as setting, while Chapters 7–12 offer apocalyptic visions written down by Daniel as seer during three successive world empires. The happy conclusion of Dan. 6 with its notice that Daniel prospered during the reigns of King Darius and King Cyrus (6:28) may once have formed the conclusion of the entire book. Earlier forms of the legends in Chapters 3 and 6 may have already circulated in the fourth or third century BCE.[1] The heroes of these tales, Daniel, Shadrach, Meshach and Abednego, are exiles from Judah who came to serve at the royal court in Babylon (Dan. 1). Dan. 3 and 6 concern dramatic episodes in these four Judaean princes' career as royal administrators at the Babylonian court. Both tales correspond to the paradigm of Ancient Near Eastern wisdom stories about the defamation of a sage by other members of the court (cf. the Story of Ahiqar, see Chapter 1).[2]

The narrative structure of Dan. 3 and 6 corresponds so closely to that of Jewish martyr stories that the tales can be considered forerunners of martyr legends from a form-critical point of view (see Introduction). The structure of both stories is quite similar. After the introductory verses offering the stories' settings (3:1–7; 6:1–3) follow accusation, condemnation and execution (3:8–23; 6:5–18). In both chapters the heroes are actually executed, but they miraculously survive because of God's intervention (3:24–7; 6:19–25). After the deliverance of the sages Nebuchadnezzar promotes this new deity to one of the recognised gods of his empire, which made its cult legitimate (3:28–30; cf. 6:26–8).

In both stories the heroes are executed for their disobedience. In fact, this penalty because of the refusal to worship a deity of state is striking in a Babylonian or Persian–Median context, because the Greek king Antiochus IV (175–164 BCE) seems to have been the first ruler who ordered Judaeans or Jews to be executed for their refusal to perform acts of worship of foreign deities (see below). This implies that the core of the stories in Dan. 3 and 6 may be inspired by Greek conventions. Indeed, Dan. 3 corresponds to Greek traditions about a trial because of ungodliness (*asebeia*). The ungodliness of the accused in these traditions from the classical period onwards could be apparent

---

1 The loan words from Persian in the lists of administrators and musical instruments in Chapter 3 support this assumption. A setting during Antiochus IV's reign, which was disastrous for the Jews, does not fit, since Dan. 3 and 6 do not reflect a persecution of all Judaeans or Jews or an attempt to suppress Jewish religion forever. For further references, see Koch *et al.* (1980); Kratz (1991); Collins (1993), 24–52.

2 Müller (1977); Collins (1975); Wills (1990) with references.

from the profanation of holy places, the contempt of state deities or the introduction of new gods, not recognised by the state. The most famous example of such a trial was the case against Socrates (see Chapter 1).[3]

In any case, the religion of Daniel and his companions is a central element of their identity. The monotheism of the four puts fundamental limits on the state authority at the moment when the king's policy and the Judaeans' religious practice run into conflict with each other. The dialogue between Nebuchadnezzar and the three men in 3:14–18 just before their execution shows their double loyalty and the tension between the authority of the king and that of God. Nebuchadnezzar offers them a second chance, which the three decline with a religious and a political motivation. They refuse not only to serve Nebuchadnezzar's gods but also to pay tribute to his golden statue (3:18). This conflict of loyalty between God and the secular authorities also underlies most Jewish and Christian martyr texts. The political dimension of both stories is highlighted by the fact that there is not only a tension between the foreign authorities and the God of these foreign subjects, but also between the ethnic identities of the young men and the people who accuse them.[4] Shadrach, Meshach and Abednego are accused as Judaeans (3:12).[5] This reference has a double meaning, since the three young men belong not only to a specific people, but are also worshippers of the God of this people. Their accusers are colleagues who are identified as 'Chaldaeans' (3:8).[6] In the Book of Daniel this name indicates a professional class of sages (e.g. 1:4; 2:2, 4, 10; 4:7) as well as an ethnic identity (5:30; 9:1). Daniel 3, therefore, creates a double opposition: the Chaldaeans oppose the Judaeans Shadrach, Meshach and Abednego as professionals, co-administrators, as well as representatives of a different people.[7]

The story of Daniel's deliverance from the lion's den in Dan. 6 is set in the court of King Darius the Mede. While this story is replete with historical details regarding this setting, there are good reasons to think that it is fictitious, dating from a much later period. No Darius was ever

---

3 Josephus lists instances of such trials in his apologetic work *Against Apion* in order to prove that the Greeks despised the deities of other peoples (2.262–7).
4 Cf. Est. 3:8–11; Tob. 1:19.
5 Cf. Ezra 4:12, 23; 5:1, 5; 6:7–8, 14; Neh. 1:2; 3:33; Est. 2:5; 3:4; 5:13.
6 The Chaldaeans were the founders of the Neo-Babylonian empire.
7 With Kuhl (1930), 20; Kratz (1991), 127 and 130 with footnotes 204 and 208.

king of a Median empire. The historical kings with the name Darius were Persians. After the fall of the Babylonian Empire, the Persians became the rulers of 'the ancient world'. The Medes were involved with this kingdom at the same time. The succession of the Babylonian by a Median empire is probably constructed in order to match the scheme of the four successive world empires of the Babylonians, Medes, Persians and Greeks, which figures prominently in Daniel 2 and 7.[8] The outcome of the stories in Dan. 3 and 6 shows that the power of the king is subordinate to that of the God of the Judaeans. The stories may have offered religious as well as political guidelines for those Judaean readers who lived under a foreign government.

1, 2 and 4 Maccabees

As indicated already above, the name 'Maccabees' can be used for a collection of books linked to the Bible, a family of freedom fighters or a group of martyrs. The Second Book of Maccabees contains three stories of noble death. The last of them is a suicide story (2 Macc. 14:37–46). 4 Maccabees has taken up and embellished the martyr stories about the old scribe Eleazar (2 Macc. 6:18–31) and the anonymous mother and her seven sons (2 Macc. 7). Later Jewish literature offers retellings of the story of the mother and her sons only (see Chapter 4). Early Christian sources from the second century CE onwards frequently refer to both legends. Even nowadays visitors to the Roman-Catholic Church of St Andrew can admire a shrine where the relics of the 'Maccabaean martyrs' are supposedly kept. Competitive traditions claim, however, that the remains of the seven brothers are in a marble sarcophagus in the church San Pietro in vincoli in Rome and those of the mother in the church of Agios Georgios of the Greek Orthodox Patriarchate in Istanbul.

The Book of 2 Maccabees is a combination of two letters of invitation to participate in a new festival (1:1–2:18) and a history of liberation of Judaea (Chapters 3–15).[9] The book's historical section basically concerns the liberation of the Judaean temple state from

---

8 Jeremiah's prophecy in Jer. 51:11 may have served as source of inspiration for this construction: 'The Lord has stirred up the spirit of the king of the Medes, because his purpose concerning Babylon is to destroy it' (cf. 51:28 and Isa. 13:17; 21:2).

9 The prologue presents the history as a summary of a five-volume work by Jason of Cyrene (2:23), of whom nothing is known apart from the reference in 2 Macc. 2:23.

the Seleucid oppression during the reigns of Antiochus IV (175–164 BCE), Antiochus V (164–162 BCE) and Demetrius I (162–150 BCE). The author tends to complement the historical reports with brief explanations that ultimately boil down to the belief that the God of Israel determines all human affairs.[10]

The history told in 2 Maccabees 3–15 is closely linked to the Jews of Jerusalem's invitation to their Egyptian fellow-Jews to participate in the festival of liberation in Jerusalem transmitted in the letters of invitation at the beginning of the work (1:1–9 and 1:10–2:18). The narrative pattern's final event in two cycles of events described in the historical part (4:7–10:9 and 14:1–15:36) concerns the institution of a holiday to commemorate Jewish victories. The first one is a feast of liberation on Chislev 25, called the festival of the purification of the temple, which later became known as the festival of Chanukka. It was founded to commemorate the victory over Antiochus IV and the deliverance and purification of the Jerusalem temple told in 10:5–8. This festival forms the occasion for the festal letters at the beginning of the book.[11] The invitation to the Egyptian Jews to participate in a feast of liberation connected with the Jerusalem temple and the explanation of this invitation imply that the work may have received its present form in Jerusalem. The Jerusalem temple is of central importance in the historical part. If the history and festal letters in fact are closely connected, the work may originate from about 124 BCE, the year mentioned in the date of the first festal letter (1:9).[12]

The stories about the noble death of the 90-year-old Eleazar, the mother and her seven sons, and the elder Razis in 2 Macc. 6:18–31, 7:1–42 and 14:37–46 are pivotal according to the narrative pattern in 2 Maccabees. Their noble deaths seem to restore the bond between the Lord and His chosen people and herald the deliverance of the Jews. The martyrdoms in Chapters 6–7 are part of a chain of horrible repressive deeds by representatives of the Seleucid king Antiochus IV.[13] The book informs us without much comment that 80,000 Jews were killed in three days (5:12–14) and that the military commander Apollonius killed many Jews on the Sabbath afterwards (5:25–6).

---

10 For a survey and references, see van Henten (1997), 163–72.
11 The second feast concerns the so-called Day of Nicanor (Adar 13, celebrated just before the date of the feast of Purim). This holiday was founded in commemoration of the Jews' victory over the Seleucid general Nicanor (15:36).
12 Bickermann (1933), 239–41.
13 Gera (1998), 141–61, offers an extensive discussion with references.

Another official, the Athenian Geron, changed the Jerusalem temple into a sanctuary to Olympian Zeus and abolished the Jewish way of life. The fate of some women who had circumcised their sons as well as those people who still celebrated the Sabbath in secret attests to the fact that the Jews were executed without mercy if they remained faithful to their own way of life (6:10–11).

The oldest Jewish writing entirely devoted to noble death is 4 Maccabees. The anonymous work is a discourse with a mixed form, a philosophical treatise on the autonomy of devout reason as well as a eulogy of the Maccabaean martyrs, the heroes of 2 Maccabees.[14] The Maccabaean martyrs are the main characters of the book. However, 4 Maccabees offers its own interpretation of martyrdom. It pays, for example, much more attention to the role of the mother of the seven brothers than 2 Maccabees does.

The detailed descriptions of the martyrdoms substantiate 4 Maccabees' philosophical proposition about the autonomy of devout reason. Scholars have suggested that 4 Maccabees is a composite work based on two different sources, a popular philosophical discourse (*diatribe*) on the autonomy of reason and a funeral oration in commemoration of the Maccabaean martyrs. The text does not offer, however, clear indications that help us to isolate the remains of literary sources. The discourse's composition and content match guidelines and practices in connection with laudatory rhetorics. The coherence between the two main sections, 4 Macc. 1:1–3:18 and 3:19–18:24, and the correspondences of vocabulary and style in both parts make it probable that 1:1–3:18 and 3:19–18:24 belong together from the outset. On the other hand, 2 Maccabees may have been a source for 4 Maccabees. The setting of the martyrdoms and the vocabulary in several sections correspond so closely to what we find in 2 Maccabees that it is very probable that 4 Maccabees' author has made use of 2 Maccabees.[15]

There are only general indications for the date and provenance of 4 Maccabees. Scholars have often suggested Alexandria or Antioch as the work's place of origin as well as a first-century CE date, but

---

14 Manuscripts of the Septuagint include 4 Maccabees, but the ancient Church historian Eusebius refers to 'About the autonomous reason' as the work's title and attributes it to Josephus (*Hist. eccl.* 3.10.3). Some manuscripts of Josephus' works also give the text of 4 Maccabees. For this reason scholars used to refer to the author as Pseudo-Josephus.

15 Van Henten (1997), 58–82, and DeSilva (1998) discuss introductory matters concerning 4 Maccabees.

recently a later date around 100 or even the second century CE has been proposed.[16] A diaspora origin is highly probable, since the references to Jerusalem and Judaea are not important and partly even incorrect. Judaea, Jerusalem and the temple seem to have no actual significance in the work. Jerusalem figures in the summary of the martyrdoms' prehistory in 3:20–4:26, but is not mentioned in the descriptions of the martyrdoms themselves. There is just one other reference to Jerusalem, in 18:5. The location for Jason's gymnasium mentioned in 4:20 ('at the very citadel of our native land') does not correspond to the data given in 1 and 2 Maccabees, and shows that the author did not have detailed knowledge of Jerusalem.[17] The author largely neglects the actual social and political history of the Jews. External cultural items are also unimportant for him, only the proper way of life counts. In particular, the martyrs' statements and behaviour demonstrate the rightness of the philosophical thesis. They lead to the tyrant's defeat, the re-establishment of the Jewish way of life and the restoration of the Jewish polity. The conflict between Antiochus and the Jewish people is narrowed down in 4 Maccabees to a prestigious competition between the martyrs and the king. There are no military battles and Judas the Maccabee does not figure in the book. The steadfastness of the martyrs, their personal conviction and deeds alone bring about the defeat of the tyrant. In this way, 4 Maccabees shows interesting correspondences to the presentation of martyrs in Christian texts.

The philosophical proposition specified in 4 Macc. 1:1–3:18 presents a solution to a basic issue discussed in Graeco-Roman philosophy: the antithesis of reason and emotions. The author uses philosophical vocabulary that frequently shows correspondences with writings stemming from the various philosophical schools in antiquity, but he puts his own views forward.[18] For example, contrary to views put forward by philosophers from the Stoa, one of these schools, the author does not focus on stamping out the emotions but on controlling them with the help of reason. Thus, 4 Maccabees seems to advocate a Jewish philosophy of its own. This is apparent from

---

16 Van Henten (1986); Klauck (1989), 668–9; Campbell (1992), 221–4. Cf. Dupont-Sommer (1939), 75–82.

17 Cf. 1 Macc. 1:33–4; 3:45; 2 Macc. 15:31, 35.

18 The author of 4 Maccabees incorporates philosophical notions deriving from several philosophical schools. For details and references, see Renehan (1972); Klauck (1989), 708–14; Weber (1991); van Henten (1997), 273–88.

explicit references to such a philosophy (5:22, 35; 7:9, 21; 8:1) as well as from a shift in the presentation of the famous four cardinal virtues. In 1:18 the author mentions these four virtues as we know them from non-Jewish philosophical writings (prudence, courage, self-control and justice); but in 5:23–4 he lists them again in Eleazar's discussion with the tyrant and replaces prudence by piety (*eusebeia*). Piety is presented as the basis of Jewish philosophy (cf. 1:4, 6; 2:6, 23; 13:24; 15:10).[19]

Philo

Despite the enormous volume of his work, the Jewish philosopher Philo pays very little attention to the theme of noble death. He does not even describe the violent deaths of the Alexandrian Jews during the pogrom in 38 CE[20] with motifs of noble death, despite his two extensive writings dealing with this pogrom: the *Discourse against Flaccus* (*In Flaccum*), and the *Embassy to Gaius* (*Legatio ad Gaium*).[21] Philo describes the theme of noble death only in his ideal presentation of Judaism in his *Every Good Person is Free* (see below).

Josephus

Contrary to Philo, the Jewish historian Josephus (37 CE – about 100 CE)[22] highlights noble death wherever he can, despite the fact that he did his best to convince his audience that he tried hard to calm down the Jews during their war against the Romans in 66–70 CE. Josephus fulfilled a prominent role in this war in Galilee as one of the Jewish generals.[23] The future emperor Vespasian besieged him in the spring of 67 in the mountains at Jotapata (Galilee). After a siege of seven weeks Jotapata was given up and Josephus was taken captive after he miraculously survived his men's collective suicide (*War* 3.141–391). The fulfilment of his prophecy that Vespasian would

19 Weber (1991); van Henten (1997), 278–84.
20 Discussions of this brutal episode are offered by Smallwood (1981), 235–50, and Modrzejewski (1997), 229–39.
21 For a survey of the content of these works and their connection with Philo's other *œuvre*, see Morris (1986), 859–64, who argues that the two writings originally were part of a collection of five books concerning persecutors of the Jews and their well-deserved punishment.
22 Rajak (1983) and Bilde (1988) offer readable introductions and many references.
23 See the persuasive argument by Cohen (1979).

become emperor prevented him from being thrown in prison for life or taken to Rome in order to participate in the march of triumph there and be executed afterwards. Vespasian released him, gave him one of his houses, lands in Judaea and an annual salary. Josephus spent the rest of his life among the elite in Rome, writing four works in thirty volumes on Jewish history and culture primarily for civilised Greeks and Romans. His extensive writings have become a major source in the study of Judaean history from 200 BCE to about 75 CE as well as the matrix of Christian origins, which explains why some have even called Josephus the fifth evangelist.

The first part of Josephus' *Jewish Antiquities* offers extensive retellings of biblical events.[24] Josephus' additions to the biblical stories show a trend to stress the nobility of the death of his heroes. His version of Isaac's Binding (Gen. 22) adds a reference to Isaac's joy about his being sacrificed to God (*Ant.* 1.223–36, especially 232). Some of Josephus' reports about post-biblical events also emphasise noble death, such as Josephus' two descriptions of the removal of the golden eagle from the temple roof. A group of young men were responsible for the removal of this despicable tribute to Rome. Josephus describes Herod's interrogation of these men and their execution afterwards (*War* 1.648–55; *Ant.* 17.156–64). This episode includes a prominent dialogue with the king. Herod acts in these passages like the foreign king in stories about martyrdom. He interrogates the young men after their arrest and asks them whether it was they who had dared to take down the golden eagle. The boys confess[25] and justify their deed in a way that reminds one of the Maccabaean martyrs' refusal to give in to Antiochus IV (*War* 1.652–3; cf. *Ant.* 17.158–60). They tell Herod that 'the ancestral law' (*ho patrios nomos*) ordered them to remove the eagle.[26] Later Herod asks why they were so cheerful even though they faced execution. They answer him that they were happy since they would enjoy even greater happiness after death, a hint at their posthumous vindication.

Josephus' apologetic work *Against Apion*, which refutes the accusations against the Jews made by the Alexandrian grammarian Apion

---

24 Bilde (1988) offers a survey of Josephus' writings.
25 On confessions in martyr texts, see Buschmann (1994), 113–14, 117–19, 193–5, 205, 229–32, 251–3; van Henten (1997), 89–90; 237–8.
26 *War* 1.653. In *Ant.* 7.159 they contrast the king's decrees to Moses' laws, which echoes the stories in Dan. 3 and 6 as well as the martyr stories in 2 and 4 Maccabees; van Henten (1997), 10–14.

and others, contains a passage that suggests that the Jewish people were unique because of their attitude towards suffering and self-sacrifice (*Ap.* 2.225–35). Josephus compares the Jews to the Spartans, who had an outstanding military reputation. They were famous for their contempt of death, obedience to the laws and particular system of education. Josephus concludes that the Jews surpassed even the Spartans, by noting that the Spartans remained faithful to their laws only as long as they were independent, while the Jews had never betrayed their laws, not even during the most extreme sufferings (*Ap.* 2.226–8). The passage about the Masada suicide translated below shows not only Josephus' tendency to highlight the noble death of Jews, but also his own ambiguity about such a death.

1 Daniel 3 in the Hebrew Bible/ the Old Testament

Nebuchadnezzar's decision to erect an enormous golden statue with rather strange proportions – it is ten times higher than it is wide – is the point of departure of the story in Dan. 3.[27] It is impossible to identify a historical core, although several particularities have parallels in non-biblical sources. Huge statues of gods, for example, were erected in Babylon for Zeus as well as in Daphne, near the source of the River Jordan, for Apollo. With its height of 70 cubits (about 105 feet) the famous Colossus of Rhodes was even 10 cubits higher than Nebuchadnezzar's statue. An exhaustive list of officials had to worship the statue as representatives of the various peoples and language groups of the Babylonian kingdom. The Aramaic text distinguishes between the god represented by the statue and the king (3:12, 14, 18), but the Old Greek translation identifies the two, which implies the veneration of the ruler.[28] The repeated references to the musical instruments and officials and their falling on their knees as a sign of the veneration[29] of the statue create the impression of a gigantic manifestation of loyalty to the king. The statue's god may be

---

27 As well as the commentaries, Kuhl (1930) is still useful for details.
28 Some scholars suggest that the story may be reminiscent of the promotion of the god Sin by the last Babylonian king Nabonidus, implying that Nabonidus has been confused with Nebuchadnezzar. Cf. Jdt 3:8 on Holophernes' orders that every people should worship Nebuchadnezzar alone and that every tribe and language group should invoke him as god.
29 Cf. Deut. 4:19; 8:19.

considered the principal state god, who protected the king and made him triumph. Its veneration, therefore, was a demonstration of loyalty to Nebuchadnezzar as well. A refusal would, of course, be a manifest act of civil disobedience.

The execution by fire is a motif that is found in many martyr stories, but there are also parallels in legal and other texts from several periods and locations in the ancient world.[30] Execution by burning is already mentioned in the *Codex Hammurabi* as a punishment for several crimes. It is a biblical punishment as well, among other things for a man and a mother with her daughter if the man had sexual intercourse with both women, and for prostitution by a priest's daughter (Lev. 20:14; 21:9).[31]

Translation[32]

(1) King Nebuchadnezzar[33] made a golden statue. Its height was 60 cubits and its width was 6 cubits. He set it up in the valley of Dura[34] in the province of Babylon. (2) And King Nebuchadnezzar sent for the satraps, prefects, governors, counsellors, treasurers, judges, police officers, (in short) all the officials of the provinces so that they would come to the dedication of the statue that King Nebuchadnezzar had erected. (3) Thereupon the satraps, prefects, governors, counsellors, treasurers, judges, police officers, (in short) all the officials of the

---

30 2 Macc. 7 and 4 Macc.; *T.B. Avodah Zarah* 17b-18a; *Sifre Deut.* 307; *Semahot* 8; *Kallah* 18c; *Mart. Pol.* 11–18. Cf. also the punishment of Harsiesis in the *Wisdom Instruction of Onchsheshonqy*, Lichtheim (1980); Herodotus 1.86; Plutarch, *De Isid.* 73; Eusebius, *Praep. ev.* 9.39.1–5, Holladay (1983), 132–3; Pseudo-Philo, *Biblical Antiquities* 6.

31 See also Gen. 38:24; Jer. 29:21–2 on the false prophets Zedekiah and Ahab executed by Nebuchadnezzar in Babylon.

32 Translation based on Elliger and Rudolph (1977).

33 The story does not contain a date. Nebuchadnezzar ruled from 606/605–562 BCE. The story in Dan. 2 is situated in his second year (2:1) and the same date may be implied for Dan. 3. The Greek translations add a reference to Nebuchadnezzar's eighteenth year (587/586 BCE), during which the major deportation of Judaeans to Babylon took place.

34 Dura derives from a Mesopotamian word meaning 'outer wall' or 'enclosure' and can also be part of a compound geographical name (e.g. Dur-Karashu). Several locations have been proposed, among others the vicinity of the large cities of Uruk, Ur and Babylon. Because of the prominent presence of court officials in Dan. 1–6, the latter option is the most likely. On the other hand, since the king is clearly apocryphal the geographical name may well be fictitious.

provinces assembled for the dedication of the statue that King Nebuchadnezzar had erected, and were standing before the statue that King Nebuchadnezzar had erected. (4) And the herald read aloud: 'You, peoples, nations and (people of different) languages, are commanded: (5) "When you hear the sound of the horn, the pipe, the zither, the *sambuke*,[35] the harp, the double-flute, (in short) all kinds of music, you shall fall down and prostrate yourself before the golden statue that King Nebuchadnezzar has erected, (6) and whoever does not fall down and prostrate himself will immediately be thrown into the furnace of blazing fire".' (7) Therefore, when all the peoples heard the sound of the horn, the pipe, the zither, the *sambuke*, the harp, the double-flute, (in short) all kinds of music, all the peoples, nations and (people of different) languages fell down and prostrated themselves before the golden statue that King Nebuchadnezzar had erected.

(8) Accordingly, at that time some Chaldaean men[36] came forward and denounced the Judaeans. (9) They said to King Nebuchadnezzar: 'O king, live forever! (10) You, O king, issued a decree that everyone who hears the sound of the horn, the pipe, the zither, the *sambuke*, the harp, the double-flute, (in short) all kinds of music shall fall down and prostrate himself before the golden statue (11) and whoever does not fall down and prostrate himself will be thrown into the furnace of blazing fire. (12) There are certain Judaean men whom you have appointed to administer the province of Babylon, Shadrach, Meshach and Abednego. These men do not pay attention to you, O king, they do not worship your god and they do not prostrate themselves before the golden statue that you have erected.'

(13) Then Nebuchadnezzar, in fury and anger,[37] ordered Shadrach, Meshach and Abednego to be brought. Thereupon these men were brought before the king. (14) Nebuchadnezzar said to them: 'Is it true, Shadrach, Meshach and Abednego, that you do not worship my god and that you do not prostrate yourself before the golden statue that I have erected? (15) Now if you are prepared at the time when you hear the sound of the horn, the pipe, the zither, the *sambuke*, the harp, the double-flute, (in short) all kinds of music to fall down and prostrate yourself before the statue that I have made, (well and good);

35 The *sambuke* was a triangular instrument of four strings which produced high notes.
36 See the General Introduction to this chapter, p. 44.
37 The anger of Nebuchadnezzar (also 3:19) corresponds to the response of kings and other officials to the disobedience by martyrs to their decrees, see, e.g. 2 Macc. 7:3.

but if you do not prostrate yourself, you shall immediately be thrown into the furnace of blazing fire. And who is the god that can save you from my hands?' (16) Shadrach, Meshach and Abednego said to King Nebuchadnezzar: 'We do not need to give you an answer on this matter. (17) If our God whom we serve is able to save us from the furnace of blazing fire, He will also save us from your hands, O King.[38] (18) Indeed, no, O King! Let it be known to you, that we shall not worship your god and that we will not prostrate ourselves before the golden statue that you have erected.'

(19) Thereupon, Nebuchadnezzar was so filled with anger at Shadrach, Meshach and Abednego that his face was distorted. And he ordered the furnace to be heated to a level seven times more than what was customary. (20) And he ordered some of the strong men of his army to bind Shadrach, Meshach and Abednego and to throw them into the furnace of blazing fire. (21) Thereupon these men were bound, wearing their trousers, shirts, hats,[39] (in short) their cloths. And they were thrown into the furnace of blazing fire.

(22) Since the king's order was urgent and the furnace was overheated, the flames of fire killed those men who escorted Shadrach, Meshach and Abednego, (23) but these three men, Shadrach, Meshach and Abednego, fell into the furnace of blazing fire while being bound.[40] (24) Thereupon King Nebuchadnezzar was amazed and rose up quickly. He said to his ministers: 'Did we not throw three bound men inside the fire?' And they said to the king: 'Certainly, O king.' (25) He said: 'Behold, I see four men, unbound and unhurt, walking in the middle of the fire without being hurt; and the fourth looks like a son of the gods.'[41] (26) Thereupon Nebuchadnezzar approached the

---

38 The Aramaic clause can be subdivided in several ways and is open to several interpretions, Collins (1993), 187–8.

39 The translation of the words indicating the clothes of the three men is far from certain. Instead of 'hats' one could, for instance, also read 'coats'.

40 Verse 23 may seem redundant and is left out by some scholars. It is missing in the Old Greek translation, which may, however, be caused by the insertion of a prose passage with an explanation of the miracle and the poetic additions of Azariah's prayer and the three men's Hymn of Thanks. From a narrative point of view, these additions fill striking gaps in the story concerning the way the three were rescued, the motives for their refusal and their feelings during the execution.

41 The verse presupposes a cluster of miracles: falling into the furnace does not harm the men, like ancient Houdinis they are quickly unbound, the fire does not harm them and 'a son of the gods' appears. The last expression matches a polytheistic context. Verse 28 interprets the figure as an angel. Christian tradition

opening of the furnace with blazing fire and said: 'Shadrach, Meshach, and Abednego, servants of the Highest God: Come out!'. Thereupon Shadrach, Meshach and Abednego came out from inside the fire. (27) And the assembled satraps, prefects, governors, and ministers of the king saw that the fire had no power over the bodies of those men and that the hair of their heads was not singed and that their trousers were not changed, and the smell of fire was not on them. (28) Nebuchadnezzar said: 'Blessed be the God of Shadrach, Meshach and Abednego, who sent His angel and saved His servants who trusted in Him, they who transgressed the edict of the king and gave their bodies so that they should not worship and prostrate themselves for any god except their own God. (29) I have issued a decree that any people, nation, or language saying something contemptuous of the God of Shadrach, Meshach and Abednego will be torn limb by limb and his house will be made into a dunghill; for there is no other god who is able to save like this.' (30) Thereupon the king promoted Shadrach, Meshach, and Abednego in the province of Babylon.[42]

2 Daniel 6 in the Hebrew Bible/ the Old Testament

As in Daniel 3 religious practice and politics go hand in hand in Daniel 6.[43] Daniel is a worshipper of the God of the Judaeans, but also a high government official, being in the second position in the kingdom. The other satraps and ministers envy him and induce the king to promulgate a decree in order to get rid of him. Ethnic tensions may be apparent from Daniel's accusation that does not mention his position at the court,[44] but refers to him as 'one of the exiles of Judah'

---

sometimes supposes that Jesus Christ was this son of the gods, which corresponds to his comforting role of martyrs in Christian martyr texts.

42 The Aramaic text continues with a few verses that form the beginning of the story in Chapter 4 despite the fact that a doxology usually comes at the end of a narrative section. The verses were assigned to Chapter 3 only by the division of chapters in the Vulgate attributed to Stephen Langton (thirteenth century).

43 Cf. Levinger (1977). The story of Bel and the Dragon, belonging to the so-called apocryphal or deutero-canonical Books of the Old Testament, shows correspondences with Dan. 6 (including the lions' den), but it focuses on the unmasking of idols.

44 The Old Greek differs from the Aramaic text and refers in 6:14 to Daniel as the king's friend, which indicates a high position in the king's service, cf. 2 Macc. 7:24.

(6:14). The king is well disposed towards his Judaean official, but lets himself nevertheless be manipulated by 'those men' (6:6), in fact, all the other satraps who use Daniel's religion to accuse him (6:5). The redundant description of the opposition of all satraps united against Daniel by the repetition of 'went in a throng to the king' (6:7, 12, 16) emphasises the foreignness and particular ethnic identity of Daniel.

The royal decree (6:13) functions as a test case for the recognition of the king's absolute authority and also has religious implications. It forbids requests from any god or human being except the king for thirty days, which may hint at a divine status for the king. As a worshipper of the God of the Judaeans, Daniel is manoeuvred into an awkward position. The trap anticipates the confirmation of his double loyalty, towards the king and towards his God. The decree carries a horrible death penalty (6:8, 13, 17–18).[45] There is no evidence that a kind of pit closed with a stone in the ancient world served as a means to execute people. The penalty may originate in a creative adoption of biblical passages about lions.[46]

Translation[47]

(1) And Darius the Mede received the kingdom at the age of about sixty-two. (2) It pleased Darius to appoint 120 satraps in the kingdom to be stationed throughout the entire kingdom; (3) and over them three royal ministers of whom Daniel was one. These satraps were accountable to them, so that the king would not be troubled. (4) Then Daniel became more successful than the other royal ministers and satraps, since a powerful spirit rested upon him, so that the king was considering appointing him over the entire kingdom.[48] (5) Thereupon

---

45 See Bentzen (1950); Cassin (1951); Haag (1983), 86.
46 In Ezek. 19:4, 8–9 the image of a pit is used to symbolise Israel as a lioness being caught by the nations. Cf. Ps. 57:4. Daniel's rescue from the lions may be inspired by Ps. 22:21: '(O Lord . . .) Save me from the mouth of the lion'. Cf. a passage in the Babylonian text *Ludlul Bel Nemeqi*: 'It was Marduk who put a muzzle on the mouth of the lion who was eating me', referred to by Collins (1993), 267.
47 Translation and numbering based on Elliger and Rudolph (1977).
48 Daniel's position reminds one of Joseph's career in Egypt. Potiphar left everything in the hands of Joseph and had no other concern than the 'food' he ate (Gen. 39:6), which may refer to Potiphar's wife. Later on Joseph became the second person in the Egyptian kingdom (Gen. 41:41–4).
49 The irrevocability of a law of the Medes and Persians is stated in Dan. 6:8, 12,

the royal ministers and the satraps sought a pretext against Daniel in connection with his work for the kingdom, but they could not find any ground or fault, since he was trustworthy. No negligence or fault was found in him. (6) Thereupon these men said: 'We will not find any pretext against this Daniel, except what we find against him in connection to the law of his God.' (7) Thereupon these royal ministers and satraps together came to the king, and so they said to him: 'King Darius, live forever! (8) All royal ministers of the kingdom, prefects, satraps, counsellors and governors recommend that the king should issue an edict strongly prohibiting anyone praying to any god or human person apart from you during the next thirty days, O king, lest they shall be thrown into the lions' den. (9) Now, O king, issue the prohibition and write the document so that it cannot be changed, like a law of the Medes and Persians which may not be invalidated.'[49] (10) Therefore King Darius wrote the document and the prohibition. (11) When Daniel learned that the document had been written, he went to his house. The windows of his upper room looked towards Jerusalem.[50] Three times a day he fell on his knees,[51] prayed and thanked his God, as he had done for a long time. (12) Thereupon these men came together and found Daniel praying and entreating his God. (13) Then they approached the king and reminded him of the prohibition: 'O king, have you not written a prohibition that every person who will pray to any god or human being within thirty days except to you, O king, will be thrown into the lions' den?' The king replied and said: 'The pronouncement is solid like a law of the Medes and Persians, which may not be invalidated.' (14) Then they replied and said before the king: 'Daniel, who belongs to the exiles of Judah, does not pay attention to you, O king, nor to the prohibition you have written. Three times a day he prays his prayer.' (15) When the king heard the statement, he was very upset and set his mind on saving Daniel. And he exhausted himself working until sunset to rescue him. (16) Thereupon these men came together to

---

15 (cf. Est. 1:19) and is implied by the context as well. It does not correspond to references to these laws in non-biblical sources.

50 Praying towards Jerusalem is already mentioned in Solomon's prayer of dedication of the temple (1 Kings 8:35–44). See also Ps. 5:7 and 138:2.

51 This description of Daniel's private prayer corresponds to data in some other texts (kneeling: cf. Ezra 9:5; Luke 22:41; Acts 9:40; three times a day: cf. Ps. 55:17), but there is no indication that there was a fixed practice of praying that Daniel followed. Several Jewish authors from the Second Temple period refer to prayers twice a day. Rabbinic passages prescribe a morning, afternoon and evening prayer and sometimes refer to Dan. 6 in this connection (*T.B. Berakhot* 31a).

the king and said to the king: 'Know, O king, that it is a law of the Medes and Persians that every prohibition and edict that the king issues cannot be changed.' (17) Thereupon the king gave the command and they brought Daniel and threw him into the lions' den. The king said to Daniel: 'May your God, whom you worship constantly, save you.' (18) A stone was brought and placed over the opening of the den and the king sealed it [the stone] with his signet ring and the signet rings of his ministers so that nothing might be changed concerning Daniel. (19) Thereupon the king went to his palace and spent the night fasting. They did not bring food[52] to him and his sleep fled from him. (20) Then, at dawn, the king rose at daylight and went in haste to the lions' den. (21) And when he approached the den the king cried out with a sad voice to Daniel and said to him: 'Daniel, servant of the living God,[53] has your God, whom you worship constantly, been able to save you from the lions?' (22) Thereupon Daniel spoke to the king: 'O king, live forever! (23) My God has sent His angel[54] and He has shut the mouth of the lions, so that they did not harm me, because I was found innocent before Him; and before you too, O King, I have done no crime.' (24) Thereupon the king was greatly pleased for him and he commanded Daniel to be brought up out of the den. And Daniel was taken up out of the den and no injury was found on him because he trusted in his God. (25) And the king commanded that these men who had accused Daniel be brought in. And they threw them with their sons and their wives in the lions' den. And before they reached the bottom of the den, the lions overpowered them and crushed all their bones. (26) Thereupon King Darius wrote to all peoples, nations and (people of different) languages that live on the entire earth: 'May your peace abound! (27) I establish a decree that in every dominion of my kingdom people should tremble and fear the god of Daniel. For He is the living God and endures forever. And His

---

52 The food may be a euphemism for bedmates (cf. n. 48).

53 This designation of God occurs already in older passages of the Hebrew Bible (Deut. 5:26; Josh. 3:10) and contrasts the Lord with the deities of the nations. The exclamation 'king, live forever!' may hint at a parallelism between God and Darius, with an acknowledgement, of course, of their principally different powers (6:7, 22).

54 A supernatural anonymous messenger of the Lord is often mentioned in the Hebrew Bible. As in Dan. 3 the angel brings about the divine rescue. The story of *Bel and the Snake* is more explicit about the angel of the Lord. It notes that this angel transported Habakkuk in one day from Judah to Babylon and back by carrying him by his hair, in order to bring Daniel a meal in the lion's den (vv. 33–9).

kingdom shall not be destroyed and His rule will be endless. (28) He saves and delivers and does signs and wonders in heaven and on earth, because He saved Daniel from the power of the lions.' (29) And this Daniel was successful during the reign of Darius and Cyrus the Persian.

3 Prayer of Azariah = Dan. 3:24–45 in the Septuagint version

The process of reinterpretation of the story of the deliverance of Daniel's three companions had already started in the second century BCE with additions to the original Aramaic text of Dan. 3 in the Greek translations. The first of these expansions, translated below, associates the execution of the three with a burnt offering. The Septuagint translation of this passage also hints at a death of atonement. This first addition is called the Prayer of Azariah. It concerns Dan. 3:24–45 in the Greek translations of the Hebrew Bible.[55] The prayer is called after Azariah, which is the Hebrew name of one of the three Judahites who were thrown into Nebuchadnezzar's furnace according to Dan. 3. The Greek translations use the Hebrew names Azariah, Mishael and Hananiah for Daniel's companions.[56]

The prayer is inserted into Dan. 3 at the moment the three are actually executed, that is, between verses 23 and 24. In this way, the reader gets the impression that the young men say the prayer when they fall into the furnace. At first sight it may look like a personal cry of despair in the three's very last seconds. The prayer actually does refer to the context of the young men in the furnace, but is strongly influenced by conventions of collective prayer as reflected in the Hebrew Bible (for example, the collective prayer and confession of sins in Neh. 9:6–37). Azariah's prayer may have originally circulated separately from the Book of Daniel. The Greek text can easily be re-translated into Hebrew, so that a Hebrew source is a serious possibility. In any case, in its present form the Prayer probably dates from the second half of the second century BCE, because the allusions to historical events in 3:28, 32 can best be explained against the background of the repression of Antiochus IV in Jerusalem (see the General Introduction).[57]

55 Unless indicated otherwise, we use the edition and numbering by Rahlfs (1935).
56 For commentary and further references, see Kuhl (1930); Moore (1977); Koch (1987).
57 So, among others, Collins (1993), 200–1, 203.

Translation[58]

(24) Thus prayed Hananiah, Azariah and Mishael. They began to sing to the Lord, at the moment when the king ordered that they had to be thrown into the furnace.

(25) And Azariah stood up and prayed as follows. He opened his mouth and praised the Lord together with his companions in the middle of the fire of the furnace, which was heated exceedingly from below by the Chaldaeans.[59] And they said:

(26) Blessed are You, O Lord, God of our fathers, worthy of praise and glory is Your name forever!

(27) Because You are just in everything that You have done, and all Your works are truthful and Your ways right, and all Your judgements are truthful.

(28) You have taken truthful decisions in everything which You have brought upon us and upon Jerusalem, the holy city of our ancestors. Since You have done all these things by a truthful judgement because of our sins.

(29) We have sinned in every respect and we have acted against the law by turning away from You. We have erred in every respect and did not obey to the commandments of Your law.

(30) We have not kept and have not done what You have commanded us, so that things would be good for us.

(31) Thus, everything which You have brought upon us and everything which You have done to us You have done by a truthful judgement.

(32) You have handed us over to our enemies, lawless people and the most hostile rebels, to an unjust king, the most wicked person on earth.

(33) So we cannot open our mouth, we, Your servants, those who worship You, have become an object of shame and reproach.

(34) Do not hand us over forever for Your name's sake.[60]

---

58 The translation is based on the Septuagint version of the Prayer. Theodotion's version of the Greek additions to the Book of Daniel proves to be secondary to the Septuagint version. It tends to solve difficulties in the Septuagint text by abridgement and/or simplification, Schüpphaus (1971); Engel (1985), 55–7.

59 For the Chaldaeans, see the General Introduction to this chapter, p. 44.

60 The appeal to God mentions three reasons that also occur in Jewish prayers of

Do not scatter (the people of) Your covenant.[61]
(35) Do not withdraw Your mercy from us
for the sake of Abraham, Your beloved,
and for the sake of Isaac, Your servant,
and Israel, Your holy one,
(36) when You have spoken to them saying to multiply their offspring
like the stars of heaven and the sand of the shore of the sea.
(37) Since, Master, we have been diminished more than any other
people,[62]
and presently we are of no account on the entire earth because of our sins.
(38) In this period we have no ruler, nor a prophet nor a leader,
no burnt offering, nor a sacrifice, nor an offering of food or incense.[63]
We have no place to offer fruit to You and to find mercy.
(39) May we be accepted with our broken heart and humbled spirit,[64]
as though we came with burnt offerings of rams and bullocks
and with thousands of fat lambs.[65]
(40) Let our sacrifice be as such before You this day.
And let Yourself be atoned[66] (from) behind You,[67]

---

lamentation and deliverance: (a) God's glorious name (3:34); (b) the covenant with
God's people (3:34–5); and (c) the appeal to God's mercy (3:35). Cf. Ezra 9:5–15;
Neh. 9; Dan. 9:3–19; Baruch 1:15–3:8 and the Greek versions of Esther 4.

61 Or: 'Do not annul Your covenant.'

62 The appeal is being upheld by the conclusion that Israel suffered more than any
other people. Cf. Neh. 9:32; *As. Mos.* 9:3; Josephus, *Ap.* 2.225–35.

63 Verses 38b–40 suggest that the temple cult did not function at the time of the
prayer and refer to something that replaces this cult.

64 Allusion to Ps. 51 (50 in the Septuagint). This psalm depicts a situation in
Judah when the walls of Jerusalem were destroyed and God took no delight in
sacrifices (51[50]:18. Cf. Dan. 3:28, 32, 37–8.

65 The prayer alludes to prophetic passages that are critical about the temple cult,
such as Isa. 1:11–20 and especially Mic. 6:6–8. Both Mic. 6 and Isa. 1 emphasise that a righteous way of life is more important than a temple offering. This
is the background of Dan. 3:39's allusion to Micah's rhetorical question whether
God would be pleased by the offering of thousands of rams or ten thousand rivers
of oil (or: fat lambs).

66 The reference to atonement in the Greek text (*exilasai*) is far from clear. The verbal
form can here only be a second person singular imperative of the aoristus middle
voice of *exilaskomai*, usually translated as 'atone for', 'make atonement' or 'propitiate'.
In the passive voice the simplex can also mean 'to be merciful', *LSJ* 594 and 828.

67 Some scholars interpret '(from) behind You' as 'before You' or assume that the
reading goes back to a corruption of the Hebrew or Aramaic source, Kuhl (1930),
146–7. The phrase may, however, just indicate the location where the atonement
was supposed to take place. God's backside is referred to in Gen. 16:13 and Exod.
33:23, Lindblom (1961), 102 n. 21; *KBL*³ I, p. 34.

because there is no disgrace to those who put their trust in You,
and consecrate[68] (from) behind You.[69]
(41) And now with all our heart we follow You and fear You,
we seek Your presence, do not put us to shame,
(42) but deal with us according to Your fairness
and the abundance of Your mercy.
(43) Deliver us in accordance with Your wonderful deeds
and bring glory to Your name, Lord.
(44) May all who harmed Your servants be put to shame,
be dishonoured and lose all their power,
and may their strength be shattered.
(45) They must know that You alone are the Lord God,
famous over the whole world.

4 1 Maccabees 6:43–6

1 Maccabees is a history of the liberation of the Jews from Antiochus
IV's tyranny. It is at the same time a success story of the dynasty of the
Maccabees whose first generations are presented as the founding
fathers of a new Judaean state. 1 Maccabees describes the deeds of
three generations of Maccabees acting as leaders of the rebellion
against the Seleucids: (a) Mattathias the priest; (b) his five sons,
named Judas, Simon, Jonathan, John and Eleazar; and (c) his only
remaining grandson John Hyrcanus. 1 Maccabees offers a clever legit-
imisation of the power of the Maccabaean rulers (also called
Hasmonaeans) and probably originated in circles close to the
Hasmonaean court of John Hyrcanus around 125 BCE.[70]

1 Maccabees depicts all five sons of Mattathias as being prepared
to die for their people and the Judaean state (1 Macc. 2:42, 50;
9:10; 11:23; 13:4; 14:29), in line with their father's wishes as presented to them on his deathbed (2:49–70). Judas dies nobly, after
many glorious fights, in a hopeless battle against the Seleucid general Bacchides (9:11–21). Eleazar also dies on the battlefield in a

---

68 In the Septuagint the Greek for 'consecrate' usually refers to the installation of
   priests.
69 Theodotion's version of v. 40 is different: 'Let our sacrifice be as such before You
   this day. Consider it as perfect, so that no disgrace shall come to those who put
   their trust in You.'
70 For introductory information about 1 Maccabees, see Schürer (1973–87),
   3.180–5; Attridge (1984), 171–6. Martola (1984) and Williams (1999) analyse
   the book's composition.

way that measures up to the *devotio* of a Roman general (see Chapter 1).[71] Eleazar sacrifices himself in an attempt to kill the Seleucid king Antiochus V Eupator during the Battle of Beth-Zechariah (162 BCE), south of Jerusalem (1 Macc. 6:32–54). The battle did not end well for the Jews. The focus is upon the king's thirty-two war elephants that were fed juice of grapes and mulberries to arouse them to fight. Eleazar attacks the largest of these elephants in an attempt to kill the king and in this way saves the face of the Jews who lost the battle.[72]

Translation[73]

(6:43) Eleazar Avaran[74] saw that one of the animals was covered with royal coats of mail.[75] It exceeded all the other animals, and he believed that the king was on it. (6:44) He gave his life to save his people and to achieve for himself an everlasting name.[76] (6:45) Boldly he ran over to the line of battle and killed soldiers right and left, and they parted before him on either side.[77] (6:46) He got unto the elephant, stabbed it from beneath[78] and killed it, but it fell to the ground on top of him and he died there.

---

71 Eleazar's death did not have, however, the beneficial outcome of a *devotio*, which may partly explain Josephus' cynical comment in the margin of his report of Eleazar's noble death (*War* 1.42–4).

72 Adinolfi (1969), 103–22, questions the interpretation of 1 Macc. 6:43–6 as a noble death story.

73 Based on Rahlfs (1935).

74 'Avaran' is Eleazar's second name, perhaps a nickname. Depending on the Hebrew root the name is associated with, it may mean 'paleface', 'agitated one' or hint at Eleazar's way of dying.

75 Elephants were part of Persian, Roman and Greek armies and depictions of them in coats of mail have been shown on coins. 2 Macc. 13:15 also suggests that Seleucid armies included elephants.

76 The reference in 6:44 implies that Eleazar followed his father's incitation in 2:51 'Remember the deeds of the ancestors, which they did in their generations; and you will receive great honour and an everlasting name'. Judas and Jonathan also die a glorious death (1 Macc. 9:10; 13:29).

77 Eleazar had to kill an unbelievable number of soldiers before he could reach the elephant, since 1 Macc. 6:35 explains that 1,000 heavy-armed soldiers and 500 horsemen accompanied every elephant.

78 The Greek is not very specific, using the same verb as in 2 Macc. 14:41 for Razis' suicide. The Lucian recension is more clear, reading 'he gave it [the elephant] the sword'.

NOBLE DEATH IN EARLY JEWISH SOURCES

5 2 Maccabees 6:18–31

2 Maccabees 6:18–31 and 7 presume a context of obligatory participation in Gentile religious activities. Eleazar and the mother with
her seven sons are forced to eat the meat of pigs (6:18, 21; 7:1)
during some sort of ritual meal (*splangchnismos*, 6:21; 7:42), which is
part of the persecution by Antiochus (see the General Introduction).
The Greek phrase referring to this ritual may imply that the martyrs
had to eat some of the inward parts of a pig, which was forbidden
according to the Jewish Law (Lev. 11:7; Deut. 14:8). 2 Maccabees
6:7 suggests that such meals were organised every month as part of
the king's birthday's celebration. 1 Maccabees 1:47 presents a different picture of the king's instructions about pigs: Jerusalem and
the other cities of Judah had to sacrifice swine and other unclean
animals. If the ritual meal in 2 Maccabees is not historical, the
detail that it concerned swine's flesh may have been added to
increase the king's monstrosity. Razis' suicide (14:37–46) occurs in
the context of an attack by the Seleucid general Nicanor
(14:1–15:36). Like the martyrs, he decides to die rather than surrender to the Greeks.

The martyr stories in Chapters 6–7 offer little information about
the arrest, interrogation and execution of the martyrs. They focus
upon the opposition between the martyrs and king or his representatives. References to the juridical procedure, verdict, judge and, in
the case of 2 Macc. 6:18–31, the king are simply missing. In 2 Macc.
7, however, the king is very much present and tries to force the
brothers to eat pork by using torture. Several of the seven young men
address their last words to him. Since 2 Maccabees' last reference to
the king before the martyrdoms tells us that the king left to go to
Antioch (5:21), several scholars assume that Antioch is the place
where the martyrs were executed.[79] This assumption does not fit
other data that strongly suggest that Jerusalem was the setting of the
martyrdoms. Jerusalem is by far the most important place within the
Judaean temple-state as depicted in 2 Maccabees. The author certainly would have told us if the executions had taken place
somewhere else.

79 See, e.g., Kellermann (1979), 16–17.

64

Translation[80]

(6:18) A certain Eleazar, one of the most important scribes,[81] a man of already advanced age and very good looks, was forced to open his mouth and eat pig's meat. (6:19) But he preferred a glorious death to a life of defilement and walked out of his own accord towards the drum,[82] (6:20) spitting out[83] the meat in a way required by those who remain steadfast in avoiding those things not right to eat for people who love (the right) life affectionately.[84] (6:21) Those who were posted at the unlawful eating of inwards took him aside because of their long acquaintance with him. They encouraged him to bring meat prepared by himself that he could take, and to act as if he were eating the sacrificial meat decreed by the king. (6:22) If he did that, he would escape the death penalty. Thus he would be granted a favour because of his old friendship with them. (6:23) But he started a civilised argument, which was worthy of his many years and superior old age, the remarkable grey hair he acquired,[85] his splendid behaviour from childhood onward, and even more of the holy law established by God. According, he quickly responded by saying that they could send him to Hades:[86] (6:24) 'Since it is not worthy of my

---

80 The translations of 2 Macc. 6:18–31; 7 and 14:37–46 are based on Rahlfs (1935).

81 The Greek word *grammateus* ('clerk' or 'secretary') can also mean 'scribe' in the sense of 'scholar', 'expert in Jewish law'. The story highlights Eleazar's faithfulness to the law of God and suggests that his prominent position among the scribes was the result of his impeccable way of life.

82 The Greek word *tympanon* is a technical phrase for an instrument of torture or a way of execution. One may think of a drum in or on which Eleazar was harnessed and stretched and then beaten to death (cf. 6:30), Vergote (1972), 118–20, 127.

83 The Greek verb given in the manuscripts is very rare and some scholars have proposed an alternative reading. Cf. the traditions about the Greek philosophers Zeno of Elea and Anaxarchus of Abdera, who spat their tongue into the tyrant's face (see Chapter 1).

84 The Greek phrase is unclear. Another interpretation, translating '(even) out of love of life' implies that transgressing the law in order to save one's life would be allowed, but that Eleazar decided not to follow this guideline. Rabbinic discussions of Lev. 18:5, 'You shall keep My statutes and My ordinances; by doing so one shall live . . .' make the choice whether to die a martyr's death in obedience to the law or to avoid this in order to save one's life explicit; see Schwartz (1993), with references.

85 Eleazar's age and splendid appearance presuppose that he enjoyed the support of God, in line with Sir. 10:5 (Greek): 'Human success is in the hand of the Lord, and it is He who makes the face of the scribe glorious.' At the same time, the verse emphasises that Eleazar's own behaviour from childhood onwards brought about his privileged situation.

86 The reference to Hades in this verse is sometimes understood in its Greek

---

years to pretend, so that many of the young people would think that Eleazar at the age of ninety had gone over to the way of life of the Gentiles (6:25) and they, because of my acting as if for a brief period of extra life, would be led astray because of me, and I (only) would win a defiled and blemished old age. (6:26) Since even if I would avoid the punishment by humans now, I cannot escape the hands of the Almighty, alive or dead. (6:27) Therefore, I will prove myself worthy of my old age by departing this life now as a man (6:28) and leave behind a noble example[87] of my dying happily,[88] eagerly and nobly for the revered and holy laws.' After he had said these things, he went straight to the drum. (6:29) They who had just previously behaved in a kind fashion, turned hostile because of the words stated, which were stupid in their opinion.

(6:30) When he was almost dead because of the blows, he sighed deeply and said: 'For the Lord who possesses the holy knowledge, it is clear that I could have been discharged of the death penalty, and that, being martyred, my body undergoes heavy tortures, but my soul gladly suffers these things out of awe for him'.[89] (6:31) And this person died in this way and left behind, not only for the young ones but also for most others of his people, an example of the greatest nobility and a distinct memory.

6   2 Maccabees 7:1–42

See for introductory remarks under no. 5 on p. 64.

mythological sense, implying that Eleazar asked to be sent to the god of the underworld. This would be ironic in the clearly anti-Greek context. On the other hand, Hades in the Septuagint is the usual translation of *sheōl* 'netherworld', having no mythological connotation whatsoever; see van der Horst (1991), 152. The reference to posthumous punishment in 2 Macc. 6:26 presupposes some kind of afterlife. 2 Macc. 7 is more explicit about the fate of the martyrs after death.

87   In Graeco-Roman sources model people often have a patriotic-propagandistic function, see Chapter 1, pp. 16, 18–19 and 21, and van Henten (1997), 210–43. 2 Maccabees suggests a similar function for Eleazar.

88   Cf. concerning the motif of joy during suffering 2 Macc. 6:30; 4 Macc. 10:20; *T.Y. Berakhot* 9.5. See also pp. 50, 124 and 129–30.

89   This phrase belongs to a well-established tradition of Israelite wisdom literature (Prov. 1:7; 9:10). Wisdom stories about righteous figures like Esther, Susanna, or Tobit exemplify how the key characters remain faithful to God despite utmost adversity. In the end, the divine deliverance follows. Cf. Sus. 2; 57; Est. 2:20; Tob. 4:21; 13:14S; 14:2, 6; Jdt 8:8. See also Wanke and Balz (1973), 194–201.

Translation

(7:1) It happened also that seven brothers and their mother were arrested and forced by the king to eat from the forbidden pig meat, while they were being tortured with scourges and cords made of sinew. (7:2) One of them became their advocate and said as follows: 'What do you intend to ask and learn from us? Since we are ready to die and won't transgress the ancestral laws.' (7:3) The king exploded and commanded men to heat up skillets and cauldrons. (7:4) While these were immediately heated up, the king also commanded them to cut out the tongue of the one who had become their advocate, to scalp him in Scythian fashion[90] and to cut off his hands and feet while his brothers and mother were watching together. (7:5) After he had become unable to do anything but was still breathing, the king ordered him to be brought to the fire place and to fry him. When the smell from the skillet had spread around amply, his brothers incited each other with their mother to die nobly. They spoke as follows: (7:6) 'God our Lord is watching and truly will have mercy with us, as Moses made clear in the song that functioned in public as a witness against (the people), saying "And He will have mercy with His servants."'[91]

(7:7) After the first one had quit his life in this manner, they brought the second one to the place of mocking and tore the skin from his head together with his hair, while asking: 'Will you eat, or rather have your body being punished limb by limb?' (7:8) He answered in his ancestral language[92] and said to them: 'No.' Therefore, this one received the same further torture as the first one. (7:9) With his last gasp of breath he said: 'You wretch, you take life

---

90 Scalping was known as a Scythian punishment for defeated enemies (Herodotus 4.64–5). The proverbial cruelty of the Scythians is also apparent from 2 Macc. 4:47.

91 2 Macc. 7:6 alludes to the Song of Moses in Deuteronomy 32 and contains a brief quotation of the Septuagint version of Deut. 32:36. Moses' Song implies bearing witness against the people of Israel (Deut. 31:19, 21, 26 and 32:46) because of Israel's unfaithfulness to the law. In the context of 2 Macc. 7 the reference functions, however, to emphasise that those who remain faithful to God's law will rejoice in God's compassion.

92 2 Macc. 7 not only highlights the martyrs' religious motivation, but also emphasises that these heroes are members of a people with its own institutions and unique identity. The ancestral language is part of 2 Maccabees' presentation of Jewish identity. The language is not specified. One may think of Aramaic or, more probably, Hebrew. See van Henten (1999).

away from us now, but the King of the world will raise us, who die for His laws, up from the dead for an everlasting renewal of life'.[93] (7:10) After this one, the third was mocked. He was asked for his tongue, exposed it quickly and held out his hands with good courage. (7:11) And he said nobly: 'I have got these from Heaven[94] and for its laws I forgo these and hope to receive them back again from it.' (7:12) Therefore, even the king and his people were struck with admiration because of the spirit of the lad, who did not care at all about the tortures. (7:13) After this one had quit his life, they maltreated and tortured the fourth one likewise. (7:14) Before he died he spoke as follows: 'It is preferable that people who have to quit life through humans[95] cherish the hope because of God to be raised again by Him. For you, however, there will be no resurrection to life.' (7:15) Subsequently, they brought the fifth one and tortured him. (7:16) And he looked at him (the king) and said: 'You have power among humans, but you are perishable. Do what you want. Don't think that our people has been forsaken by God. (7:17) Wait and you will see the magnificence of His power, how He will torture you and your descendants.' (7:18) After this one, they brought the sixth one. At the moment of dying he said: 'Don't lead yourself astray, since we suffer these things having sinned before our own God. Therefore, amazing things have happened. (7:19) But don't think that you will go scotfree having joined battle with God.'

(7:20) The mother was exceedingly admirable. She deserves to be well remembered. She watched how her seven sons perished within one day and bore this with good courage because of her hope in the Lord. (7:21) She incited every one of them in the ancestral language, full of a noble spirit. She aroused her female way of reasoning with male courage[96] and said to them: (7:22) 'I don't know how you have appeared in my womb, nor have I graciously given the breath of life

---

93 The Greek may emphasise the everlasting result of the renewal of life. The resurrection of the martyrs (see also 7:11, 14, 23, 29, 36; cf. 14:46) is their posthumous vindication. God is aware of the martyrs' sufferings (6:30; 7:6, 35–6) and rewards those who have sacrificed their life for His sake and His laws after death.

94 According to 2 Macc. 15:3–4 God is located in heaven and the priests call upon him there in 3:15.

95 An alternative translation, reading the preposition *apo* instead of *hypo*, would be: 'who pass away from human life'.

96 Like some early Christian female martyrs the mother demonstrates the courage and virtues which are usually associated with males in ancient sources, which becomes clear if the Greek is translated literally here. The author of 4 Maccabees

to you, nor have I made the elementary forms of every one of you into a harmonious whole. (7:23) Therefore, the Creator of the world,[97] who has moulded the genesis of humans and invented the genesis of everything, will give you back again the breath of life with mercy, since you forgo yourselves because of His laws.'

(7:24) Antiochus, however, thought that he was being humiliated since he assumed that he heard a reproaching voice. He exhorted the youngest, the only one left, not only with words, but also made promises under oath to make him rich and very happy, as well as to consider him one of his friends and entrust him a high office if he would drop his ancestors' practices. (7:25) Since the young man did not pay any attention to him, the king called the mother and encouraged her to advise the lad so that he would be saved. (7:26) After he had encouraged her urgently, she agreed to persuade her son. (7:27) She leaned towards him, scoffed the cruel tyrant and spoke in her ancestral language: 'Son, have mercy with me who has carried you around in her belly for nine months, who has suckled you three years, has educated and raised you to this age and fed you. (7:28) I beg you, child, to look up to heaven and earth, look at everything contained by them, and know that God did not make them out of existing things and that the human race came into being this way. (7:29) Don't fear this executioner, but be worthy of your brothers and accept death, so that I will get you back through God's mercy, together with your brothers.' (7:30) She had not finished speaking when the young man said: 'What are you waiting for? I do not obey the king's decree, but I obey the decree of the law given to our ancestors by Moses. (7:31) You have become the inventor of all evil for the Hebrews, you will not escape the hands of God. (7:32) We suffer namely because of our own sins. (7:33) If the living Lord is angry with us for a short period in order to punish and discipline us, He will let himself be reconciled again with His servants. (7:34) But you, O godless and most abom-

---

gives the gender aspect even more emphasis, see 4 Macc. 14:11; 15:23, 30; 16:24 and also *1 Clem.* 6.2; *Pas. Perp.* 10.7 and *Acts of Paul and Thecla* 40; Moore and Anderson (1998).

97 The creative power of God is the basic argument in the mother's statements of incitement. Her sophisticated reasoning in 7:22–3, 28–9 suggests that if God was able to create humankind and universe and made her conceive her sons, he would be capable to re-create them as well. The repeated references to the breath of life in 7:22–3 and 14:46 allude to Gen. 2:7 and suggest that God not only would re-create the heroes' bodies but also revive them by breathing life into their nostrils.

inable of all humans, don't think that you can be so insolent to have the idle hope that you can raise your hands against the children of heaven. (7:35) Since you have not yet escaped the punishment of the almighty overseeing God. (7:36) My brothers have undergone now a brief period of suffering, but they belong to the covenant of God which brings eternal life. And through the verdict of God you will receive the right punishment for your arrogance. (7:37) I, like my brothers, surrender my body and my life for the laws of our ancestors. I call upon God that He will show mercy speedily to the people, that you will confess because of trials and tortures that He alone is God, (7:38) and that you because of me and my brothers will make an end to Almighty's anger that was deservedly brought upon our entire people.'[98] (7:39) The king exploded and treated this one worse than the others, since he felt aggrieved by the sneering. (7:40) And this one, therefore, quit his life being pure, trusting completely in the Lord.[99] (7:41) The mother of the sons died last.[100] (7:42) Thus far the events during the sacrificial meals and the outrageous tortures will be made known.

7 2 Maccabees 14:37–46

Razis is introduced as a very prominent Jew and a great patriot as well. Verse 37 implies that he was a member of the Judaean council of elders with representatives from the city of Jerusalem as well as from its countryside. Razis' name is unparalleled and may be symbolical. It can derive from several Aramaic or Hebrew roots and may hint at his dedication to the Lord, his bringing atonement or his

---

98 The intercessory prayer of the youngest son builds upon 7:33 referring to the reconciliation between God and His people in the near future (cf. 5:20; 8:29). The invocation consists of three elements: (a) that God may soon be merciful again to the people; (b) that Antiochus will be punished and confess that He is the only God; and (c) that the divine anger will stop with the martyrs. The prayer is answered, as is apparent from Judas the Maccabee's victory and Antiochus' painful death and confession described in Chapters 8–9. Apparently, the intercessory prayer and the sacrificial death together brought about God's atonement.

99 The last verse about the youngest emphasises again the martyrs' unconditional faithfulness to God (cf. Dan. 3 and 6).

100 Compared to the mother's elaborate statements, the description of her death is very brief. 4 Maccabees notes that she threw herself into the flames in order to prevent Antiochus' guards from touching her (17:1). 4 Maccabees elaborates her praise at length (14:11–16:25).

rejoicing God's favour. 2 Macc. 14 tells us that Razis' suicide follows upon the high priest Alcimus' betrayal of the Jewish cause. This leads to the royal appointment of Nicanor as governor of Judaea, who was ordered to kill the freedom fighter Judas the Maccabee (2 Macc. 14:12–13). Nicanor tries to arrest Razis in order to show the Jews what plans he had in mind for them. Razis' successive attempts to kill himself are described in painstaking detail. The literal meaning of the Greek indicating his first act means that Razis consigned himself to a death by the sword by a thrust or a blow (14:43). This attempt failed. His next steps involve his opponents and resemble the self-sacrifice of the Theban prince Menoeceus and Roman generals, who brought about the defeat of the enemy by their ritual suicide (see Chapter 1). Razis tries to throw himself upon the multitude of soldiers, but his fall takes some time, so that they can avoid being hit by his body. But he finally succeeds in involving them physically in his death by the blood that he loses running through the crowd and by hurling his entrails upon it.

Translation

(14:37) A certain Razis, one of the elders from Jerusalem, was denounced to Nicanor.[101] He loved his fellow-citizens, had a very good reputation and was called 'father of the Jews' because of his goodwill towards them. (14:38) In the bygone period of the secession he had been convicted because of fighting for Judaism.[102] Eagerly, he risked his body and his life for the cause of Judaism.[103] (14:39) Since Nicanor wanted to make clear beforehand the hostility he felt towards the Jews, he sent more than 500 soldiers to arrest him. (14:40) It seemed to him that he would strike them a heavy blow by arresting Razis. (14:41) When the multitude was on the point of capturing the fortified house,[104] having forced

---

101 Chapter 8 highlights Nicanor's earlier attempt to solve Antiochus IV's financial problems because of the tribute to the Romans by selling Jews as slaves. Judas the Maccabee had defeated him then in a humiliating way (8:9–36).

102 An alternative translation of the highly unusual Greek would be: 'because he brought about a decision for Judaism', see Risberg (1918), 30–1.

103 The text suggests in rather general terms that Razis had engaged himself in the past in a struggle to maintain Jewish practice and identity, and that he had been convicted but, apparently, not punished. Since Razis is not mentioned elsewhere in the book, we can only speculate about this earlier event.

104 The information about Razis' house has many lacunae and allows for several

the gate of the courtyard, having been ordered to bring fire and having set the gates on fire, Razis understood that he was trapped and thrust himself upon his sword. (14:42) He wanted to die nobly rather than be in the power of the criminals, being maltreated in a way unworthy of his noble birth. (14:43) But he did not hit exactly right in the heat of the struggle. When the mob was forcing its way in through the gates, he nobly ran up to the wall and threw himself straight down upon the mob, as a real man. (14:44) Since the mob quickly stepped back, a space became vacant and he landed in the middle of the opening. (14:45) While he was still breathing he stood up with blazing anger. The blood spouted from his painful wounds, but he went at a run through the mob and placed himself upon a precipitous piece of rock. (14:46) Having lost all his blood, he exposed his bowels, took them with both hands and hurled them into the mob, while he called upon the One[105] who has the mastery over the breath of life to give them back again to him. In this way he quit his life.[106]

8 4 Maccabees 5

4 Maccabees dates from the beginning of the second century CE and may originate in Asia Minor (see the General Introduction). The philosophical thesis about the autonomy of devout reason (4 Macc. 1:1), which is proved by the martyrs, is discussed primarily in the first main section (1:1–3:18).[107] Later passages repeat the thesis in connection with the acts of the martyrs in highly rhetorical formulations (6:31–5; 7:16–23; 13:1–5; 16:1–4; 18:2).[108] The section of the book can be subdivided as follows:

interpretations. The relevant Greek word *pyrgos* (literally 'tower') may refer to a stronghold (cf. 2 Macc. 10:18, 20, 22), a house with a wall around it or a tower. Razis' fall described in vv. 43–4 presupposes, in any case, that the building was quite high.

105 Razis calls upon God at the moment of dying. Cf. the *devotio* formula with which a Roman general dedicated himself and his enemies to the gods, see p. 37. The reference to God's returning his sacrificed bodily parts echoes phrases in 2 Macc. 7 about the posthumous re-creation of the martyrs (7:11, 22–3).

106 The closing formula is similar to the one in 2 Macc. 6:31 and associates Razis' noble death, therefore, with that of the martyrs (see also 7:7, 13, 40).

107 4 Macc. 3:19–18:24 can be considered the demonstration (*apodeixis*, 3:19) of the philosophical thesis presented in 1:1–3:18, Aristotle, *Rhet.* 1414a lines 31–7; Menander, see Soffel (1974), 170.

108 Breitenstein (1976), 91–130, analyses the rhetorical style.

3:19–4:26:	the historical setting of the martyrdoms
5:1–7:23:	martyrdom and praise of Eleazar
8:1–14:10:	martyrdom and praise of the seven brothers
14:11–17:1:	suicide and praise of the mother
17:2–18:24:	summary and consolation of the survivors.

The passage translated below follows directly after the subsection describing the historical setting of the martyrdoms. Antiochus had decided to force every Hebrew to switch from the Jewish to the Greek way of life. He tried to realise this by compelling all of them one by one to eat some unclean food and sacrificial meat in order to show obedience to the king's decree (4:26; 5:2). The description of the setting evokes the picture of a contest between the king and the Jewish people. The martyrs, who act as the king's actual opponents, represent the people. Athletic vocabulary as well as the passage looking back upon the martyrdoms in 17:11–16 confirm the image of a contest between tyrant and Jews: 'Eleazar was the first contestant, the mother of the seven brothers competed, and the brothers contended as well. The tyrant was the antagonist, and the world and the human race were the spectators' (17:13–14). This view of the conflict between the tyrant and the Jewish people explains why the author can argue that the martyrs alone defeated Antiochus (1:11; 17:15; 18:4–5).

Eleazar is the first Jew who had to demonstrate his loyalty to the king by eating unclean food. Antiochus not only threatens him with torture, but also does his best to persuade Eleazar, acting as a real tyrant, being gentle and brutal alternately. He uses arguments often brought up in the dialogues between martyrs and the representatives of the secular authorities. He appeals to Eleazar's old age, his common sense, the harmlessness of eating the food, the fact that he had salvation in his own hands and that the divinity Eleazar adhered to would understand the necessity of eating. The dialogue surpasses these conventional arguments, however, since Antiochus also comes up with arguments that have a philosophical background.[109] He derides Jewish philosophy and argues that one should seek what is pleasant and beneficial, and avoid pain.[110] Eleazar's response offers philosophical arguments and is

---

109 Cf. also the dialogue between Antiochus and the seven brothers in 8:1–9:9.

110 The king emphasises the pleasures brought by nature and implies that one should enjoy these instead of rejecting them (5:8–9, 11). He seems to advocate ideas attributed to the well-known Greek philosopher Epicurus (342/341–271/270 BCE), who aimed at being safe and without pain and advocated the virtue of calmness (*ataraxia*).

part of 4 Maccabees' consistent presentation of Jewish religion as the philosophy that turns important non-Jewish philosophical notions into reality. In 5:20 Eleazar incorporates the Stoic view that small or large sins are equally bad to make his point that even the smallest transgression of the law is not allowed. In 5:22–4 he counters the tyrant's criticism of Jewish philosophy as irrational by stating that this philosophy teaches the Jews the four basic virtues of self-control, courage, justice and piety. Finally, he refutes Antiochus' argument based on nature by suggesting that nature and law have to be in line with each other, since God has created them both (5:25–6). Thus, anybody who wants to live according to Jewish law would live in agreement with nature as well.[111]

Translation[112]

(5:1) Sitting in public with his assessors at a certain high spot[113] and his soldiers standing around him, the tyrant Antiochus (2) ordered each and every Hebrew to be dragged there and forced them to eat swine's flesh and sacrificial meat. (3) If, however, some of them were unwilling to eat unclean food, they would be broken on the wheel and killed. (4) After many had been seized and carried off, the first of the flock was brought near to the tyrant. His name was Eleazar. He was of priestly origin,[114] learned in the law, of advanced age, and because of his age well known by many of the tyrant's people.

(5) When Antiochus saw him, he said: (6) 'Before I start torturing you, old man, I would like to advise you this, that you eat from the swine's flesh in order to be saved. (7) I respect your age and grey hairs. Having these for such a long time, you do not seem to me to philosophise according to the religious practice of the Jews.[115] (8) Since why would you abhor the wonderful flesh-diet of this animal, a

---

111 Eleazar incorporates in this way a non-Jewish philosophical notion in his articulation of Jewish philosophy, since living in agreement with nature was an ideal of Cynic as well as Stoic philosophy.

112 Based on Rahlfs (1935).

113 The location is not specified. Since no change of place is indicated from Chapter 4 up to the reference about Antiochus leaving Jerusalem in 18:5, a location in Jerusalem seems to be implied.

114 Also 7:6, 12; 17:9. This detail is not given in 2 Macc. 6:18–31, but a scribal profession and a priestly origin may well have gone together.

115 4 Maccabees suggests like 2 Macc. 6:18–31 that Eleazar's old age and respectable appearance are the result of a virtuous life.

welcome gift of nature? (9) It would be foolish not to enjoy pleasant things without blame. And it would be wrong to turn oneself away from the gifts of nature. (10) You would seem to act even more foolishly, if you hold a vain opinion of the truth and still look down on me at the price of your own punishment. (11) Should you not awake from this silly philosophy of yours? Should you not throw away these nonsense arguments, and take up a kind of thinking worthy of your age? Should you not philosophise about the truth in an advantageous way, (12) respect my humane advice and have mercy with your own old age? (13) Consider that, if there is some overseeing power connected with this religious practice of yours, it will pardon you in every case of transgression of the law which happened out of necessity.'

(14) After the tyrant had tried to persuade him in this way to follow the lawless flesh-diet, Eleazar asked to have a word. (15) He received permission to speak and began to address the people present as follows: (16) 'Our way of life, Antiochus, is based upon obedience to the law, and we believe that no necessity is more forcible than the ready obedience to our law. (17) Therefore, in no way do we deem it worthy to transgress the law. (18) And yet, if our law is, as you assume, not truly divine – anyhow, we believe it is divine – we are still not allowed to deny the validity of the glory which leads to piety. (19) You should not think that it is a small sin if we eat unclean food. (20) Small and large transgressions are equally sinful. (21) Since in either way the law is being treated with arrogance alike. (22) You scoff at our philosophy as if we do not live with circumspection by it. (23) You should realise that it teaches us temperance thoroughly, so that we control all pleasant lusts and desires. It trains us in courage, so that we endure any pain willingly. (24) It teaches us justice, so that we act in a well-balanced way, no matter what state of mind we are in, and it teaches us piety thoroughly, so that we worship the only living God magnificently. (25) Therefore, we do not eat unclean food. We believe that God has established the law and we know that the creator of the world sympathises with us, having given the law in accordance with nature. (26) The food familiar to our souls he allowed us to eat, but the meats adverse to them he prevented us from eating. (27) You act like a tyrant by forcing us not only to transgress the law, but also to eat, so that you could laugh about our most hateful eating of unclean food. (28) But you will not laugh with such laughter about me. (29) I will not disregard the sacred oaths of my ancestors about keeping the law. (30) Not even if you gouge out my eyes and melt away my bowels. (31) I am not so old and unworthy a man that I would not be able to make my reason young again on behalf of piety. (32) Therefore, make the wheels ready

and blow up the fire more vehemently. (33) I do not pity my old age so much that I would break the law by my own act. (34) I will not deceive you, my law and teacher,[116] nor will I renounce you, beloved self-control. (35) I will not put you to shame, my reason and philosopher, nor will I deny you, dear priesthood and learning of the law. (36) You will not defile my revered old mouth or my lifelong lawful life. (37) The patriarchs will receive me as holy,[117] because of my not being afraid of your deadly violence. (38) You can rule as a tyrant over godless people, but you will not gain mastery over my arguments on behalf of piety by words or by deeds.'[118]

9 Philo, *Every Good Person is Free (Quod omnis probus liber sit)* 88–91

Philo of Alexandria was born about 25 BCE and died around the year 45 CE. Scholars have labelled him either a philosopher or an exegete of the Pentateuch, but he definitely was both.[119] His family must have been part of the Greek elite in Alexandria. Philo had a great interest in Greek culture, which is apparent from his allusions to theatre, concerts, sports, games and quotations from Greek literature.[120] He incorporated and re-interpreted Plato's famous parable of the cave in his philosophical work. No matter how learned he was, Jewish culture and religion remained the basics in his life.

Philo's discussion of the 'good person' (*spoudaios*) in his *Every Good Person is Free*[121] includes a passage about Jewish philosphers, the Essenes, who withstood every brutal ruler.[122] Philo argues in this

---

116 The personification of abstract concepts like law, reason and priesthood mentioned in 5:34–5 is a trope in ancient rhetorics called *fictio personae*; Klauck (1989), 713.

117 This reference to Eleazar's afterlife with the patriarchs may be an allusion to Gen. 15:15.

118 The final verse of Eleazar's speech expresses the ideal of the freedom of the philosopher, who does not give in to any pressure, not even torture or execution by tyrants. See Chapter 1 on Socrates, Zeno and Anaxarchus, and p. 79 about the Essenes.

119 See Borgen (1984), Morris (1986) and Mach (1996).

120 Philo quotes Euripides on Heracles' endurance of suffering (*Prob.* 99; Euripides *Fragm.* 687, see Nauck (1955); the quotation can also be found in *All.* 3.202; *Jos.* 78; cf. *Prob.* 25.

121 Petit (1974) offers a detailed introduction.

122 The name 'Essenes' may derive from Aramaic *hase'* 'pious'. For a discussion on

work that every good person is a free person. The 'good person' is not interested in external matters like possessions or secular political power. Like the martyrs in 4 Maccabees, the 'good person' is not influenced by emotions (*Every Good Person* 17–18; 45; 107; 159)[123] and realises the four cardinal virtues of prudence, justice, courage and self-control.[124] The 'good person' should, if necessary, even defy death (22–25; 111; 146). Philo offers a long list of examples of persons who demonstrated the ideal attitude of the 'good person'.[125] The Essenes, a large group of Jewish philosophers,[126] are his most important example. His extensive discussion in *Every Good Person* 75–91 describes the Essenes as being initiated in divine philosophy. They live as true brothers in a holy community (75; 79). Their philosophy does not deal with logic. Only that part of physics that concerns the existence of God and His creation of the world interests them (80). They devote themselves to ethics based on God's law revealed by Moses.[127] Their ethical views made them decide to have only communal property. Philo considers the Essenes the ideal philosophers because of their way of life. Their deeds demonstrate that they are truly free and virtuous.

The passage below is a rather abstract and stereotypical description of periods of horrible sufferings for the Jewish people. Philo distinguishes two types of tyrants who cause these sufferings: 'animals' who immediately show their savageness by their cruel deeds, and tyrants in disguise, who behave gently first, but are as devastating as the former.[128] From the context it is apparent that the Essenes stood

---

the Essenes, see Schürer (1973–87), 2.555–97; Vermes and Goodman (1989), 1–17.

123 Josephus, *War* 2.120, notes that the Essenes considered self-control (*engkrateia*) and disregard of the emotions important.

124 *Prob.* 70; 159; cf. 67; 72 and 107.

125 The list includes many famous non-Jewish examples: the seven sages of Greece, the Persian *magi*, Heracles and the philosophers Anaxarchus, Zeno and Kalanus the Indian (*Prob.* 73–4; 92–109). Cf. Philo, *Prov.* 2.8–11.

126 Philo notes that there were more than 4000 Essenes (*Prob.* 75; cf. Josephus, *Ant.* 18.21), who lived in many towns of Judaea (*Hyp.* 1). Josephus describes the Essenes as one of the four philosophical schools of contemporary Judaism (*War* 2.117–66; *Ant.* 18.9–25; cf. 13.171–3).

127 Moses as writer of God's revealed law is the 'lawgiver' of the Jewish people (*Vit. Mos.* 1.3, 49; *Op.* 1–12; *Ebr.* 1; *Prob.* 43. Cf. also *Ep. Arist.* 31; Josephus, *Ant.* 12.37).

128 Philo may have used motifs of traditional characterisations of tyrants here. Cf. Berve (1967), 1.476–509; 2.747–53.

up against these tyrants, but their sufferings are not described.[129] The Essenes triumphed over the tyrants[130] because of their nobleness and superior way of life (*Prob.* 91).

Translation[131]

(88) Such are the athletes of virtue[132] this philosophy produces, which is very different from the futile Greek playing with names.[133] It advances as exercises praiseworthy deeds, deeds that secure unsubdued liberty. (89) An example: many rulers have risen against our country[134] in various periods, with different characters and policies. Some did their best to outdo the savageness of wild animals to the point of sheer ferocity.[135] They did not omit any of the cruelties imaginable. They slaughtered their subjects in herds or cut up their flesh while they were still living, the way butchers do it, in portions, limb by limb. They did not stop until they underwent the same fate at the hands of Justice that watches over human affairs.[136] (90) Others[137] replaced this violent and mad behaviour by other evils. They practised indescribable bitterness.[138] Although they spoke quietly, they displayed a character filled of anger through the hypocrisy of their mild speech. They fawned like

---

129 Josephus, referring to the Essenes undergoing heavy torture during the war against Rome (66–70 CE), writes in *War* 2.151–3 that they despised danger, triumphed over pain with the help of their conviction and considered a glorious death better than the preservation of life, Toki (1981). Cf. 4 Macc. 6:5–9; 9:5–7, 21–2; 10:14; 11:26; Josephus, *War* 7.418; *Ant.* 18.23–4; *Asc. Is.* 5:14; *T.Y. Berakhot* 9.5 (R. Aqiva); *Mart. Pol.* 2.2–3; *Mart. Lugd.* 23; Eusebius, *Hist. eccl.* 8.6.2–4.

130 This corresponds to the triumph of the Maccabaean martyrs over Antiochus IV in 4 Maccabees, see p. 73.

131 Translation based on Cohn and Reiter (1915).

132 I.e. the Essenes. Philo also uses athletic vocabulary concerning the Essenes in his *Hypothetica*, of which Eusebius has transmitted some fragments (*Praep. ev.* 8.6–7).

133 This negative characterisation of Greek philosophy may have been due to one of the Greek philosophical schools, the Sophists, who got a reputation for hairsplitting discussions.

134 Judaea, where Philo locates the Essenes, see n. 126.

135 Cf. 4 Macc. 7:27; 9:15, 30, 32; 12:13; 18:20.

136 The 'Justice' is an indirect reference to the God of Israel. Philo assumes like the authors of 2 and 4 Maccabees that God punished the tyrants for their wickedness towards the Jews.

137 The second type of tyrants, see p. 77.

138 Cf. 4 Macc. 18:20.

venomous dogs, causing incurable evil. In the cities they left behind the unforgettable calamities of their victims as reminders of their own wickedness and hatred of humans.[139] (91) Yet, no one either from the horribly savage-hearted characters or from the thoroughly deceitful and underhanded creatures was capable of laying a charge against this group of Essenes or holy ones[140] we spoke about. All of them turned out to be weaker than the nobility of these men. They dealt with them as people being independent and free by nature.[141] They praised their communal meals and their fellowship[142] that no word can describe adequately, the clearest proof of a perfect and very happy life.

10 *Assumptio Mosis* 9:1–10:10

The *Assumption of Moses*, sometimes called the *Testament of Moses*, is a farewell discourse by Moses. A dialogue with his successor Joshua forms the framework of Moses' revelation about Israel's history from the moment of its entrance into the Promised Land until the end of days. The *Assumption* is linked to the last chapters of the biblical book of Deuteronomy that describe the last period of Moses' life (Deut. 31–4). The Latin text of the only extant manuscript is incomplete, but there are serious reasons to assume that the work originally contained a description of Moses' ascent to heaven after his death.[143] The group that produced the *Assumption* is unknown. A Palestinian provenance is probable, because Jerusalem is the only city mentioned in the entire work. *As. Mos.* 6 refers to a petulant king who will rule for thirty-four years and to children who will rule a shorter period (6:6–8).[144] These detailed references exactly match the duration of the

---

139 These two phrases reverse the brutal accusations levelled against the Jews as in the king's decree in the Greek versions of Esther (Addition B to Chapter 3 or Chapter 13 according to other numberings); Apollonius Molon (first century BCE) according to Josephus, *Ap.* 2.148; Diodorus Siculus (first century BCE) 34–35.1.1, and Tacitus, *Hist.* 5.5.1, see Stern (1974–84), nos. 49, 63 and 281.

140 There is a word-play in the Greek here (*Essaioi/hosioi*), as in *Prob.* 75 and *Hyp.* 1.

141 Cf. 4 Macc. 5, p. 72.

142 The Essenes' communal meals are also highlighted in Philo, *Hyp.* 5. The Essenes had common ownership (*Hyp.* 4; Josephus, *War* 2.122–3), like the Qumran community (1QS 1:11–13; 6:17, 19–20; 1QpHab 12:9–10).

143 Tromp (1993), 115–16; 281–2.

144 For criticism of the view of Licht (1961) and Nickelsburg (1972), 43–5, 97–102, 109, and (1973) that Chapter 6 is an addition to a second-century BCE writing, see Tromp (1993), 109–11.

reigns of Herod the Great (37–4 BCE) and fit the reign of one of his sons as well.[145] A date between Herod's death in 4 BCE and 70 CE seems to be probable, because the temple cult is very much a reality in the *Assumption*.

As. Mos. 9:1–10:10 is part of the last cycle of events of Moses' prophecy, which starts in 7:1. The intervention of the Herodian rulers triggers the beginning of the end of time. Incredible sinfulness (7:3–10) precedes a divine revenge unheard of, executed by the 'king of kings' (Chapter 8). This is the context of the appearance of Taxo and his seven sons (Chapter 9). The name Taxo is unique and probably symbolical. Many attempts have been made to give an explanation of this name, but none is satisfactory.[146] Taxo and his sons seem to represent the very few that remained of Israel after its incredibly harsh punishments at the end of time. They retreat to a cave and await their death, because they refuse to transgress the Lord's commandments (9:4). The prayer of father and sons suggests that their death had crucial consequences for both Israel and its enemies. This becomes more obvious when one notes the web of allusions to Scripture that underlies the prayer.[147]

The coherence of 9:1–10:10 strongly suggests that Taxo and his sons' death brings about the end of time. Their faithfulness to God's commandments leads to salvation for Israel and eternal punishment for its enemies. *As. Mos.* 10:1–10 describes the events of the end of time. Three sections can be discerned in this scenario:

10:1–2: the manifestation of God, the disappearance of the devil and the vindication of the faithful by a heavenly messenger;

10:3–7: God's manifestation in His creation, the nations' punishment and the destruction of their idols;

10:8–10: salvation for Israel and its exaltation to heaven.

God's manifestation in 10:3–7 effects the three major parts of creation: heaven, earth and waters. Their transformations are described with images that recall passages in the Hebrew Bible about God's revelation of Himself.[148]

---

145 Archelaus succeeded Herod the Great as ruler of Judaea and ruled from 4 BCE to 6 CE.
146 For a survey, see Tromp (1993), 124–8.
147 See the notes to the translation.
148 Jeremias (1965).

Translation[149]

(9:1) Then, on that day,[150] a man from the tribe of Levi,[151] whose name will be Taxo and who will have seven sons, will speak to them and ask: (9:2) 'You must notice, my sons, that another cruel and impure punishment has come upon the people.[152] It is merciless and surpasses the first one. (9:3) What nation, region or godless people that has committed evil actions against the Lord has suffered so many terrible things as those that have come over us?[153] (9:4) Now then, my sons, listen to me: 'For you should see and know that neither our parents nor our ancestors have ever tempted God by transgressing His commandments.[154] (9:5) Beware that our strength lies here.[155] And this is what we shall do. (9:6) We will fast for three days[156] and on the fourth day we will enter a cave in the field. And we will die rather than transgress the commandments of the Lord of lords, the God of our ancestors. (9:7) For, if we will do this and die, our blood will be revenged before the Lord.'[157]

---

149 Based on Tromp (1993).

150 With Tromp (1993), 16. The MS reads 'while this one speaks', which is unclear. The day mentioned refers to the terrible period of repression caused by the king of kings described in Chapter 8. Apparently these horrors will be followed by a second and even worse period of suffering.

151 Taxo's levitic descent is important, since he and his sons appeal to God to act according to the blessing of Levi in Deut. 33:8–11, because the behaviour of Taxo and his sons matches the behaviour mentioned in the blessing.

152 As in 2 and 4 Maccabees, the Gentiles act as God's instruments of punishment, but are sinners themselves who deserved to be punished (cf. *Jub.* 23:23; *Ps. Sol.* 2:1, 24; 17:5). This punishment will take place at the end of time, see *As. Mos.* 10:2, 7, 10.

153 Allusion to Deut. 32:36, which indicates that Israel's vindication will take place at the moment when it is almost extinguished. Cf. Azariah's Prayer (Dan. 3:37).

154 Taxo and his sons emphasise that they, contrary to other Israelites, have not sinned and that their ancestors also have not tested or tempted God. They allude to Moses' blessing of Levi in Deut. 33:8–11 (with a brief paraphrase of Israel's episode near the Waters of Massa and Meriba during the forty years in the desert as told in Exod. 17 and Num. 20). The blessing suggests that Moses/Levi was tested at Massa and Meriba and that he remained faithful to the Lord (Deut. 33:8).

155 'Here' (*haec*) is ambiguous, it may refer to the ancestors' being without sins or to the ancestors' and Taxo and his sons' faithfulness to the commandments.

156 For other fastings of three days see Est. 4:16; Tob. 3:10 (Vulgate); 2 Macc. 13:12 and *Testament Joseph* 3:5. Cf. Jdt 12:7–9.

157 Taxo and his sons allude to God's vindication of His children as indicated in

(10:1) And then His Kingdom will appear throughout His entire creation. And then the devil will find his end and sadness will be carried away together with him.[158] (10:2) And then the hands of the messenger,[159] who will be in heaven, will be filled.[160] Thereupon He will avenge them on their enemies. (10:3) For the Heavenly One will rise from His royal seat.[161] He will leave His holy habitation with indignation and anger because of His children. (10:4) And the earth will tremble and it will be shaken as far as its ends. And the high mountains will be made low, and they will be shaken. And the deep valleys will sink even further.[162] (10:5) The sun will no longer give light and the horns of the (crescent) moon will turn into darkness and they will be destroyed. And the entire moon will turn into blood. And the cycle of the stars will be deranged.[163] (10:6) And the sea will retreat unto the abyss, the sources will lack water and the rivers will dry up.[164] (10:7) For the Most High, Eternal and Only God will rise and manifest Himself in order to take vengeance upon the nations and destroy all

---

Deut. 32:43 (according to the Septuagint and 4Q45): 'for He will avenge the blood of His children, and take vengeance on His adversaries'. 2 Kings 9:7; Ps. 79:10 and Rev. 6:10; 19:2 also refer to the vindication of the blood of God's servants. Cf. Gen. 4:10.

158 The disappearance of sadness may come because the devil is no longer able to execute his role as prosecutor of humans in God's courtroom. The passage may, however, more generally suggest that sadness caused by the devil will disappear because he will not be part of the Kingdom of the Lord, as several apocalyptic passages suggest (*Jub.* 23:29; 50:15; *1 Enoch* 10:6; Rev. 20:10).

159 The messenger (*nuntius*) is probably a human figure and not an angel (*angelus*) as argued by Nickelsburg (1972), 28–31, and Carlson (1982). Tromp (1990) suggests that Taxo himself is the messenger, turning him into a suffering righteous or martyr who is vindicated after death in heaven. Moses himself, however, is called messenger in 11:17 and his role as intercessor for Israel was well known (Exod. 32:11–14, 28–35; Ps. 106:19–23; Philo, *De vita Mosis* 2.166; *As. Mos.* 12:6).

160 A technical phrase for the consecration of priests.

161 God's rising is the first step of His help of those who suffer, cf. Num. 10:35(34); Ps. 3:7(8); 7:6; 68:1.

162 Similar events are described in Judges 5:4–5; 2 Sam. 22:8; Isa. 24:19; 63:19; Joel 2:10; Nah. 1:5; Hab. 3:6, 10.

163 The celestial bodies will no longer give light, cf. Isa. 13:10; Joel 2:10; 3:15; Ezek. 32:7–8. The image of the moon turning into blood is reminiscent of Joel 2:31(3:4).

164 Reading the verb *exaresco* with R.H. Charles instead of *expavesco* in the MS, which would imply a translation like 'and the rivers will recoil out of fear'. See for parallel views about the retreat of the waters Joel 1:20; *1 Enoch* 101:7; *4 Ezra* 6:23–4; *Ps. Sol.* 17:19; *Sib. Or.* 3:675–7.

their idols. (10:8) Then you will be happy, Israel. And you will mount the neck and the wings of an eagle, and they will be filled.[165] (10:9) And God will exalt you and make that you remain in the heaven of the stars,[166] the place of His (own) habitation. (10:10) And you will look down from above and you will see your enemies on the earth[167] and recognise them, rejoice, thank and confess your Creator.

11 Josephus, *Jewish War* 7.389–406

The collective suicide of the Jewish rebels at Masada during the aftermath of the War against Rome (66–70) is a world-famous episode, not least because the location of the suicide has been developed into a site easily accessible to tourists. Masada has been one of the great icons of Israeli national identity since the 1930s and the excavations with Yigael Yadin's preliminary publication in 1966 about them caused a new wave of interest.[168] Young Israelis hiked to the mountain fortress and saw the sun coming up sitting on top of it. Soldiers swore their oath of allegiance during a ceremony at Masada, quoting a line of Yitzaq Lamdan's 1927 poem about Masada: 'Masada shall not fall again'.[169]

The Masada episode is part of book 7 of Josephus' *Jewish War*, which may have been completed in the early years of Trajan (98–117 CE).[170] Eleazar ben Yair and his fellow *Sicarii* ('dagger-people', carrying a *sica* 'dagger' under their coat)[171] became masters

---

165 In Exod. 19:4 the image of Israel mounting the neck and/or the wings of an eagle refers to God's bringing the Israelites from Egypt to Himself. See also Deut. 32:11; Ob. 4; 1 Enoch 96:2.

166 Israel's exaltation to the stars (10:8–10) is mentioned in several biblical scenarios of the end of times (Isa. 14:13; Jer. 51[28]:9; cf. *Ps. Sol.* 1:5). Some passages suggest that Israel would live among the stars after the end of time (cf. Dan. 12:3; 4 *Ezra* 7:97, 125; 2 *Baruch* 51:5, 10; 1 *Enoch* 51:4; 104:2, 6), others that Israel would be like stars or angels (*Biblical Antiquities* 33:5; *Testament Levi* 14:3; 18:4).

167 Other apocalyptic passages suggest that Israel's enemies would be thrown into darkness (1 *Enoch* 108:14) or swallowed by the earth or the underworld (1 *Enoch* 56:8; 90:18, 25–7).

168 Yadin (1966).

169 Zerubavel (1995), 60–76, 114–37 and 192–213, and Ben-Yehuda (1995) offer fascinating discussions of recent Israeli interpretations of the Masada episode.

170 S. Schwartz (1986). Others tend to date the book slightly earlier, e.g. during Titus (79–81 CE) or Domitian (81–96).

171 The *Sicarii* joined the rebellion against Rome in 66–70 CE, see C.T.R. Hayward in Schürer (1973–87), 2.598–606; Stern (1982–83). Yadin (1966) and several

over Masada by using deceit, probably against fellow Jews who occupied the fortress (*War* 2.408, 433). They made raids on settlements in Masada's neighbourhood, such as Ein Gedi, where they killed 700 fellow Jews (*War* 4.402–5), but they stayed at Masada until the siege by the Roman governor Flavius Silva in the spring of 73 or 74.[172] Josephus describes the site and the Romans' siege in detail (*War* 7.275–319).[173] Two speeches by Eleazar, inciting his fellows to collective suicide (7.320–36; 340–88), and the report of the suicide itself (7.389–406) precede the brief reference to the Roman capture of the fortress. Scholars have questioned the credibility of Josephus' transmission of Eleazar's speeches and suicide report, pointing to the discrepancies between the archaeological data and Josephus' report as well as to the highly improbable chain of events in Josephus.[174] The Romans, for instance, must have been quite stupid to let Eleazar deliver two grand speeches and to allow him and his fellows to commit suicide and burn their possessions after they had gained access to the fortress.[175]

Josephus' report of the suicide seems to be enthusiastic on the surface, but ambivalent on closer inspection.[176] This ambivalence increases, when one compares the report as well as the preceding two speeches by the rebels' leader (*War* 7.320–80) with that other famous

other scholars argue that *Sicarii* is a name indicating all participants in the war against Rome. A group of *Sicarii* fled to Egypt in the aftermath of the Jewish War and Josephus describes their execution in *War* 7.416–19.

172 See the n. to 7.401.

173 Roth (1995) discusses Josephus as well as archaeological data and argues that the siege lasted only about seven weeks.

174 Josephus mentions only one of the two palaces excavated, refers to just one fire while many buildings show severe damage because of fire, refers to 960 people who were killed while only 28 bodily remains of people have been found, etc.; Cohen (1982), 394–5. See about Masada's buildings, Netzer (1991). Carbon 14 research confirms a date around Masada's fall for the twenty-five skeletons found in a cave, Zias *et al.* (1994). Nikiprowetzky (1971), Ladouceur (1980; 1987) and Stern (1982–1983) also discuss the Masada episode.

175 Cohen (1982), 386–92, emphasises that Josephus' report was not unique in the ancient world by discussing sixteen Graeco-Roman reports about collective suicide that show many correspondences with Josephus' passage. See also Stern (1982–83).

176 The contemporary Masada traditions in Israel have been greatly influenced by Yitzhaq Lamdan's poem (a fragment of it is presented in Masada's new visitors' centre). The suicide often plays a minor role in modern readings of the event. The medieval Hebrew version in *Josippon* reports that the male rebels found death in a final attack by the Romans and not by killing themselves.

episode during which Josephus himself was supposed to commit suicide with his soldiers in Jotapata, but surprisingly escaped this fate. Josephus' own speech at Jotapata is highly critical of suicide even in a hopeless military situation (*War* 3.361–82). Apparently, Josephus was not embarrassed by this inconsistency.

Translation[177]

(389) While he [Eleazar][178] still wanted to encourage them, all cut him off and jumped to the deed, fully taken by an urge that could not be stopped. They went away as if they were mad,[179] striving to be first one after the other and thinking that the fact that one was not seen among the last would be a demonstration of their courage[180] and prudence. Such a desire to slaughter[181] their wives, children and themselves had seized them. (390) Moreover, they were not disheartened when the deed came nearer, what one would expect. They kept clinging to the opinion they had when they listened to (Eleazar's) words. All kept their affectionate feelings for their relatives, but reason prevailed, as if it was planning the most excellent things for their dearest. (391) They said goodbye, embraced their wives and took their children in their arms. They stuck to them with their last kisses and cried. (392) But on that same spot, they fulfilled their plan, as if working with different hands. Thinking about the evil they would have suffered through their enemies, they found the encouragement that death was necessary.[182] (393) At last nobody

---

177 Translation based on Michel and Bauernfeind (1959–69), vol. 2.2.

178 Eleazar ben Yair is clearly meant because of the reference to his speeches. Eleazar was a relative of Menahem, son of Judas, the Galilaean, the founder of the so-called fourth philosophy. He escaped to Masada in August/September 66. Cotton and Geiger (1989, 3–7) discuss the Jewish presence at Masada.

179 Another translation would be 'as if they were possessed by a demon'. In both cases the phrase may show some criticism about the act, Ladouceur (1987), 102–3.

180 The original meaning of *andreia* is 'manliness', and this seems appropriate as well. Cf. above n. 96 to 2 Macc. 7:21.

181 There is no reason not to stick to the literal meaning of the Greek. Corresponding non-Jewish stories about collective suicides, which may have influenced Josephus' articulation of the report, use the same terminology. This makes it less probable that the suicide was a cultic sacrifice, as some scholars argue, like Michel and Bauernfeind (1959–69), 2.2.280. Cf. Cohen (1982), 393 n. 22.

182 This matches the argument of Eleazar's first speech, see above.

appeared to be unable to commit this daring act, but all went by their dearest relatives.[183] They were unhappy out of necessity and thought that killing their own wives and children was the smallest evil. (394) Now at this point they were no longer able to endure the pain because of what they had done. They thought that it would not be just if they lived only a bit longer than those already killed. They quickly made one pile of their possessions and set that on fire. (395) They chose ten of them by lot who would slaughter all others.[184] Everyone concerned positioned himself next to his wife and children, lying flat on the ground and putting their hands over them. They held themselves ready to be slaughtered for those who had to execute this unhappy service. (396) They murdered all without trembling and determined to apply the same rule to one another, so that the one who would get the lot would kill the nine others and kill himself near all the dead. In this way, all were confident with each other that no one would do or feel something different than the other.[185] (397) At last they undertook the slaughter and the final one inspected the multitude of dead persons. Since there was no one left at this deadly scene who would need his hand, he started a large fire in the royal buildings[186] as soon as he found out that all were killed. With a massive thrust he drove the sword fully through his body and fell down close to his relatives. (398) They had died in the assumption that no living soul of them would be left behind to fall in the hands of the Romans. (399) But an old woman and a certain female relative of Eleazar,[187] who differed greatly in prudence and education from most women, as well as five children escaped notice by hiding themselves in the underground areas that carried drinking water, while the others were only thinking

---

183 The males kill their wives and children before they die at the hand of those assigned by lot.

184 A similar procedure is followed at Jotapata (*War* 3.387–91). Selecting persons by lot was a common practice in early Judaism, cf. Josephus, *War* 4.153–5; Acts 1:26. Cohen (1982), 397–8 and J. Naveh in Yadin and Naveh (1989), 28–31, discuss Yadin's view that he had found the ten lots mentioned by Josephus. This view is problematic, since Yadin actually found twelve potsherds with names and not ten, and the place where they were found contained many other potsherds that may have functioned as lots.

185 It is interesting to compare this with Josephus' own behaviour at Jotapata (see above).

186 There were two palaces at Masada, one in the north and one in the west; Netzer (1991).

187 The two women help to explain why Josephus was able to give a detailed report.

of the slaughter. (400) The number of those killed was 960, women and children included.[188] (401) The calamity was executed on Xanthikos 15.[189] The Romans were still expecting a combat. They prepared themselves at dawn, entered from the earthen dams with the help of ladders and made an attack. (403) But they saw none of their enemies, only a terrible desolation, fire in the buildings and silence. They could not understand what had happened. Finally, they shouted their war cry as when a missile is discharged, to see whether they could call some of those inside out to fight. (404) When the women heard the shouts, they arose from their underground hiding places and revealed to the Romans what was done, just as it happened. One of the two reported clearly and in detail everything that was said and in what way it was done. (405) It was not easy for them to pay attention to her, because they did not believe the magnitude of this bold act. They attempted to extinguish the fire and quickly made a passage through it into the royal buildings. (406) When they arrived at the host of dead, they did not see them as enemies, but admired the nobility of their decision and contempt of death[190] displayed by so many who did not change their mind during the deed.

---

188 The archaeologists found skeletons of three humans on the lower terrace of the northern palace and twenty-five in a cave, see n. 174.

189 The Greek month Xanthikos roughly coincides with the month of March in the common calendar. Josephus' last date given before the Masada episode concerns the year 72 (*War* 7.219, 252). One should not read his account as a strictly chronological report, since geographic and thematic interests seem to have been more important than a chronological one. The traditional date of Masada's fall in the spring of 73 has been questioned by Eck (1970), 93–111, who argues on the basis of two inscriptions that the Roman governor Flavius Silva could only have arrived in Judaea in the spring of 74. Cotton (1989) offers a discussion of the old and the new date and more references.

190 See pp. 50–1 and 104 for discussion of this motif.

3

CHRISTIAN MARTYRS
FROM THE FIRST TO THE
THIRD CENTURY CE

The early Christian writings discussed in this chapter date from the end of the first to the beginning of the third century. Although the earliest among them are not yet called Martyrdoms, Passions or Acts, that is writings entirely devoted to martyrdom (see Introduction), the theme of martyrdom figures prominently in these early writings (Clement's Letter to the Corinthians and Ignatius' Letters). The theme is important as well for one of the later documents, the *Writing to Diognetus*, which is not a martyrdom but an apologetic writing that presents the Christians as a people of martyrs. The other passages selected for this chapter do belong to one of the three types of Christian writings about martyrdom mentioned above.

General Introduction

1 Clement

The earliest Christian passages on the theme of martyrdom are part of very different writings. Clement's *Letter to the Corinthians*, also called *1 Clement*, dates from the last years of the first century CE. It is probably the oldest early Christian writing outside the Christian Bible that refers to martyrs. The letter is attributed to the Clement who was the third bishop of Rome. Scholars have often assumed that the general reference to a persecution of Christians in the introductory part (1.1) reflects an actual persecution instigated by the Emperor Domitian (81–96 CE) and is a clue to the letter's date. In fact, the description in 1.1 is not specific at all, and external evidence about a persecution ordered by Domitian is scanty.[1] However, the information about

---

1   Thompson (1990), 95–185, offers a recent discussion.

functionaries within the Christian communities and the references to *1 Clement* from the second century confirm a date at the end of the first century. Clement was an intellectual with a rhetorical training. He had a considerable knowledge of popular philosophical ideas as well of what became the Hebrew Bible/Old Testament. The letter consists basically of two sections: (a) a general one about jealousy, envy and strife and their consequences, and admonitions to act in a harmonious way towards each other (4.1–39.9); and (b) a section that focuses on the immediate reason for the letter, the conflict within the Corinthian community, because a few younger members stood up to the presbyters who had led the community for a considerable time (40.1–59.2).

1 Clem. 5.1–6.2 presupposes that the apostles Peter and Paul died as martyrs in Rome.[2] Its references to the apostles' sufferings and posthumous vindication strongly suggest that their martyr deaths had taken place in the recent past. Many scholars assume that Nero's persecution of the Christians after the fire in Rome in 64 forms the historical background for the rather general description of the sufferings of Peter, Paul and other Christians in *1 Clem.* 5–6.[3] The Roman historian Tacitus reports on the disastrous event in 64 that those Christians who had already confessed their religion were executed after the fire. Subsequently a great multitude of others were killed (*Ann.* 15.44). Tacitus does not give us names, but gradually a fixed tradition was established that Peter and Paul died a martyr's death during Nero's reign in Rome. The Church historian Eusebius confirms this tradition by reporting that Peter was crucified and Paul was decapitated (*Hist. eccl.* 2.25.5). According to an old tradition the site of Paul's execution and burial was along the Via Ostiense at the place where the church St. Paul without the Walls stands. By emphasising that Peter and Paul were paragons of perseverance until death, Clement already seems to suggest that Christian martyrs demonstrate the special character of the Christian stock.

Ignatius, Letter to the Romans

Ignatius was bishop of Antioch in the first part of the second century CE[4] and wrote about his own future martyrdom. On his way to the

---

2 John 21:18–19 alludes only to the violent death of the apostle Peter.
3 Tajra (1994), 1–32, reconstructs Paul's trial and execution and argues that Paul died before the fire in Rome.
4 The church historian Eusebius notes in his *Chronicon* concerning the 212th

amphitheatre in Rome he wrote seven letters to local Christian com-munities.[5] In these letters one finds unusually personal and emotional passages, expressing somebody's almost desperate longing for a death at the hands of Roman executioners. Surprisingly, the letters offer little substantial information about his personal circumstances and arrest as many later Christian writings about martyrdom do, which look like trial reports or eyewitness accounts, but are primarily liter-ary texts.[6]

Ignatius indicates that he was bishop of the Christian community of Antioch, the capital of the Roman province of Syria, one of the largest cities of the empire. His self-deprecating remarks have been inter-preted as evidence that he had great difficulties in maintaining his leadership of the Antiochene community. This, moreover, has been connected with the hypothesis that Ignatius saw his death as a martyr as the possibility to make up for his shortcomings as bishop with one grand gesture.[7] This theory seems attractive, but there is no explicit reference by Ignatius himself to support it. Ignatius expresses joyfully that he was convicted *ad bestias*, to fight the wild beasts in Rome. The journey can be reconstructed from the seven authentic letters written during a very brief period, perhaps two weeks, as Ignatius made his way to Rome in the company of ten Roman soldiers. In Smyrna, close to Asia Minor's West coast, he met the local bishop, Polycarp, who would die as a martyr several decades later. Several Christian commu-nities sent representatives to Ignatius in Smyrna. From Smyrna he himself sent a letter to them as well as to the Roman Christians, asking them not to prevent or obstruct his execution. Ignatius continued his journey from Smyrna to Troas in the North West of Asia Minor. Polycarp's *Letter to the Philippians* shows that he reached Philippi in the East of Macedonia, but from here we are in the dark again.

William Schoedel compares Ignatius' journey to a victor's proces-sion, which is an attractive reading. In that case, Ignatius' journey

---

Olympiad (*GCS* 20.218) that Ignatius was bishop of Antioch from the first year of the Emperor Vespasian up to the tenth year of Trajan (107–108 CE), which may imply that Ignatius died a martyr's death in that year.

5 Mellink (2000), 5–50, discusses the authenticity of the seven letters and their recensions.

6 The description of Ignatius' execution is only found in legendary writings that are considerably later than his death. The *Martyrdom of Ignatius* dates from the fifth or sixth century CE. Cf. Polycarp's *Letter to the Philippians* (1.1; 9.1). See dis-cussion on the *Martyrdom of Polycarp*, p. 95.

7 Harrison (1936), 79–106; Schoedel (1985), 10 and 212–13.

would have been a triumphal march, applauded by many and ending with the execution as the martyr's victory.[8] Indeed, representatives of various communities waited for Ignatius to greet him on the way to Rome or travelled ahead of him.[9] Ignatius and his friends arranged embassies, escorts and letters in order to gain recognition and support.[10] In any case, this view helps us to understand how Ignatius could idealise his death and present it as the beginning of real life.

How did Ignatius interpret his sufferings at hand? His statements seem to underlie a dualism that radically relativises his existence on earth and focuses on life in or after death. Matter, earth, secular things and the present age are of no importance at all for Ignatius, but attaining God through death is everything for him, since it implies real life. One of the images Ignatius uses to indicate this is that of becoming a disciple.[11] The paradoxical outcome of Ignatius' reasoning is that the learning process to live according to Christ comes to fulfilment only in death. The same is true for other images referring to his ultimate goal, like becoming an imitator of God or Christ, a word of God or a true human being (cf. *Rom.* 6.2).

Clearly for Ignatius, violent death is the road to this goal. The passages with his language of attaining God (or Christ) seem to have a double meaning, referring to reaching God as well as acquiring God.[12] Ignatius thinks he will reach God at the moment of his death. The notion of 'acquiring God' is also implied, since the spatial reaching of God will lead to perfection, which is having God within oneself. Other believers can also reach God, but this will happen at the end of time (*Eph.* 10.1; *Mag.* 1.3; *Smyr.* 9.2). What reaching and acquiring God means remains rather vague, which is striking in the light of Ignatius' passionate desire to reach this stage.[13] Ignatius' resurrection seems to take place after death, but the moment is not specified.[14] On the basis of passages about the resurrection of martyrs in other documents one could argue by way of analogy that Ignatius

---

8   Cf. Ignatius, *Rom.* 2.2; 5.1.
9   See *Rom.* 9.3; 10.1–2; cf. *Eph.* 2.1; *Phil.* 11.1; *Smyr.* 10.1.
10 Schoedel (1985), 11–12.
11 See *Rom.* 4.2 and p. 109, n. 101.
12 *Eph.* 12.2; *Mag.* 14.1; *Tral.* 12.2; 13.3; *Rom.* 1.2; 2.1; 4.1; 5.3; 9.2; *Smyr.* 11.1; Pol. 2.3; 7.1. Ignatius speaks twice about 'attaining Christ' in *Rom.* 5.3.
13 As emphasised by Bommes (1970), 164.
14 The only thing that is specified by Ignatius about being resurrected is that it is not spiritual only, cf. *Smyr.* 2–7.

expected an immediate posthumous revival.[15] His passionate longing for reaching God becomes rather awkward if Ignatius did not expect that he would be resurrected immediately after his death. Why take all this trouble if he only would arise with the other faithful Christians at the end of time?

The Ascension of Isaiah

Jewish and Christian passages tell us that the biblical prophet Isaiah was sawn in two on the orders of the wicked Manasseh, king of Judah. One of the more elaborate versions of Isaiah's martyrdom is a section in the *Ascension of Isaiah*, one of the so-called Pseudepigrapha of the Old Testament.[16] Only Ethiopic manuscripts have preserved this book entirely and given it the title *Ascension of Isaiah*.[17] The writing as we have it is a composite Christian work from the second century CE, combining several sources. Chapters 6–11 describe the visions about Isaiah's ascent to the firmament and the seven heavens and his encounter with God, God's Beloved and the Holy Spirit. This section may have been added to Chapters 1–5 that tell the events that lead up to Isaiah's martyrdom.[18] Several Italian scholars have recently called for a setting of the document in a context of competing Christian prophetic groups in the area of Antioch during the first decades of the second century CE.[19]

The depiction of prophets from the Hebrew Bible as martyrs is an elaboration of the theme of Israel persecuting or murdering these messengers of the Lord. In the Hebrew Bible this theme is restricted

---

15 Mellink (2000), 251–87, rejects this, referring to *Eph.* 11.2 and *Rom.* 4.3.
16 Several Christian passages refer to an extra-biblical writing about Isaiah's death or his ascension to heaven: Origen, *Ep. ad Afric.* 9 (*PL* 11, col. 65); *Com. Mat.* 13:57 (*GCS* 40, p. 24); Didymus, *Com. in Eccl.* 329; Jerome, *Com. Is.* 64:4–5 (*PL* 24, col. 622).
17 Greek, Latin and Coptic fragments have been found and Latin and Slavonic translations belonging to a separate textual tradition. Knibb (1985), 144–6; Norelli (1995).
18 Norelli (1994), 66–7 argues the opposite, taking Chapters 6–11 as the oldest part. Scholars have argued that part of Chapters 1–5 ultimately go back to an independent Jewish source and have sometimes called this section the *Martyrdom of Isaiah*, but this view has recently been rejected; Pesce (1983), 17–29; 40–1 and (1984).
19 Acerbi (1983), especially 210–53; Pesce (1984); Norelli (1993, 1994, 1995). See also Hall (1990), 292–306. Knibb (1985), 149–50, argues that the original part of Chapters 1–5 dates from the first century CE and originates in Palestine.

to only a few passages (e.g. 1 Kings 19:1, 14; Jer. 26:20–3; 2 Chron. 24:20–2; Neh. 9:26), but later writings suggest that more and more prophets have undergone such a fate.[20] The New Testament reflects this expansion in several passages like 1 Thes. 2:16 and Hebr. 11:32–8. Many traditions about the violent death of Israel's prophets have been collected in a hagiographic writing called the *Lives of the Prophets*.[21] This collection, transmitted and adapted by Christians like the *Ascension of Isaiah*, combines twenty-three reports concerning prophets figuring in the Hebrew Bible.

Isaiah was sawn asunder by the Judaean king Manasseh according to the *Lives of the Prophets* (*Vit. Isa.* 1). The *Ascension of Isaiah* offers a more elaborate version of this brutal execution. The tradition itself may partly have been triggered by the alleged cruelty of the idolatrous king Manasseh (*c.* 687–642 BCE). 2 Kings 21:16 describes his murderous behaviour in words not to be mistaken: 'Moreover Manasseh shed very much innocent blood, until he had filled Jerusalem from one end to another.' The passages that refer to Isaiah's execution by a saw characterise Manasseh as a persecutor and murderer of prophets.[22] Sawing the convict in two was a very rare form of execution in the ancient world, but not totally without precedents.[23] Some of the versions of the martyrdom state that Isaiah was sawn asunder from his head downwards.[24] The instrument used for this horrible punishment was a wood saw, not a wooden saw, as the later *Legend of Isaiah* suggests.[25]

A second reason for Isaiah's unbelievably harsh execution may be the seriousness of the accusation against him. The execution by a saw seems to be connected with accusations of blasphemy of God and false prophecy.[26] The prophet Belkira from Samaria accuses Isaiah and his followers of false prophecy and lying (*Asc. Is.* 3:6–10). He

---

20 Schoeps (1943) and Steck (1967) offer surveys of the relevant passages in the Hebrew Bible and early Jewish and Christian literature.
21 Satran (1995); Schwemer (1995–96).
22 *Vit. Isa.* 1; *Asc. Is.* 5; Josephus, *Ant.* 10.38; Hebr. 11:37 (anonymously); Justin, *Dial.* 120.5; Tertullian, *De pat.* 14; *Scorp.* 8; *Legend of Isaiah*; *T.Y. Sanhedrin* 10.2; *T.B. Yevamot* 49b.
23 Suetonius reports that the Emperor Caligula brought this punishment over from the East (*Hist. aug. Cal.* 27.3). Cf. Amos 1:3; 1 Chron. 20:3 in the Septuagint translation and Sus. 54–5. Norelli (1994), 11–21.
24 *Asc. Is.*, Justin and translations of *Vit. Proph.*, see Schwemer (1995–96), 114–15.
25 Knibb (1985), 146; Schwemer (1995–96), 1.114–15; Norelli (1995), 2.289–90.
26 Cf. Sus. 58–9. Engel (1985), 123–31; van Henten (1990), 4–5.

could lay his hands on several alleged prophecies. Isaiah not only prophesied that Jerusalem would be laid waste, but also claimed that he would see more than Moses and see God Himself. Belkira counters this claim by quoting Moses' own words: 'There is no man who can see the Lord and live' (Exod. 33:20).[27] Belkira's accusations are a major blow in the confrontation between the right and the false prophets, led by Isaiah and Belkira respectively, and highlighted in the first part of the *Ascension of Isaiah*.[28]

The passage about Isaiah's martyrdom in Chapter 5 takes up Belkira's accusation of false prophecy. Belkira and the other false prophets rejoice in Isaiah's execution. Belkira acts as the devil in human form in 5:4–9. He tempts Isaiah like the devil tempted Jesus (5:8). When Christian prophets have interpreted the martyrdom of Isaiah as a reflection of their own rejection and persecution, the combination of the martyrdom with the visions of Chapters 6–11 makes sense.[29] In that case, the situation of the Christian prophets would have been part of an eschatological scenario. Their sufferings would become understandable, since they belonged to the disastrous events of the last generation (9:13; 11:38), when the final confrontation between Jesus Christ and Beliar (the devil) would take place. The final chapters encourage and reassure the righteous by describing their blessings in heaven, their heavenly robes, thrones and crowns of glory (11:40; cf. 4:16; 9:24–6).

The Martyrdom of Polycarp

The *Martyrdom of Polycarp* may be the oldest Christian document fully devoted to martyrdom, if the early date of 155–160 CE is correct.[30] It is a letter from the Christian community in Smyrna to the community

---

27 *Asc. Is.* 3:8–9. Cf. *Par. Jer.* 9:21–2.

28 *Asc. Is.* 2:9; 3:1, 6; 5:2, 12. Cf. 6:3–7 and 7:1. Belkira had many followers in Jerusalem, but dwelled in Bethlehem, as Isaiah did for some time (2:12; 3:1).

29 Several passages in Ch. 5 show traces of Christian adaptations (e.g. 5:1a, 15–16).

30 Scholars who defend the authenticity of the *Martyrdom of Polycarp* have suggested no less than three different dates: (a) 155–160 CE, based on the reference to the proconsul Statius Quadratus in Chapter 21, whose term of service is known through inscriptions; (b) 167 CE in line with Eusebius' dating of the *Martyrdom* in the seventh year of the Emperor Marcus Aurelius' reign (*Hist. eccl.* 4.14.10–15.1; *Chron.* to the year 167); (c) 177 CE, assuming that Eusebius' date has been transmitted incorrectly. See Dehandschutter (1993), 497–502, for discussion and further references.

of Philomelium and all other Christian communities about the martyrdom of Bishop Polycarp of Smyrna.[31] The narrative about Polycarp's death may ultimately go back to a trial protocol or a Christian eyewitness report. The work as transmitted to us, though, clearly has a literary character. Polycarp's behaviour leading to his execution has been embellished in several ways. There is a structural correspondence with Jewish stories about martyrdom and the narrative shares significant motifs with these stories.[32] Furthermore, there are many parallels with the passion narratives of Jesus. Polycarp is being arrested because of betrayal by his own set, like Jesus (1.2; 6.2). Most of the correspondences between Polycarp and Jesus are significant but do not match completely, probably because the author wanted to keep a clear distinction between the status of both holy persons. Thus, one of Polycarp's opponents is named Herodes, but this Herodes is not a king like Herodes Antipas in the Gospels (Luke 23:6–12), but a police officer (*Mart. Pol.* 6.2). Another striking parallel is that Polycarp enters Smyrna on an ass just as Jesus entered Jerusalem. Like Jesus, Polycarp states in connection to his arrest that God's will had to be fulfilled (*Mart. Pol.* 7.2–3; Mark 14:32–42; Mat. 26:36–46; Luke 22:39–46).[33]

The reason for Polycarp's arrest is not given explicitly. Yet, the narrative presupposes a decree implying that Christians brought before the Roman governor were required to call the emperor Lord (8.2), to offer a sacrifice (8.2; 4; 12.2), to curse their own group as 'atheists' (9.2),[34] to taunt Christ, and, last but not least, to swear to the Fortune of the emperor (9.2–10.1; cf. 4). In the dialogues of Chapters 8–12 the police officer Herodes, his father Nicetes, as well as the governor emphasise time and again that Polycarp's refusal to obey the authorities will be punished by a terrible death penalty (8.2; 9.3; 11). Nevertheless, Polycarp prefers death to conceding to the Romans (8.2; 9.2–3; 10–11). Chapters 13–16 describe the execution on the stake in detail. The author notes that the Jews eagerly collected wood for Polycarp's stake (13.1), but it is far from certain that this detail is historical. It may, in fact, have been inspired by anti-Jewish

---

31 Dehandschutter (1993) offers discussion and references. See also Buschmann (1998).
32 Perler (1949), 66–7, and Baumeister (1980), 295–8, argue that the author of *Mart. Pol.* has used 2 and 4 Maccabees. Cf. van Henten (1993), 714–23.
33 Dehandschutter (1979), 233–58, offers a long list of such parallels.
34 Atheism is one of the frequent accusations against the Christians, Frend (1965), 259–60; Lampe (1987), 82; 166–72. See also *Mart. Lugd.* 5.1.9.

passages in the New Testament like Mat. 27:25 or Rev. 2:9.[35] Chapter 18 reflects the beginning of Polycarp's martyr cult. It reports that the Smyrnean Christians took his burnt bones and put them away in a suitable place with the hope of celebrating his 'birthday' together, commemorating the ones who had 'triumphed' before and preparing those who had to face martyrdom in the future.

Polycarp died in his eighty-sixth year. His name 'Fruitful one' matches his significance for the Christian movement. A passage in *Mart. Pol.* 12 illustrates this. A crowd of pagans and Jews living in Smyrna shout after Polycarp's confession of being a Christian that he was 'the teacher of Asia, the father of the Christians, the destroyer of our gods and the one who is teaching many to abstain from sacrificing and worshipping' (*Mart. Pol.* 12.2). In their immediate context these epithets imply that Polycarp was considered a very important Christian, which would justify his execution. However, the author must have adapted this passage, since it is highly improbable that Jews would have supported these exclamations with a clearly polytheistic tenor. The passage is very much in line with the patriotic purport of the *Martyrdom of Polycarp*. Polycarp's surname 'the father of the Christians' and other epithets function foremost as honorary titles in a Christian context, expressing Polycarp's significance for them as an exemplary figure.

The Acts of Justin

The *Acts of Justin* is a brief document about the trial and conviction of the early Christian philosopher and apologist Justin, as well as some of his fellow Christians living in Rome. It is probably the oldest specimen of the acts form of Christian martyr texts and seems at first glance rather close to official acts of trial.[36] The greatest part concerns the dialogue between Justin and the Roman prefect Rusticus. Justin was a well-known Christian apologetic author who was born in Flavia Neapolis in Samaria (present-day Nablus).[37] He has travelled as a teacher of Christianity. His writings present Christianity in philosophical terms, using, among other things, concepts from Middle Platonism. He probably worked as a freelance teacher in Rome until

---

35 See Lieu (1996), 63–70.
36 See the Introduction about the various Christian documents concerning martyrdom, pp. 3–5.
37 Barnard (1967); Lampe (1987), 219–45.

his arrest. Some of his pupils were executed with him. This execution probably took place during the sixties of the second century CE, shortly after Polycarp's martyrdom. Justin's judge was the prefect of Rome Q. Iunius Rusticus, who acted as consul in 162 and may have become prefect of the city of Rome shortly after his consulate.[38] As the local head of police, the prefect of Rome was responsible for law and order in Rome and its neighbourhood up to a distance of 100 miles from the city. He also represented the emperor in legal matters in this area. Rusticus remained prefect until about 168. This implies that Justin's martyrdom can be dated between 162 and 168 CE.

The simple form of the *Acts* with its focus on the interrogation of the martyrs seems to imply that the document is authentic. Gary Bisbee's comparison of the *Acts* with Roman trial reports, however, notes several discrepancies with these official reports.[39] The introduction and conclusion must have been added and the text must have been reworked in several passages. The passage with Justin's confession is clearly an expansion of the simple question and answer structure of most of the document (2.5–7). Justin's statements in this confession do not always match what he has written in his own works.[40] The other Christians seem to be presented as his pupils (4.7).[41] Their mostly Greek names may be another reason to doubt the authenticity of the document in its present form. If these names are to be interpreted in a symbolical way,[42] which is rather obvious in most cases, would the names Chariton and Charito refer to the grace (*charis*) of God and Eu(h)elpistus to the expectation (*elpis*) of Christians. The document even invites the reader to make such associations, because the responses of Charito, Euelpistus and Hierax clearly play with the meaning of their names (4.2–4).[43] These findings hardly fit in with the content and aim of an

38 Hilhorst in Bastiaensen *et al.* (1987), 391.
39 Bisbee (1988), 94–118.
40 In his writings Justin does not refer to Jesus Christ as child (*pais*) of God, nor to Jesus as herald. The vocabulary about God as creator used in *Acts* 2.5 is also different from what Justin himself writes, Bisbee (1988), 109–11.
41 Freudenberger (1968), 27; Lampe (1987), 238–40.
42 Most of these names are attested at Rome in the early imperial age and some of them have been frequently used for slaves or freed-persons, Freudenberger (1968), 28; Solin (1982), 60–1; 451–3; 591 and 1049. The female name Charito was extremely rare, though. Bartelink (1961) discusses the symbolic character of early Christian names.
43 One wonders, therefore, whether all names have a symbolical meaning. Liberianus can be associated with *liber* 'child' and hints at the importance of having Christian parents (cf. 4.5–8). The second part, however, is identical with

official trial report. Whatever the Christian embellishment of this document precisely has been, it certainly enhanced its didactic significance for other Christians.

The Martyrdom of Lyon and Vienne

The *Martyrdom of Lyon and Vienne* is transmitted by Eusebius (264–340 CE) in the fifth book of his *History of the Church* (5.1.1–63; 2.1–7).[44] It is a letter about the martyrdom of prominent members of the Christian communities of Lyons and Vienne to their fellow Christians in Asia Minor. The letter describes endless tortures in painstaking detail and presents martyrdom as a battle between the devil and the martyrs. The martyrs come from two Christian communities in the South East of France, Lyons and Vienne, both located on the river Rhône. Close to the ancient city of Lyons stood a huge temple of the imperial cult of the three Roman provinces of Gaul.[45] This area was the location of the amphitheatre, where the martyrs fought.[46] In the introduction to the martyrdom Eusebius refers to the Emperor Marcus Aurelius' seventeenth year (177 CE, *Hist. eccl.* 5 pref.). Most scholars accept this date of 177 CE for the martyrdom.[47] The *Martyrdom* is usually taken as an authentic report by a Christian eyewitness.[48] However, some of the details are simply too good to be true, such as when Sanctus' body, after his weakest parts had been scorched and he had been heavily mutilated, fully recovers during a new session of torture (*Hist. eccl.* 5.1.20–4). We do not know whether Eusebius has adapted the report considerably.[49]

Ianus, the name of a Roman god. Paeon may hint at the martyr's Christian education (*paideia*) by way of alliteration.

44 Discussions and references are offered by Frend (1965), 1–30; Rougé and Turcan (1978); Löhr (1989); Farkasfalvy (1992).

45 Fishwick (1987–92).

46 Chevallier (1975), 913–39, offers a survey of ancient Lyons.

47 Eusebius offers an earlier date in his *Chronicon* (*GCS* 20, p. 222. Cf. Jerome, *Chronicon*, *GCS* 47, p. 205), where he links the martyrdoms of Polycarp and the Christians in Gaul to the 236th Olympiad and the reign of Marcus Aurelius and his co-ruler Lucius Verus (who died in 169). Barnes (1968), 518, considers the first date as probable as the second. Barnes in Rougé and Turcan (1978), 139–41, defends a date of 175 or some years later on the basis of Eusebius' preface to the martyrdom.

48 See, for example, Frend (1965), 1; Barnes (1968), 517.

49 In any case, Eusebius has not fully copied the document, which is apparent from his own comments in the margin. See Löhr (1989).

The *Martyrdom* has been linked to a joint decision of the emperor and the Roman senate in 176 or early 177 to relieve the sponsors of gladiatorial games by allowing them to use condemned criminals at the price of six *aurei* per head. This was a bargain compared to the price of hiring a gladiator.[50] The priests of the imperial cult in Gaul may have been tempted to use convicted Christians instead of gladiators on the basis of this decision, but unfortunately the *Martyrdom* does not inform us about this. On the contrary, the references to the persecution start with a brief description of a pogrom-like situation (5.1.5–7).[51] The mob brings the martyrs to Lyons' market-place, where the head of the local garrison decides to put them in jail and await the return of the province's governor (5.1.8). Most of the martyrs' tortures take place in connection with their interrogation by the governor, whose questions aim at the confirmation of their Christian identity. At a certain stage, the document does refer to gladiatorial games (5.1.50, 53), which may have been linked to 1 August, the date of the commemoration of the dedication of the altar of Rome and Augustus, which marked the beginning of the imperial cult in Gaul.[52] The document does not say so, however, and notes that the Christians had to fight in the amphitheatre over several days (5.1.50; 53).[53] In any case, the *Martyrdom* is much more interested in the heroic behaviour of the martyrs than in a detailed description of the persecution.

The martyrdoms are presented as a spectacular show, with the martyrs in the role of gladiators and the devil as orchestrator of the mob and the torturers.[54] For the onlookers the battle takes place in the arena. For the martyrs themselves, their bodies seem to be the battlefield. The battered body is evidence of the martyrs' triumph

---

50 Frend (1965), 5. The senate's decision is preserved in *CIL* 6278 = *ILS* 5163.

51 Barnes (1968), 518, suggests that the pogrom may partly have been the result of a shortage of gladiators. L. Gracco Ruggini in Rougé and Turcan (1978), 77–8, 81, 90–1, suggests that Lyon's professional corporations (*collegia*) were highly suspicious of the Christians, who could be seen as a threat to the *collegia* because of their refusal to participate in the manifestations of loyalty to the emperor. In combination with the robberies and raids in this period this anxiety may have led to outbursts of aggression against Christians.

52 M. le Glay in Rougé and Turcan (1978), 19–31; Fishwick (1987–92), 1.1, 97–149.

53 *Mart. Lugd.* 5.1.37 notes that an earlier day of games, during which the martyrs had to face wild animals, was organised especially for the martyrs.

54 Cf. the reference to 1 Cor. 4:9 in 5.1.40, see p. 123.

and their participation in Christ's suffering (5.1.23; 41–42; 59). Jesus Christ supports the martyrs during their battle (5.1.22–4; 27–8). Blandina communicates with Him during her final suffering,[55] not feeling the wounds caused by the horns of the bull (5.1.56). The devil appears to be the martyrs' principal opponent.[56] He tries to make them blaspheme God and is behind the denial of the Christian faith of the weaker members of the group, who finally manage to succeed on the road of martyrdom because of the example of the others.[57]

Perpetua's Passion

Another document that presents martyrdom as a spectacle is the Passion of the North-African women Perpetua and Felicitas and other Christians. It offers everything that one expects of a martyr story: an exceptional autobiographical section, a father desperately trying to save his daughter brought up for trial, intriguing visions and a spectacular death scene.[58] Together with their tutor Saturus, the two women are the key figures of the martyrdom. By the conversion of the Emperor Constantine (315 CE) Perpetua and Felicitas' 'anniversaries' were already incorporated into calendars of martyrs on 7 March. Later sources mention 7 March 203 as the date of the martyrdom of Perpetua and her group. Scholars usually take the writing as authentic, but the symbolical meaning of the combination of the names of the two female martyrs cannot be missed: 'perpetual happiness' is the reward after their victory, as the *Passion* indicates several times.[59] Prophecies and visions as gifts of the Holy Spirit are characteristic of *Perpetua's Passion*. Through her visions Perpetua demonstrates that she had direct contact with the divine. In this respect the *Passion* corresponds to the prophetic movement of the Montanists, which originated in Phrygia and for which the famous early Christian author Tertullian had a great admiration. Some scholars, therefore, have

---

55 Cf. *Pas. Perp.* 4.6.
56 See also Ignatius, *Rom.* 5.3; 7.1; *Mart. Pol.* 2.4; 17.1; *Pas. Perp.* 3.3; 10.14; 21.10; *Mart. Pauli* 1. Dölger (1933); Baumeister (1980), 254–5.
57 *Mart. Lugd.* 5.1.16; cf. 5.1.11–12, 25, 32–5, 45–8.
58 For detailed discussion and references see Dronke (1984); Habermehl (1992); Shaw (1993); and Salisbury (1997).
59 Augustine already reflects on these names and notes that all martyrs who withstood their trials rejoiced in perpetual felicity: 'with the names of these two the eternity of all is signified' (*Sermo* 2 and 3).

assumed that Tertullian was the one who edited and transmitted the *Passion*.[60]

Perpetua's family name Vibius suggests that her family had received Roman citizenship many generations ago. Her father is presented as a person of high rank. Perpetua's excellent education is emphasised in 2.1. According to 13.4 she knew not only Latin but also Greek. The place of trial and execution was very probably Carthage, which was re-colonised by Julius Caesar and Augustus with thousands of colonists from Rome and served as the capital of the Roman province of North Africa. In the second century CE it was one of the greatest and wealthiest cities of the empire. The amphitheatre in the north-west of the city, the location of the martyrs' execution, was just one of its magnificent buildings.

The martyrs' arrest and execution were probably connected with the Emperor Septimius Severus' attempts to strengthen the imperial cult. Septimius Severus (193–211 CE) tried to integrate the so-called mystery cults into the ceremonies of the imperial cult and propagated the cult of the Graeco-Egyptian god Serapis. He considered himself to be the incarnation of this god. Shortly after 201 he forbade conversion to Judaism or Christianity, which led to a persecution of Christians in Alexandria and other places in North Africa. By emphasising their Christian identity and undergoing baptism Perpetua's group violated Septimius Severus' edict. The *Passion* indicates that they were executed in the amphitheatre during the festivities at the occasion of the emperor's son Geta's birthday (7.9; 15.4; 16.3).[61]

The *Passion* can be read as a story about conflicting values and identities, the old Roman as opposed to the new Christian, with the dialogues of Perpetua and her father as a *leitmotiv*. Family relations figure prominently in the *Passion of Perpetua and Felicitas*, but they are consistently rejected by Perpetua.[62] Perpetua is married and is breast-feeding her young son in the first part of the martyrdom. Surprisingly, we hear nothing about her husband and hardly anything about her mother and brothers. Likewise, the marriage of Felicitas and Revocatus, which results into the untimely birth of a daughter, does not get any attention in the text (2.1; 15), which is focused upon the martyrs awaiting their road to heaven. By way of

---

60 Bastiaensen in Bastiaensen *et al.* (1987), 418.
61 Ibid., 428–9.
62 Frend (1965), 321–2; Shaw (1993), 20–6; Perkins (1995), 104–13; Salisbury (1997), 5–11.

exception, however, Perpetua's father plays a prominent role as representative of the old order and traditional identity. He clearly is a contrast figure to Perpetua, who embodies the new way of life (3.1–3; 5.1–6.8; 9).[63] The power of Perpetua's father as the head of a Roman household and the traditional role of a mother nursing and raising children to continue the family line clash with Perpetua's behaviour during trial, in prison and, finally, in the amphitheatre. The pitiful aristocratic father fights a losing battle for the Roman deities against his Christian daughter. Perpetua as well as Felicitas destroy traditional family structures and their Christian group in prison functions as an alternative family. Perpetua's ambiguous attitude towards her son exemplifies the tension between old and new values and identities. This tension dissolves when Perpetua accepts that her son should no longer stay with her in prison. Like the mother of the seven Maccabaean brothers she overcomes her motherly love for her child.

The Writing to Diognetus

The so-called *Writing to Diognetus* erroneously attributed to Justin Martyr is not entirely devoted to martyrdom.[64] In fact, the issue of martyrdom is not even its central theme, but the author highlights the willingness to die a noble death as a greatly admired Christian virtue. The *Writing*'s usual name, *Letter* or *Epistle to Diognetus*, is inadequate. The *Writing* does not show the literary characteristics of a letter at all, and serves a double purpose. Like Christian apologetic writings from the second century CE it responds to pagan questions and criticisms concerning the Christians. It also incites the primary addressee, Diognetus, to become a Christian. This implies that the work can be considered a *logos protreptikos*, a discourse aimed at persuading the audience to accept the view presented by the author. Diognetus, called 'most excellent' in the *Writing*'s opening, can be compared to Theophilus, the addressee of the prologues of the Gospel of Luke and Acts. Both were members of the elite and may have been involved in the distribution of the writing dedicated to them. Several attempts have been made to identify this privileged

---

63 The fact that Perpetua remains in his power and household after marriage may be explained by the assumption that her marriage was contracted.
64 For discussion and references, see Marrou (1951); Brändle (1975); Wengst (1984).

Diognetus, but these are good guesses at best.[65] The anonymous author also remains very much in the dark. The date of the writing is difficult to determine. The references to persecutions of Christians seem authentic and imply, therefore, a date before the Constantine era, when Christianity became the state religion.[66] The correspondences with other apologetic Christian writings and the self-evident way in which the apologetic arguments are being presented seem to point roughly to a date between the late second and the late third century CE.

The *Writing*'s brief passages about noble death of Christians concern the relation of Christians to others. The outside world is supposed to be hostile to the Christians out of ignorance. The Christian attitude towards the world as described in the *Writing to Diognetus* can be characterised as a distanced but serious participation in world affairs.[67] The distance from the world results from the tensions between Christians' loyalty to the outside world and their Christian belief. The author emphasises that Christians should be loyal to the authorities up to the moment when this affects their belief (5.10; 7.7).

The statement of 1.1 about the newness of the Christian race seems to be a clue to the meaning of the *Writing* 1–6. In the eyes of the ancients, Christianity was a new and unimportant phenomenon. Other apologetic Christian writings tackle their opponents' questions about this newness by referring to the history of Israel as the pre-history of the Christians or to the prophecies about Christ in what became the Old Testament.[68] The author of the *Writing to Diognetus* argues differently here. In his opinion, all history develops according to a predestined divine plan with no special place for Israel as God's chosen people. The Christians seem to have taken over Israel's role. Therefore, the compositional scheme of Chapters 1–6 with the succession of pagans, Jews and Christians is rather telling. History seems to be divided in three periods that are each connected with a specific people. The Greek era is followed by the era of the Jews, and history comes to its fulfilment, so to speak, with the era of the

---

65 Marrou (1951), 265–7.
66 Baumeister (1988). *Writing* 1.1; 5.5, 11–12, 14–17; 6.5–6, 9; 7.7–9; 10.7–8 refer to persecutions.
67 Cf. other apologetic passages, like Aristides 16; *Kerygma Petri* Frag. 5, see n. 69.
68 See also *Act. Just.* 2.6, p. 118.

Christian people.[69] Like Clement of Rome and the author of the *Martyrdom of Polycarp*, the author considers the Christians to be a people. He does not directly refer to martyrs in this connection, as Clement and the author of the *Martyrdom of Polycarp* do,[70] but comes up with the extraordinary way of life of Christians. The Christians' contempt for death becomes their major characteristic.[71]

The *Writing to Diognetus* mentions this contempt for death in its introduction.[72] The author seems to connect this 'virtue' with the peculiar observation that the more the Christians are punished, the more their number grows (7.9). This reminds one of the famous statement made probably a little later by Tertullian: 'the blood of the Christians is seed' (*Apol.* 50.13).[73] This paradoxical growth of the Christians[74] demonstrates God's power (7.7–9). It also supports the author's view that history has come to fulfilment with the arrival of the Christians. The power of the Christians becomes apparent in their steadfastness when confronted with those having great political power.[75]

1 *1 Clement* 5–6

Clement's notes about martyrdom of Christians (late first century CE) are part of his discussion of envy, the divisive element of the Corinthian community (see the General Introduction). The martyrs belong to a list of famous people (4.1–6.2) that starts with persons from Israel's

---

69 Other apologetic writings describe the Christians as the third race of humankind: Aristides 2.2; 16.4; *Kerygma Petri* Frag. 5 (Clement of Alexandria, *Strom.* 6.5.41); Tertullian, *Ad nationes* 1.8; Origen, *Contra Celsum* 1.26; 8.43; Harnack (1924), 259–89; Oepke (1950), 266–7; Lieu (1996), 164–77.

70 *1 Clem.* 5–6; *Mart. Pol.* 3.2; cf. 12.2; 17.2.

71 Cf. Josephus, who emphasises the Jewish contempt for death in *War* 3.475; 5.315, 458; 7.406; *Ant.* 17.256; *Ap.* 1.42–3; 1.191; 2.146; 2.218–19; 2.294. See p. 51. Cf. 4 Macc. 15:9.

72 Other Christian apologetic writings highlight this motif as well: Justin, *1 Apol.* 11.2; 57.2; *2 Apol.* 12.1; Tatian, *Or.* 11.1; *Acta Apollodori* 37; Origen, *Contra Celsum* 2.15, 56, 73; 3.78; Minucius Felix 8.5; Eusebius, *Hist. eccl.* 8.14.13.

73 Cf. 21.25; Justin, *Dial.* 110.4; Origen, *Contra Celsum* 1.3.27; 2.8; 8.43. Pellegrino (1955–56).

74 This motif also occurs in other apologetic writings, see Justin, *Dial.* 110.4; Minucius Felix 37.6; Origen, *Contra Celsum* 3.8; 5.50; Lactantius, *Div. inst.* 5.13.1.

75 A related motif in martyr texts is God's or Christ's support of martyrs during their last moments: Mat. 10:18–20; Acts 7:55; *Mart. Pol.* 2.2; *Mart. Lugd.* 5.1.22; Ignatius, *Smyrn.* 4.2; *Pas. Perp.* 15.3. Campenhausen (1936), 90.

history who either committed crimes out of envy or suffered because of envy. Cain and Abel (Gen. 4) are mentioned as the first examples. In 5.1–6.2 the focus changes from exemplary figures from Israel's past to Christian martyrs.[76] The apostles Peter and Paul are clearly the greatest exemplars that Clement can present to the rebellious Corinthians (cf. the repetition of 'greatest' in 5.2, 7 and the phrase 'the greatest model of steadfastness', 5.7).[77] Clement notes that they had to pay for their preaching with their own life because others were envious of them (5.2, 5). Peter's manifold sufferings are emphasised in 5.4. Paul experienced multiple torments, all of which are familiar from traditions concerning the violent death of prophets: being in bonds, exile and stoning.[78] After referring to the holy way of life of Peter and Paul (cf. 44.6), Clement moves on to the anonymous martyrs (6.1). In the light of the short and general information about a recent persecution in 1.1, perhaps during Domitian's reign, it is surprising that he speaks of so many martyrs. By emphasising the physical weakness of the women among them, on the one hand, and glorifying the martyrs on the other, the special character of the Christians and their dedication to their belief is highlighted. The outrageous undeserved suffering of these Christian 'athletes' is indicated by a comparison by contrast with the very lamentable punishment of pagan females, the Danaids and Dirce, women well-known from Graeco-Roman mythology.

Translation[79]

(5.1) But let us stop with the old exemplary figures[80] and turn to those who have become athletes in the most recent period. Let us take the noble examples from our own stock.[81] (5.2) Because of envy and

---

76 See Beyschlag (1966), 207–353. Also Dehandschutter (1989).

77 Cf. *1 Clem.* 16.17; 33.8 (cf. 1 Pet. 2:21) and Polycarp, *Phil.* 8.2; 10.1.

78 Cf. *1 Clem.* 17.1; 45.4, and Hebr. 11:36–7. Apparently, Clement did not know the tradition that Paul was decapitated, which became the standard view of his execution, see above, *Mart. Pauli* 5 (late second century CE) and Tajra (1994), 23.

79 Translation based on Bihlmeyer (1956).

80 Similar phrases in 6.1; 46.1 and 55.1. In Chapter 55 Clement suggest that the Christian martyrs stand in a tradition of pagan and Jewish model figures who had sacrificed themselves for their people.

81 Alternative translations are 'our own generation' or 'our own people', see *LSJ* under *genea* 342; *Bauer-Aland* 308; Beyschlag (1966), 207 and 214–15. Cf. *Mart. Pol.* 3.2.

jealousy the greatest and most righteous pillars[82] have been persecuted and have contended until death. (5.3) Let us take before our eyes the eminent apostles. (5.4) Because of unjustified envy Peter has endured not one, not two, but many sufferings. Having given testimony[83] in this way he went to the place of glory he deserved.[84] (5.5) Because of jealousy and quarrels Paul displayed the prize for endurance.[85] (5.6) He was chained seven times and was banished as well as stoned. Having become a herald in the East and the West, he won the genuine glory for his faith. (5.7) He taught righteousness to the entire world and went to the farthest limits of the West.[86] He gave testimony before rulers and departed after all this from the world. He was taken up to the holy place, having become the greatest model of endurance.

(6.1) Around these men who have lived holy lives a great multitude of chosen ones assembled, who have suffered many insulting treatments and tortures because of jealousy and have become a wonderful example among us. (6.2) Because of jealousy women[87] were persecuted like the daughters of Danaos or Dirce.[88] Notwithstanding their

---

82 Peter and Paul's designation in 5.2 as 'the most righteous pillars' (cf. *Mart. Lugd.* 1.6 and 1.17) may indicate their role as leaders or their representative meaning for their group. Cf. 4 Macc. 17:3 about the Maccabaean mother as the roof on the pillars of her sons.

83 Testifying and death go hand in hand, but 'testifying' (*martyrein*) does not mean 'die as a martyr' in *1 Clem.* 5.4, 7 as in the *Martyrdom of Polycarp*, see Introduction, pp. 2–3.

84 After their death the martyrs go to a place where the righteous stay, while other believers had to wait for the resurrection at the end of times. See also 5.7, Baumeister (1980), 242; Holleman (1996), 140–52.

85 I.e. Paul displayed his trophy like an athlete after his victory.

86 The Greek is difficult to interpret. Some scholars think that a location in Spain or even the pillars of Heracles (i.e. Gibraltar) as the western border of the world are meant, since Paul himself refers to a future trip to Spain in Rom. 15:24. Yet, he probably did not make it further west than Rome. New Testament sources do not report a trip to Spain. Therefore Rome could be hinted at in this passage. See Tajra (1994), 102–17.

87 The reference to female Christian martyrs in *1 Clem.* 55.3 may hint at the anonymous women mentioned in 6.2.

88 The daughters of Danaos had murdered their spouses during the wedding night. By way of punishment they continuously had to fill a bucket with a broken bottom with water in the underworld. Mythic traditions tell that Dirce was bound on the horns of a bull and dragged around until she was dead. Cf. the torture of Blandina by a bull in *Mart. Lugd.* 5.1.56 and *Pas. Perp.* 20.1–2. See Brennecke (1977) and p. 126.

weak bodies,[89] they suffered terrible and godless outrages, came to the secure finish in the race of faith and received a noble reward.

2 Ignatius, *Letter to the Romans* 1.1–7.3

The passage translated below is the body of Ignatius' *Letter to the Romans* (beginning of the second century CE), the letter in which he discusses his imminent death most intensely. The reason for writing to the Roman Christian community is his passionate longing for his execution, which he sees as a fast and secure way to attain God. The entire letter petitions the Romans not to interfere or to do anything that would prevent his execution.

The two sections of the letter not translated concern its beginning and end. The letter's inscription opens by addressing the Roman Christian community in highly honourable terms and conveying Ignatius' abundant greetings. In Chapter 8 Ignatius starts rounding the letter off by repeating his petition to the Romans. The first part of the phrase in 8.2 'Through a few letters I ask you: "be faithful to me"' is a conventional way of introducing the concluding section of a letter.[90] The second part 8.2 repeats Ignatius' wish: being faithful to him means to let him finish his mission in the amphitheatre in the mouth of the wild beasts.

Translation[91]

(1.1) Since I succeeded by prayer to God to see your faces worthy of God, as I asked to receive even more . . .[92] For being in bonds united with Christ Jesus, I hope to greet you, if it is God's will to be found worthy to reach the end.[93] (1.2) For the beginning is well arranged, if I attain the grace to receive my lot[94] unimpeded. For I fear your love,

---

89 Cf. 2 Macc. 7:21; *Ep. Arist.* 250; Philo, *Vit. Mos.* 1.8; *Ebr.* 55; 1 Pet. 3:7; 4 Macc. 16:2.
90 White (1972), 24–5; Schoedel (1985), 188.
91 Translation based on Bihlmeyer (1956).
92 Ignatius does not finish this sentence.
93 A general phrase meaning 'dying a violent death', which may have been associated with the performance of athletes, Mellink (2000), 169–71. The Greek can mean 'end', 'goal', or 'decisive event in the future'. Ignatius assumes he will reach the end at his execution in Rome, for other Christians it will come in a more remote future (*Eph.* 14.2; *Rom.* 10.3).
94 Believers are rightful heirs of the divine heritage, either at death as for Ignatius, or at the eschaton; Mellink (2000), 241–51.

that it will wrong me. Since for you it will be easy to do what you want. But for me it will be hard to attain God, if you do not spare me.

(2.1) For I do not want you to please humans, but rather to please God, as you do please Him. For I will never again have such an opportunity to attain God. Nor can you be accredited a better deed, if you remain silent. For if you remain silent and let me be, I will be a word of God. But if you love my flesh, I will be a (mere) voice again.[95] (2.2) Grant me nothing more than to be poured out as an offering to God, as long as an altar is still prepared, so that you become a choir in love and sing to the Father in Jesus Christ, because God has considered the bishop of Syria worthy to be found at the place where the sun sets[96] after having sent him from where the sun rises. It is beautiful to set from the world to God, so that I rise towards Him.

(3.1) Never have you grudged somebody something. You have instructed others. But I want those things to be fixed which you command while you are teaching. (3.2) I only ask that I may have the inward and outward strength that I not only say but also want, that I am not only called a Christian, but that I also am found to be one.[97] For if I am found to be one I can also be called one and then be faithful, when I am not visible to the world. (3.3) Nothing that is visible (in the world) is beautiful. For our God Jesus Christ is all the more visible by being in the Father.[98] Christianity is not a matter of persuasion; (to the contrary) it is great when it is hated by the world.[99]

95 The contrast between 'word' and 'voice' (word of God/a mere voice) is connected with a contrast between word and deed and opposes right to wrong testimony to God (right, i.e. presupposing that one realises one's words). Ignatius may follow Aristotle's view of 'voice' as mere sound and 'word' as sound conveying meaning; Schoedel (1985), 170–1.

96 I.e. Rome.

97 Ignatius contrasts saying and doing several times (e.g. *Eph.* 15.1; *Mag.* 4), emphasising that one should carry out what one says. The contrast here is slightly different. Ignatius does not only want to be called a Christian, but also to be one, which implies undergoing his violent death in Rome.

98 Ignatius' elliptic and brief phrases seem to underlie a dualistic view: the world is opposed to the sphere of God and appearance in the world is opposed to being with God. This may explain the statement that Jesus Christ, being physically invisible, is visible to the Christians as their God while being with the Father. Ignatius may be building upon early Christian traditions claiming that the divine truth concerns things unseen (Rom. 8:24; Hebr. 11:1 and 2 Cor. 4:18).

99 Ignatius frequently uses the term 'Christian' (*Christianos*, *Rom.* 3.2; *Eph.* 11.2; *Mag.* 4; *Pol.* 7.3), which also occurs in two of the later writings in the New

(4.1) I write to all communities in order to make it very clear that I will die voluntarily for God, if you do not hinder me. I urge you not to be kind at the wrong moment. Let me be food for the wild beasts, through whom I can attain God. I am God's grain, I am being ground by the beasts' teeth in order to be found to be the pure bread of Christ.[100] (4.2) Rather entice the beasts, so that they become my grave and leave behind nothing of my body and I may burden nobody after my death. I will truly be a disciple of Jesus Christ[101] when the world will not even (be able to) see my body. Entreat Christ for me that I may be found a sacrifice for God through those means. (4.3) I do not command you as Peter and Paul. They were apostles, I am a convict. They were free; I am until now a slave. But if I suffer death,[102] I will become a freedman of Jesus Christ and I will arise being free in Him. And now, being in bonds, I am learning to desire nothing.

(5.1) I am fighting wild beasts from Syria to Rome, through land and sea, night and day, being bound to ten leopards, by whom I mean a body of soldiers, who become worse when they treat me kindly.[103]

Testament (Acts 11:26; 26:28; 1 Pet. 4:16). The name derives from Christ (*Christos*) and may have originated in pagans' wishes for a name to differentiate between followers of Jesus Christ and (other) Jews (cf. Tacitus, *Ann.* 15.44.2; Pliny, *Ep.* 10.96). The confession of Jesus as the Messiah (Christ) may have given outsiders the motivation to start using this name. Ignatius uses it already as an insider name and applies it to his own situation of an imminent noble death. He expresses Christianity as a way of life culminating in martyrdom. In the Acts of Christian martyrs the confession 'I am Christian' often leads to the conviction and execution of the martyrs; Merkelbach (1975); Bremmer (1991).

100 The food imagery might refer to the Eucharist, as several scholars have argued. But the term 'pure bread' is perfectly understandable in the light of Ignatius' images deriving from the production of bread. The implication would be that Ignatius is 'bread of high quality' after his execution. Schoedel (1985), 175–6.

101 The execution in Rome is the way to become a true disciple of Christ (*Eph.* 1.2; 3.1; 11.2; *Rom.* 4.2; 5.1, 3; *Tral.* 5.2; *Pol.* 7.1). He presents his arrest as only the beginning of his discipleship in *Eph.* 3.1 and *Rom.* 5.3, but in *Rom.* 5.1 he suggests that his imprisonment makes him more of a disciple. Apparently, discipleship is a goal to strive for. Since Ignatius' arrest is only the beginning of the process of becoming a disciple, his execution must form the completion of it.

102 The verb 'to suffer' (*paschō*) is sometimes synonymous with 'to die', see also *Rom.* 8.3 and *Pol.* 7.1.

103 Other translations offer usually something like 'who become worse when treated well', but the middle voice of *euergeteō* can mean 'be a benefactor' (*LSJ* s.v. 1). If we assume a similar meaning here, Ignatius' passage becomes more poignant.

I become more of a disciple by their wrongdoings, but 'I am not for that reason justified'.[104] (5.2) I wish to profit from the wild beasts that have been prepared for me and I pray that they will be quick with me. I will even entice them to devour me quickly, not like some whom they, being cowards, did not touch. But in case they do not want to act out of free will, I shall force them (to do so). (5.3) Pardon me, I know what is good for me. Now I start to be a disciple. May nothing of things visible and invisible[105] seduce me, so that I may attain Jesus Christ. Let fire, cross, groups of wild beasts, the scattering of bones, the cutting up of limbs, the grinding of the entire body, and the devil's evil punishments come upon me, only that I may attain Jesus Christ.

(6.1) The ends of the world or the kingdoms of this age are of no use to me. It is better for me to die for Jesus Christ,[106] than to be king over the ends of the earth. I seek that one who died for us. I want that one who arose for us. The pains of birth are upon me.[107] (6.2) Agree with me, brothers. Do not beg me to live, do not want me to die. Do not give graciously to the world that one who wants to be God's, nor deceive Him with matter. Let me receive pure light. When I arrive there, I will be a human being.[108] (6.3) Allow me to be an imitator of the suffering of my God. If somebody carries Him within him- or herself, let him or her understand what I want and sympathise with me, knowing what constrains me.

(7.1) The ruler of this age wants to carry me away and to destroy my orientation to my God. Therefore, let none of you present help him, rather take my side, that is God's side. Do not speak about Jesus Christ and desire things of the world. (7.2) Do not let malignant influences be among you, not even when I, being present, incite you to obey me.[109] Obey the things that I write to you. For I write you being alive, but desiring passionately to die. My passionate desire has

---

104 Quotation of 1 Cor. 4:4, which continues with 'the Lord is the one who judges me'.
105 Reference to Col. 1:16.
106 Ignatius may quote part of 1 Cor. 9:15 here, but the context of that passage is very different.
107 The image of labour pains may either refer to Ignatius' day of birth (that is the day of his death) or to his own birth pains; Schoedel (1985), 182–84. The day martyrs were executed is frequently referred to as their birthday, see already *Mart. Pol.* 18.3.
108 See footnote 101.
109 Ignatius probably indicates the possibility that he will ultimately become afraid and urge the Roman Christians to prevent his execution.

been crucified and there is no matter-loving fire[110] in me, but water living and speaking within me,[111] saying from my inside: 'this way to the Father'. (7.3) I do not enjoy perishable food, or the pleasures of this earthly life. I want the 'bread from God',[112] which is the flesh of Jesus Christ, the seed of David, and I want to drink His blood, which is incorruptible love.[113]

3 *Ascension of Isaiah* 5

The *Ascension* is a composite Christian work dating from the second century CE. Christians belonging to a group of prophets, maybe from Syria, have combined and reworked the two sections, Chapters 1–5 and Chapters 6–11.[114] The introduction of the *Ascension* tells us that King Hezekiah of Judah (*c.* 715–687 BCE) provides his son Manasseh with the words of righteousness that Hezekiah himself had seen and those that Isaiah, the son of Amoz, had given Hezekiah. This happened in the twenty-sixth year of Hezekiah's reign. Isaiah's prophecy, dated in Hezekiah's twentieth year, tells us that Manasseh's rule would be wicked and that he would kill the prophet (*Asc. Is.* 1:6–7, 9). Chapters 2–5 describe how this prophecy comes true. Isaiah leaves Jerusalem, first for Bethlehem and than for the wilderness, where he stays with other prophets (2:7–11). The false prophet Belkira, or Malkira, as other manuscripts have it, accuses Isaiah of being a false prophet (3:1–12), which leads to Isaiah's execution described in

110 The Greek refers to the original matter of the earth. The fire may also be an image for earthly desires. That would strengthen the notion of repudiating earthly things.

111 'Living water' is a Johannine image for water implying real life coming from Jesus (John 4:10–14; 7:38–9, interpreted as the Spirit of God). 'Speaking water' is an image for God's Spirit in *Odes of Solomon* 11.6. The *Martyrdom of Lyon* 5.1.22 opposes 'living water' to the fire of the torturers.

112 Ignatius may refer to John 6:33, which in its turn refers to the 'mannah', the food given by God to His people wandering in the desert (Exod. 16:4; Ps. 78:23–5).

113 Eucharist and love are essential elements of Christian identity for Ignatius.

114 Brief explanatory notes and a shorter visionary section about the reign of Beliar-Antichrist and the Second Coming of Christ (1:5–6a; 2:9; 3:13 and 4:13; 3:13–4:18) have been added to the first section and connect it with the visionary second part. See the discussion by Knibb (1985), 143–7; also Acerbi (1983), 254–68; Norelli (1993), 39–59; 68–78; Hall (1990), 290–2.

Chapter 5.[115] The visionary section in *Asc. Is.* 6–11 is also dated in Hezekiah's twentieth year and refers in its conclusion once again to Isaiah's execution: 'Because of these visions and prophecies Sammael Satan sawed Isaiah the son of Amoz the prophet in half by the hand of Manasseh' (11:41; see the General Introduction, p. 93, about execution by a saw).

One other key figure has to be mentioned here. As in several other Christian martyrdoms, the devil acts as the principal opponent of the martyr. Beliar is the devil's most common name in the *Ascension*. He is called 'the ruler of this world' in 10:29 and 'the adversary' in 11:19.[116] He manipulates King Manasseh (1:7–13). He is the superhuman leader of the evil forces and the commander of a host of evil angels. He is identical with Sammael (1:8, 11; 2:1; 5:15–16) and Satan (2:2, 7; 5:16).[117] In the end it is his anger with Isaiah that causes the prophet's execution. Isaiah's prophecy of the coming of the Beloved (Jesus Christ) and his own exposition make Beliar so angry (3:13–20).[118]

Translation[119]

(5.1) Because of these visions, therefore, Beliar was angry with Isaiah, and he dwelt in the heart of Manasseh, and he sawed Isaiah in two with a wood saw.[120] (5.2) And while Isaiah was being sawn in two, his accuser, Belkira,[121] stood alongside, with all the false prophets, who were laughing and (maliciously) joyful because of Isaiah.[122] (5.3) And

---

115 The two names may derive from a conflation of two Hebrew names, *Bᵉḥîr-raʿ* 'the Elect of evil' and *Malkira* 'the King of evil'; Knibb (1985), 163. Norelli (1995), 2.291 argues that Malkira should be identified with the evil spirit Melki-resha mentioned in Qumran writings.

116 Cf. *Mart. Lugd.* 5.1.38, 42 and see p. 121.

117 Norelli (1994), 79–92; Sperling (1995). Beliar is mentioned once in the New Testament (2 Cor. 6:15).

118 Beliar instigates Jesus' crucifixion (9:14), but is defeated after the return of Jesus to earth (4:14–22). He is also responsible for the persecution of Jesus' followers before His return to earth (4:1–13).

119 The translation is that of Knibb (1985) with minor changes. We warmly thank Professors M.A. Knibb and J. H. Charlesworth for allowing us to use this translation.

120 See discussion of the sawing asunder of Isaiah above.

121 Reference to Belkira's accusation of Isaiah in 3:1–12, see above.

122 The ridiculing of the martyr is a traditional motif in martyr texts; Norelli (1995), 2.291–2.

Belkira, instigated by Mekembekus,[123] stood before Isaiah, laughing and deriding him. (5.4) And Belkira said to Isaiah, 'Say, I have lied in everything I have spoken; the ways of Manasseh are good and right, (5.5) and also the ways of Belkira and those who are with him are good.' (5.6) And he said this to him when he began to be sawn in two. (5.7) And Isaiah was in a vision of the Lord,[124] but his eyes were open, and he saw them.[125] (5.8) And Belkira spoke thus to Isaiah, 'Say what I say to you, and I will turn their heart and make Manasseh, and the princes of Judah, and the people, and all Jerusalem worship you.'[126] (5.9) And Isaiah answered and said, 'If it is within my power to say, "Condemned and cursed be you, and all your hosts, and all your house!"[127] (5.10) For there is nothing further that you can take except the skin of my body.'[128] (5.11) And they seized Isaiah, the son of Amoz, and sawed him in half with a wood saw. (5.12) And Manasseh, and Belkira, and the false prophets, and the princes, and the people, and all stood by looking on. (5.13) And to the prophets who (were) with him he said before he was sawn in two: 'Go to the district of Tyre and Sidon,[129] because for me alone the Lord has mixed the cup.'[130] (5.14) And while Isaiah was being sawn in two, he did not cry out, or

---

123 Mekembekus is a corruption of Matanbukus (2:4), which is another name for Beliar.

124 Visionary experiences during the execution also happen to Stephen (Acts 7:55–6), Alexander and Blandina (*Mart. Lugd.* 5.1.51, 56) and R. Hanina ben Teradion (*T.B. Avodah Zarah* 17b-18a). Also *Mart. Pol.* 2.2.

125 The 'them' are probably Belkira and the Holy Spirit. Isaiah speaks to them in 5:8, 14. The two may have thought to be competing over the soul of the dying Isaiah; Norelli (1993), 119.

126 In stead of the ruler's attempt to persuade the martyr to give in, Belkira tempts Isaiah in a way that reminds one of Jesus' temptation by the devil in Mat. 4:8–10 and Luke 4:5–8.

127 Isaiah would like to curse Beliar and his subordinates, whom Belkira represents here. One of the Qumran texts concerns a ritual cursing of Belial (4Q 286 10 ii).

128 Cf. Anaxarchus' and Heracles' attitude towards physical suffering, see pp. 27–8, and 4 Macc. 10:4.

129 This statement may be read in connection with the association by Christian prophets of their situation with the one of Elijah described in 1 Kings 17:7–24, who fled, commanded by God, from King Ahab to Zarephath near Sidon. These prophets may even have linked Isaiah's command to Jesus' journey to Sidon and Tyre (Mark 7:24; Mat. 15:21).

130 The cup may be an image for the wrath of God or for the suffering that is one's destiny. The latter is much more probable here. The image also occurs in Mark 10:38–9; 14:36; Mat. 20:22; 26:39; Luke 22:42; John 18:11; *Mart. Pol.* 14.2; *Apocalypse of Peter*, Fragm. Rainer; *Letter of the Apostles* 15 (26).

weep,[131] but his mouth spoke with the Holy Spirit until he was sawn in two.[132] (5.15) Beliar did this to Isaiah through Manasseh, for Sammael[133] was very angry with Isaiah from the days of Hezekiah, king of Judah, because of the things he had seen concerning the Beloved, (5.16) and because of the destruction of Sammael, which he had seen through the Lord, while Hezekiah his father was king. And he (Manasseh) did as Satan wished.[134]

4 *Martyrdom of Polycarp* 14–15

Martyrdom of Polycarp 14–15 (155–160 CE) describes the miraculous events connected with the execution of the elderly bishop of Smyrna. *Mart. Pol.* 14 reports Polycarp's prayer just before his execution. The prayer offers an interpretation of the events. It takes up a formula that we find in Jewish thanksgiving prayers as well as Christian prayers connected with the Eucharist.[135] Polycarp invokes and praises God and expresses thanks that he will be numbered among the martyrs in heaven.[136] Allusions to Dan. 3 suggest that Polycarp considers his situation at the stake analogous to that of Hananiah, Mishael and Azariah.[137] In 14.1 he compares his death to a burnt offering. This reminds one of the story about Daniel's three companions, although Polycarp's allusions to Dan. 3 do not focus on the invocation of God to rescue His people, which is the central theme in Azariah's prayer. The explicit analogy with Dan. 3 underlines Polycarp's individual fate, a deliverance after death. Hananiah, Mishael and Azariah were miraculously rescued because of their perfect obedience to the Lord and Polycarp deserved a vindication like theirs. In line with Jewish and early Christian sources about martyrdom the deliverance is transposed from earth to heaven.[138]

---

131 Cf. *Mart. Pol.* 2.2–4; *Mart. Lugd.* 5.1.51.
132 See n. 124. Baumeister (1980), 298–301, and Weinreich (1981) discuss the martyrs' conversation with the Holy Spirit.
133 Sammael, Beliar and Satan are identical, see p. 112.
134 Cf. 2.2.
135 Buschmann (1998), 227–90, offers a detailed discussion.
136 Several other Christian martyr writings share the important element of the martyr's thanks during a prayer; see *Mart. Pol.* 14: *Act. Scil.* 2; 15; *Pas. Perp.* 3; *Acta Theclae* 24; *Acta Carpi* 41.
137 Their prayer also starts with praise of God (Dan. 3:24–7). See p. 60.
138 See van Henten (2001) for discussion of the reception of Daniel 3 and 6 in early Christian literature.

The spectacular aftermath of Polycarp's prayer as described in Chapter 15 also echoes the Greek version of Daniel 3. In Dan. 3 an angel moves the fire in the furnace upward so that Daniel's companions at the furnace's bottom can even enjoy a cool morning breeze (Dan. 3:46–50 in the Greek versions). The description of Polycarp's miracle in the fire refers to a furnace as well as to wind. The fire does not affect the martyr's body, in the same way that Daniel's companions' bodies were not affected. The fire surrounds Polycarp like a vault or a sail bellying out. The wind may be an indirect reference to God's interference.

Translation[139]

(14.1) They did not fix him with nails, but bound him.[140] He put his hands behind his back and was bound. He was like an eye-catching ram, taken from a great flock for sacrifice, a well-prepared burnt offering,[141] welcome to God. He looked up to heaven and said: 'O Lord, Almighty God, Father of Your beloved and blessed servant[142] Jesus Christ, through whom we have received knowledge about Yourself.[143] You are the God of angels and powers and the entire creation as well as every generation of righteous ones who live in Your sight. (14.2) I praise You that You have deemed me worthy this day and hour, to be numbered among the martyrs by drinking the cup of Your Messiah,[144] leading to a resurrection to eternal life of soul and body,[145] in everlasting communion with the Holy Spirit. May I be

---

139 Translation based on Bihlmeyer (1956).

140 For a recent discussion of the parallels between *Mart. Pol.* 14 and the New Testament, see Buschmann (1998), 226–90. The cup of Christ mentioned in *Mart. Pol.* 14.2, for example, may echo NT passages related to Jesus' passion (see n. 130). *Mart. Pol.* consistently distinguishes Polycarp's death from that of Jesus, as the first line of 14.1 shows: Jesus was nailed to the cross according to Col. 2:14 and John 20:25.

141 See above.

142 The Greek *pais* in 14.1 and 14.3 can be translated by 'child' ('son') or 'servant'. Both translations are possible here.

143 Jesus is the mediator of the knowledge about God (John 10:38; 14:7 and 16:3).

144 The passage may refer to the Gethsemane episode (Mark 14:36), to Jesus' response to the apostles James and John, who want to sit on the right and left of Jesus in his glory (Mark 10:38–9; Mat. 20:22–3), or to Jesus' statement to Peter in John 18:11 during his arrest: 'Put your sword back into its sheath. Am I not to drink the cup that the Father has given me?'

145 The phrase echoes John 5:29, but also 2 Macc. 7:9, 14. As in 2 Maccabees, the

received among them, today in Your sight, as a rich and acceptable sacrifice, as You Yourself have prepared earlier, revealed beforehand and fulfilled, O unerring and truthful God. (14.3) Therefore I praise You in every respect,[146] I bless You and honour You through the eternal and heavenly high priest[147] Jesus Christ, Your beloved servant. Through him be glory to You, with Him and the Holy Spirit, now and in coming ages. Amen.'

(15.1) After he had sent up the amen and had finished his prayer, the people at the stake kindled the fire. A great flame flashed forth and then we saw a miracle.[148] To us it was given to see, and we were also saved to tell the others the events. (15.2) The fire took the form of a vault and bellied out through the wind like the sail of a ship. It walled all around the body of the martyr. He was in the middle of it, not like burning flesh, but like bread being baked or gold or silver being refined in the furnace. And we perceived an overwhelming sweet smell, like the smell of frankincense or another of the costly aromatic herbs.[149]

5 *Acts of Justin*

The main part of the *Acts of Justin* (162–168 CE) is the dialogue between judge and martyrs during their trial. A brief introduction and a conclusion have been added to the trial report. In version A,[150] which is translated below, the *Acts* start with a very brief reference to

---

notion of resurrection seems to imply a revival of body and soul directly after the martyr's death, cf. the next phrase 'May I be received among them (i.e. the other martyrs) . . . today.'

146 With den Boeft and Bremmer (1991), 109–11.

147 Cf. Heb. 6:20.

148 Cf. also Abraham's deliverance from Nimrod's furnace, see Ginzberg (1967–68), 1.201. Thecla's spectacular survival of the stake is an interesting parallel. In her case God directly interferes by causing a subterraneous noise below and a cloud full of rain and hail above the stake, which extinguished the fire (*Acta Theclae* 22–3).

149 A pleasing odour indicates a welcome sacrifice, as passages in the Hebrew Bible suggest (e.g. Exod. 29:18, 25; Lev. 2:2). Thus, the passage evokes the image of a burnt offering in Chapter 14. Rabbinic passages refer to a pleasant smell coming from the furnaces with Abraham and Daniel's companions, see, for example, *Midrash Genesis Rabbah* 34.9.

150 Three versions of the *Acts of Justin* have been preserved. The short version (A, represented by only one manuscript from Paris from 890 CE) is usually taken as the most original one. However, some independent readings of the middle edition (B) should be taken into account also. Bisbee (1988), 97–118, discusses the connections between versions A and B.

Roman orders concerning idolatry and the resulting arrest of the holy martyrs (*Act. Just.* 1). No general persecution is known to have taken place during the reign of Marcus Aurelius, the emperor who took such great interest in philosophy. There is evidence, though, that during his reign Christians were more regularly exposed to a test of their loyalty to the emperor, which required a sacrifice to the emperor.[151] The introduction to the *Acts* may refer to such a sacrifice, but the body of the writing in version A offers no substantial information about the order to sacrifice.[152] Eusebius suggests that Justin's death was the result of machinations by the Cynic philosopher Crescens.[153] In any case, Justin's opponent, the city prefect Rusticus (see General Introduction), does not confront Justin directly and asks him about the life he lives. In this way, he may have offered his fellow-philosopher a way out, since Justin could have responded that he was a teacher of philosophy, avoiding a reference to Christianity all together.[154] Rusticus was a follower of Stoicism and acted as Marcus Aurelius' teacher.[155]

Justin's interrogation ends when he confesses he is a Christian. Thereafter the prefect seeks confirmation that the others are Christians as well (Chapters 3–4). A second brief interrogation of Justin focuses on the vindication of the martyrs after their execution and ends with the announcement of the verdict (Chapter 5). The brief conclusion notes that the martyrs went to their place of execution while glorifying God (Chapter 6). Justin and his co-religionists' preference for execution over obeying the Roman authorities is apparent from the staccato-like dialogue resulting in the prefect Rusticus' verdict (*Act. Just.* 5.4–6).

Translation[156]

(Title) The Martyrdom of the holy ones Justin, Chariton, Charito, Euelpistus, Hierax, Paeon, Liberian and their community.

---

151 Bisbee (1988), 99, with references.
152 Freudenberger (1968), 24 and 29, assumes that the introduction and conclusion of this version, which refer to the command to sacrifice, have been added by an editor in the fourth century CE.
153 Eusebius, *Hist. eccl.* 4.16.7–9, adapting a statement by Tatian, Barnes (1968), 516.
154 Barnes (1968), 516.
155 In version B Rusticus demands obedience to the Roman gods and the emperor right at the start of the interrogation (B 2.1).
156 The translation is based on the edition by A. Hilhorst in Bastiaensen *et al.* (1987), 47–57.

(1) In the period of the godless ordinances about idolatry,[157] the afore-mentioned holy ones were arrested and brought before[158] Rusticus, the prefect of Rome.[159] (2.1) When they were brought in, the prefect said to Justin: 'What kind of life do you live?'[160] (2.2) Justin said: 'A blameless life, not to be condemned by any human.' (2.3) The prefect Rusticus said: 'What kind of teaching do you offer?' Justin said: 'I tried to learn all teachings, but I became involved in the true teachings of the Christians, even if these don't please those who adhere to false opinions.' (2.4) The prefect Rusticus said: 'So these are the teachings that please you?' Justin said: 'Yes, I follow them, since they match my belief.' (2.5) The prefect Rusticus said: 'What kind of belief is this?' Justin said: 'The very thing that we revere, the God of the Christians, whom alone we consider the creator[161] of the entire universe in the beginning, as well as the Child of God,[162] Jesus Christ, whom the prophets have proclaimed in advance as the one who would stand by the human race as herald of salvation and teacher of beautiful lessons. I believe that I say very little about His divinity when I acknowledge that He has a prophetic power,[163] (2.7) because proclamations have previously been made about this one of whom I have just said that He is the Son of God. Know that the prophets have said long ago that He would come to humankind.'[164]

(3.1) The prefect Rusticus said: 'Where do you assemble?' Justin said: 'Wherever each of us plans and is able to. You don't think that it is possible that we assemble all together (at the same place), do you?' (3.2) The prefect Rusticus said: 'Tell me, where do you assemble

---

157 See p. 117.
158 The Greek verb translated by 'brought before' is a technical phrase meaning 'bring into court'; Hilhorst in Bastiaensen *et al*. (1987), 391. Official trial records would have given information about the date, location, name and precise function of the judge, as well as the name(s) of the accused.
159 See p. 97.
160 Rusticus may have offered Justin a way out by this indirect question, see p. 117.
161 The Greek *demiourgos* meaning 'maker', 'creator' is already used for God as creator in Heb. 11:10. Justin uses this phrase frequently in his *Apologies*.
162 Hilhorst in Bastiaensen *et al*. (1987), 392–3, rejects the other possible translation of *pais* ('servant') here, because Justin uses 'son' (*hyios*) later on (2.7).
163 With Hilhorst in Bastiaensen *et al*. (1987), 393. Another translation would be: 'I acknowledge that there is a certain prophetic power . . .'
164 That Jesus Christ forms the fulfilment of the prophecies of Israel's prophets about the Messiah constitutes the central part of Justin's first *Apology* (Chapters 31–52). Cf. *1 Apol.* 56; 61; *Dial.* 78.4; 84.2; 91.4; 106.1; Skarsaune (1987).

or to what place do you go?' (3.3) Justin said: 'I live above the bath of Myrtinus[165] throughout my second sojourn in the city of the Romans. I don't know of any other meeting place than this one. And if anybody wants to come over to my home, I will share the teachings of the truth[166] with him or her.' (3.4) Rusticus said: 'Thus, you are a Christian?' Justin responded: 'Yes, I am a Christian.'

(4.1) The prefect Rusticus said to Chariton: 'Chariton, are you also a Christian?' Chariton said: 'I am a Christian by command of God.' (4.2) The prefect Rusticus said to Charito: 'What do you say, Charito?' Charito said: 'I am a Christian by the gift of God.'[167] (4.3) The prefect Rusticus said to Euelpistus: 'And who are you?' Euelpistus said: 'I am also a Christian and share the same hope.'[168] (4.4) The prefect Rusticus said to Hierax:[169] 'Are you a Christian?' Hierax said: 'Yes, I am a Christian, I venerate the same God.' (4.5) The prefect Rusticus said: 'Has Justin made you into Christians?' Hierax said: 'I have been a Christian for a long time.' (4.6) Paeon[170] stood up and said: 'I am also a Christian.' Rusticus said: 'Who has taught you?' Paeon said: 'We have inherited it from our parents.' (4.7) Euelpistus said: 'I enjoyed listening to Justin's teachings, but I inherited being a Christian from my parents.' Rusticus said: 'Where are your parents?' Euelpistus said: 'In Cappodocia.'[171] (4.8) The prefect Rusticus said to Hierax: 'Where are your parents?' Hierax said: 'They have died: I

165 The name of Myrtinus may refer to a person but has not been identified. Hamman (1975) suggests that Justin indicates a location where Christians met, but Justin's next remarks make it more probable that he indicates his own lodgings, where he could also do his teaching, Hilhorst in Bastiaensen (1987), 393–4. Den Boeft and Bremmer (1991), 114, n. that the space above small baths was frequently rented out and suggest that Myrtinus may be a corruption of the well-known name Myrtilus.

166 Cf. 2.3 and Justin, *Dial.* 121.2.

167 This answer in the form of the symbolic explanation of Charito's name (see General Introduction, p. 97) may allude to Eph. 3:7 and Rom. 5:15. Cf. also *Mart. Pol.* 2.3 and *Mart. Lugd.* 5.1.6, 24.

168 The hope may either refer to having the expectation to be resurrected or the item hoped for itself, that is the special resurrection of the martyrs, cf. 5.1–3 and 2 Macc. 7:14; den Boeft and Bremmer (1981), 43–4.

169 The name Hierax derives from the Greek name of the hawk or falcon.

170 Paeon is a geographical name indicating somebody from Paeonia in the north of Macedonia.

171 Rusticus may have been interested in tracking the parents down if they also lived in Rome. Cappadocia is the name of a region in the eastern part of Asia Minor, stretching from north to south from the Black Sea to the mountains of the Taurus.

was drawn away from Phrygia a long time ago.' (4.9) The prefect Rusticus said to Liberian: 'You are not a Christian, are you?' Liberian said: 'I am a pious Christian.'

(5.1) The prefect Rusticus said to Justin: 'If you are whipped and beheaded,[172] you believe that you will ascend to heaven?' (5.2) Justin said: 'I hope so on the basis of my endurance, if I endure. I know that it will remain ready for those who live properly until the conflagration.'[173] (5.3) The prefect Rusticus said: 'So you suppose that you will ascend to heaven?' Justin said: 'I don't suppose it, but I truly believe it.' (5.4) The prefect Rusticus said: 'If you don't obey, you will be punished.' (5.5) Justin said: 'This is exactly what we pray for, that we will be saved through punishment.'[174] (5.6) The prefect Rusticus declared:[175] 'Those who were not willing to sacrifice to the gods have to be whipped and carried away in conformity with the laws.' (6.1) The holy martyrs praised God, went out to the customary place and completed their martyrdom, confessing our Saviour, to whom be glory, power with the Father, and the Holy Spirit, now and in the ages of ages. Amen.

6 Martyrdom of Lyon and Vienne (Martyrium Lugdunensium, Eusebius, Hist. eccl. 5.1.36–47)

The *Martyrdom of Lyon* (177 CE) has a loose structure. Several attempts to break the martyrs' spirit by horrible tortures are described (5.1.7–56). The main heroes are named: Vettius Epagathus, Sanctus, Maturus, Blandina, Attalus and the local bishop Pothinus, who was even older than the 90-year-old scribe Eleazar from 2 and 4 Maccabees (5.1.29).[176] In particular, Vienne's deacon Sanctus and the slave

---

172 The punishments of whipping and beheading are also mentioned together in *Mart. Lugd.* 5.1.47–8. Tajra (1994), 20–4, discusses the capital punishment of decapitation, which was used for Roman citizens.

173 Stoic and other philosophers assumed that the world would be destroyed because of a huge fire and this became a popular view of the end of the world; van der Horst (1994). Justin refers to this concept in *1 Apol.* 20.1–4; 60.8–9 and *2 Apol.* 7.2–3.

174 Justin ridicules the prefect with this answer, which matches, however, his belief in his current resurrection; den Boeft and Bremmer (1981), 44.

175 This is the martyrs' verdict.

176 Frend (1965), 19, wrongly states that Pothinus was ninety like Eleazar. See discussion on the names and social status of the martyrs by G. Thomas in Rougé and Turcan (1978), 96–106.

woman Blandina suffer several sessions of tortures.[177] Even the martyrs' death does not satisfy the mob (see General Introduction) and the governor. They prevent the burial of the martyrs' bodily remains at the instigation of the devil (5.1.57–63). They burn the bodies and throw the remains into the Rhône, assuming – wrongly, of course, in the view of the author – that they had eliminated every possibility for the martyrs to be resurrected in this way. In the second chapter Eusebius adds some scattered information, including a note that the martyrs refused to apply the title 'martyr' to themselves and reserved it for Christ and heroes who had died before.

The passage translated below largely concerns the slave woman Blandina, whose insignificant physical appearance is stressed in order to highlight her heroic behaviour as a martyr. Like Sanctus Blandina undergoes several rounds of torture. Her final scene is described in 5.1.50–53. She dies on the horns of a bull, recalling the anonymous female martyrs mentioned in *1 Clem.* 6.[178] Several scholars have associated Blandina with the mother of the Maccabaean martyrs and suggested that this mother functioned as a prototype for Blandina.[179] There are indeed a few striking correspondences between the two women, who encourage their fellow martyrs to remain steadfast and die last of all.[180] Both women function as model figures for the other martyrs. Whereas the mother of the Maccabaean martyrs is praised as the mother of the Jewish people because of her faithfulness to the Jewish law and her exemplary piety (4 Macc. 15:29; 16:20), Blandina functions as a spiritual mother only (5.1.41, below). Perhaps the figure of Blandina can be connected with the imagery of the Church as virgin-mother, giving birth and educating her children (5.1.45–6).[181] This imagery is used in connection with the 'fallen' Christians, harshly called an abortion, who first refuse to stand up to the governor but finally make it because of the example set by others. Blandina, hanging on a beam in the figure of a cross (5.1.41), shows them the road to Jesus Christ and, as a consequence, to martyrdom as the fastest way to salvation. The translated passage begins with a new round of tortures.

177   Sanctus: 5.1.17; 20–3; 24; 37–40; Blandina: 5.1.17–19; 36–42; 53–6.
178   See *1 Clem.* 6.2 and n. 88 and cf. p. 126 concerning *Pas. Perp.* 20.1.
179   Frend (1965), 18–19; Guillaumin (1972).
180   *Mart. Lugd.* 5.1.53–5; 2 Macc. 7:21–3, 25–9, 41; 4 Macc. 12:7; 15:12; 16:13, 16–24; 17:1. Both women are motivated by the expectation of the resurrection, *Mart. Lugd.* 5.1.34, 56, 63; 2 Macc. 7:14, 20; 4 Macc. 11:7; 17:14.
181   Plumpe (1943).

Translation[182]

(36) (After some remarks in the margin they continue again.)[183] These things were followed by the testimonies of their martyrdom[184] that had many different forms. They plaited a wreath from various colours and flowers and presented it to the Father. Having endured a complex contest and triumphed greatly, these noble athletes had to receive the big wreath of immortality.[185] (37) Maturus, Sanctus, Blandina and Attalus[186] were brought to the beasts for a public and common spectacle of the pagans' hatred of humankind,[187] because the day for the games with the beasts was fixed on purpose in connection with us.[188] (38) Maturus and Sanctus went again through every kind of punishment in the amphitheatre, as if they had suffered nothing at all before; or, rather, as if they had forced their adversary[189] out already in several rounds and were fighting the game for the wreath only. When they moved to the arena,[190] they underwent again the usual lashes of whipping, the violence from the beasts, as well as all other kinds of tortures that people invoked and encouraged from all sorts of places – since the mob was raging. They asked especially for the iron chair and were filled with the smell of the fried bodies coming from that chair.[191] (39) They did not stop here, but went even more out of their mind, because they wanted to triumph

---

182 The translation is based on Schwartz and Mommsen (1903).

183 These are Eusebius' own words, who apparently has skipped something.

184 Literally 'departure', a euphemism for the martyrs' death.

185 See also 42, 4 Macc. 17:12, 15; *Mart. Pol.* 17.1; 19.2; *Mart. Pion.* 22.2; *Mart. Fruct.* 4.1; *Mart. Max.* 3.2; *Mart. Agap.* 2.1, 4. The wreath or crown as the martyrs' reward is an adaptation of the golden or olive wreath or crown of honour for athletes and other honourable persons; Brekelmans (1965); Stewart (1984).

186 Three names may have been given after the martyrs' conversion to Christianity and clearly have a symbolic meaning. Maturus means 'Ripe one', Sanctus 'Holy one' and Blandina 'Charming or Persuasive one', which may be associated with her prayer of exhortation (5.1.41). The name is attested in Gaul; G. Thomas in Rougé and Turcan (1978), 99. Attalus indicates a provenance from Pergamum in Asia Minor.

187 This is a reversion of a well-known accusation against the Christians.

188 The account presents itself to the reader as an eyewitness account.

189 Similar phrases occur in 42, where the reference to Satan as the martyrs' adversary is more explicit.

190 Literally 'there'.

191 The 'iron chair' was an instrument of torture that led to a fast death of burning, Vergote (1972), 135. Cf. concerning the 'frying' of the martyrs 5.1.56; 2 Macc. 7:3, 5; 4 Macc. 8:13; 10:10, 19.

over the steadfastness of those (Christians). Yet, from Sanctus they did not hear anything other than the confession he used to say from the beginning onwards.[192] (40) Finally, these were sacrificed, after their soul had endured the huge contest for a long time and they had become a spectacle for the world[193] during that day with all its variety of gladiator shows.

(41) Blandina was hung on a wooden beam[194] and set as food before the beasts driven in the arena. Because she was seen hanging in the form of a cross and because of her energetic prayer she caused a great enthusiasm among those who were combating. During their contest they looked with their physical eyes through the mediation of their sister to the one who was crucified for them,[195] so that she[196] persuaded those who believed in Him that everyone who suffers for the glory of Christ[197] always has communion with the living God.[198] (42) When none of the beasts touched her,[199] she was taken from the wooden beam and taken back to the prison. There she was preserved for another contest in order to make the condemnation for the crooked snake[200] incontrovertible through her victory in several exercises.[201] The small, weak and easily despised woman urged her brothers forward. She was clothed with Christ,[202] the great and

192 This confession is given in 5.1.20: 'I am a Christian'.
193 Allusion to 1 Cor. 4:9.
194 The obvious association of this beam with a cross, on the basis of New Testament references, is, perhaps, too simple. Vergote (1972), 120–3; 135, argues that the Greek *xylon* can refer in Christian writings about martyrdom to a well-known Roman instrument of torture by stretching the limbs, the *eculeus*.
195 The beneficial significance of Jesus' crucifixion is obvious in several NT passages, but there is no close parallel with the phrase used here.
196 Or 'He', that is Christ.
197 In 1 Pet. 2:21; 3:18, referring to Jesus Christ, the verb 'suffer' implies death. Followers of Jesus suffer for Him or His name according to Phil. 1:29 and Acts 9:16.
198 The 'living God' is one of the names for the God of Israel, used in the Hebrew Bible as well as in the New Testament, see, for example, Hos. 1:10 quoted in Rom. 9:26 and Mat. 16:16.
199 Cf. *Pas. Perp.* 19.
200 Allusion to Isa. 27:1 in the Septuagint translation.
201 This athletic phrase is a euphemism for the martyrs' suffering here. In early Christian literature it can also refer to ascetic practices, Lampe (1961), 324.
202 The imagery of being clothed with Christ probably alludes to Rom. 13:14 and Gal. 3:27. The latter passage indicates that the imagery is linked to baptism. Early Christian baptismal liturgies imply that newly baptised persons put on white garments.

unconquerable athlete. She forced the adversary out in several rounds and wore during the contest the wreath of immortality for herself.

(43) Attalus too was in great demand from the multitude, because he was famous. He entered as an eager competitor because his conscience was clear. He was properly trained in the Christian army[203] and had always appeared to be a witness of the truth among us.[204] (44) He was led around the amphitheatre and a tablet accompanied him on which was written in Latin: 'This is Attalus the Christian'.[205] While the mob could not wait (to see him executed), the governor learned that he was a Roman citizen and ordered to return him to the others who were in prison. For the governor had sent a message to the emperor about them and awaited the emperor's sentence. (45) The interval was neither useless nor fruitless, but displayed through their steadfastness the immense mercy of Christ. Since 'because of the living the dead were made alive again'.[206] Martyrs gave graciously to nonmartyrs and great joy sprang up in the virgin-mother, who received alive those whom she had brought forth stillborn as dead.[207] (46) Since through them the most of those who refused were taken into account again. They were made fruitful and brought to life again, and learned to confess. Living again and braced up they proceeded to the platform to be questioned again by the governor. Because God removed the bitterness, not willing the death of the sinner and being merciful with respect to repentance.[208] (47) After the emperor had given his written orders to beat some of them to death, but to let the rest go if they refused, this assembly started to convene. A huge crowd from all kind of nationalities came together for this event. The

---

203 Military imagery and athletic vocabulary go hand in hand in this description of martyrdom, as in 4 Macc. 9:23–4; 11:22–3; 13:16; 16:14, van Henten (1997), 119–22; 238; 287; Emonds (1938).

204 'Witness of the truth' and similar phrases occur frequently in the Johannine corpus in the New Testament (John 5:31–3; 8:13–14, 17; 18:37; 19:35; 21:24; 3 John 3; 12).

205 The condemned went to the place of execution preceded by a board, plank or placard called *titulus* (*pinax* in Greek) on which the reason for the execution was written, Tajra (1994), 21. Cf. John 19:19–22.

206 The imagery of birth is used in connection with those Christians who first refused to confess their belief (the 'dead') but apparently followed the example of the martyrs afterwards. See 5.1.11.

207 The imagery of birth in connection with those Christians who first refused to confess their belief in 5.1.11 is taken up again, see p. 121.

208 Allusion to Ezek. 33:11.

governor[209] brought the happy ones to the platform, mocking them and letting them parade for the masses. Therefore he examined them again with the help of torture. All those who appeared to have Roman citizenship he cut off their heads and the others he sent to the beasts.[210]

7 *Perpetua's Passion* 6 and 10

The central section of the *Passion of Perpetua* (beginning of the third century CE) is an autobiographical account, written by Perpetua and including visions of her and Saturus (3–13). It is expanded with an introduction and a description of the martyrs' final days by an anonymous editor (1–2; 14–21). The central part has a highly personal flavour and is without any doubt a very important document about Christian self-identity in the beginning of the third century CE: indeed, no other woman's diary from antiquity has been given to us. The editor passed the writing on to other Christians so that they could participate in the martyrs' experiences and enter into fellowship with Christ through them (1.6). He presents the martyrs as model figures (*exempla fidei*) who yield in nothing to the old models of faith (1.1–2; 21.11). The reading about the model figures of this *Passion* would strengthen the building of the Church (21.11).

Two sections have been selected from the *Passion*. The first concerns the trial scene in Chapter 6. The acting prosecutor is the *procurator* Publius Aelius Hilarianus, who was known as a deeply religious person with conservative Roman views about religion.[211] During the trial scene Perpetua confirms that she was a Christian (*christiana sum* 6.4; cf. 3.2), as martyrs usually do in Christian martyr texts. The trial scene, however, also incorporates an unusual dialogue between Perpetua and her father, who tries to persuade her to sacrifice for the safety of the emperor (6.3–4). This dialogue revolves around the choice between Perpetua's traditional and her new identity as a Christian.

The second section, Chapter 10, concerns Perpetua's vision of her own death.[212] She sees herself fighting a contest against an Egyptian

---

209 Literally 'he'.
210 The distinctive punishment of beheading in the case of Roman citizenship is explicitly noted here, cf. p. 120 with n. 172.
211 Salisbury (1997), 81 n. 150.
212 Cf. *Mart. Pol.* 5.2.

man and is herself turned into a man before the fight. The Egyptian is a representation of the devil, who turns out to be Perpetua's real opponent in the martyrdom (3.3; 10; 21.10).[213] Remarkably, Perpetua and Felicitas' death scene in Chapter 20 does not match the vision of Chapter 10. There the young women have to confront a mad heifer as animal of punishment.[214] The choice of this animal is attributed to the devil, who is, however, clearly associated with the Egyptian of Chapter 10.[215]

Translation[216]

(6.1) The next day, when we were having lunch, we were suddenly taken for interrogation. As soon as we arrived at the market place,[217] a rumour spread through the neighbourhood of the market place and a huge crowd gathered. (6.2) We climbed the platform. The others were interrogated and confessed. Then it was my turn. Immediately my father appeared with my son and he pulled me aside saying: 'Pray to the gods, have pity on your baby.' (6.3) And the procurator Hilarianus,[218] who at that time had received the power of life and death instead of the late governor Minucius Timinianus, said: 'Spare the grey hairs of your father, spare the early youth of your child.[219] Sacrifice for the well-being of the emperors.'[220] (6.4) I responded: 'I will not do that.' Hilarianus said: 'Are you a Christian?' And I responded: 'I am a Christian.' (6.5) When my father kept standing

---

213   The devil acts as the martyrs' principal opponent in several Christian passages about martyrdom: Ignatius, *Rom.* 5.3; 7.1; *Mart. Pol.* 2.4; 17.1; *Mart. Pauli* 1.
214   Bastiaensen in Bastiaensen *et al.* (1987), 447, notes that a heifer was highly unusual at games during which Christians were executed.
215   The gender of the animal will not be a coincidence, since the femaleness of both martyrs is stressed by taboo-breaking particularities that must have had an eroticising effect on many onlookers and readers.
216   The translation is based on the edition by A.A.R. Bastiaensen in Bastiaensen *et al.* (1987), 107–47.
217   The market-place (*forum*) was also the place where the Roman governor usually administered justice.
218   Hilarianus obviously replaced the late governor as judge. As the highest Roman administrator on the spot (*procurator*), he would have been responsible for the revenues of the emperor in the province.
219   Cf. the references to Eleazar's grey hairs in 2 Macc. 6:18–31 and the affection of the Maccabaean mother for her sons, especially in 4 Macc. 14:11–17:1; also *Passio Carpi* 6.2–3 (Latin version).
220   I.e. the Emperor Septimius Severus and his son Caracalla.

there and attempted to remove me, Hilarianus ordered his men to kick him out, and he was struck with a rod. The fate of my father hurt me as if I was struck myself. I was hurt much because of his miserable old age. (6.6) Then he (Hilarianus) passed sentence and condemned all of us to the beasts.[221] In a happy mood we descended and went back to prison. (6.7) Since my baby was used to being breast-fed by me and to staying with me in prison, I immediately sent the deacon Pomponius to my father to ask for the baby. But my father did not want to give him to me. (6.8) And as God wanted it, he did not long for my breasts any more nor did they become inflamed. Therefore, I did not suffer out of concern for the baby or because of pain in my breasts.[222]

(10.1) The day before our fight I saw the following in a vision: Pomponius the deacon came to the prison's door and hammered strongly on it. (10.2) I went out to him and opened the door for him. He was wearing a white robe without girdle and had richly wrought sandals. (10.3) And he said to me: 'We are waiting for you: come.' And he held my hand and we started to walk through bumpy and tortuous country. (10.4) Gasping we at last managed with great difficulty to reach the amphitheatre. He led me to the arena's centre and said to me: 'Do not be afraid, I will be here with you and I will suffer alongside with you.' And he left. (10.5) And I saw a huge crowd watching eagerly. Since I knew I was condemned to the beasts, I was amazed that no beasts were set at me. (10.6) A certain Egyptian, with terribly ugly looks, came out with his assistants to fight me.[223] And to me came handsome young men, my assistants and supporters. (10.7) My clothes were taken off and I was turned into a man.[224] And my helpers started to rub me down with oil, as

221 Thus Perpetua and her fellow martyrs received the same sentence as Ignatius.
222 Normally, Perpetua would have needed to express milk to prevent her breasts from being inflamed. The miracle is attributed to God as Felicitas' untimely delivery (Chapter 15).
223 Several commentators suppose that the horrible looks of the Egyptian refer to a black colour of skin, implying that he was the devil. For a detailed discussion, see Habermehl (1992), 130–70. In 10.14 Perpetua identifies the Egyptian as the devil.
224 This passage has been interpreted in very different ways, Habermehl (1992), 109–19. A simple explanation is that an athletic combat like a *pankration* contest could only be fought by men. The fact that Perpetua is a woman again after the contest imagery confirms this reading.

one does for a combat.[225] Opposite to me, I saw the Egyptian wallowing in the dust.[226] (10.8) And a certain man came forward, who was so remarkably tall that he rose above the highest point of the amphitheatre.[227] He was wearing a robe without girdle but with purple running down the middle of his chest between two strips, richly wrought sandals, made from gold and silver, a rod as if he was a trainer, and a green branch with golden apples. (10.9) He asked for silence and said: 'If this Egyptian triumphs over her, he will kill her with the sword. If she triumphs over him, she will receive this branch.' And he stepped back. (10.10) And we approached each other and started to punch. He tried to grab my feet, but I kicked his face with my heels. (10.11) And I was lifted in the air and started to kick him as if I was no longer treading the earth. And when I saw that the fight had stopped for a moment, I joined my hands, linking the fingers of the one with the fingers of the other, and caught hold of his head. He fell on his face and I stamped on his head. (10.12) And the crowd started to shout and my assistants began singing psalms. I went to the person in charge and received the branch. (10.13) He kissed me and said: 'Peace be with you, my daughter.'[228] And I started to walk gloriously to the Gate of Life.[229] (10.14) And I woke up and understood that I would not fight against beasts but against the devil. But I knew that I would be victorious. (10.15)

225 The details about the combat are not completely consistent, but the combination of punching, kicking and wrestling points to the athletic contest of a *pankration*, one of the sports of the Olympic games; Finley and Pleket (1976), 40–4; Habermehl (1992), 99. At the same time, there are links with a fight of gladiators as well; ibid., 164–5.

226 Augustine already suggests that Perpetua's opponent was the same as Eve's adversary (*Sermo* 2; 4). Perpetua's stepping on the head of the Egyptian is a sign of her victory but also echoes Gen. 3:15 telling that Eve's descendants will step on the head of the serpent. Even the apples in 10.8 may be considered an echo of Gen. 3.

227 This figure may be associated with the deacon Pomponius (10.2) who says that he will suffer together with Perpetua. The robe without girdle and the richly wrought sandals remind one of Pomponius' description in 10.2. The vocabulary and imagery used in connection with this figure, however, are not consistent. The phrase *lanista* (10.8) suggests that he was a trainer of gladiators, but 10.9 presents him as the referee or even the organiser of the contest; Habermehl (1992), 100; 164.

228 The *Passion* refers twice to the kiss of peace (see also 12.5), which was an established custom in early Christian circles.

229 Gladiators who were victorious left the arena through the Gate of Life. The others were carried away through the Gate of Death.

This I did until the day before the games. Let the one who would like to write about the events during the games, write about those.

8 *Writing to Diognetus* 1.1; 5.11–17; 6.7–10; 7.7–9

The *Writing to Diognetus* 1–10 (late second or third century CE) consists of two sections: (a) Chapters 1–6 concern the religions of the Greeks, the Jews and the Christians, as well as the reasons for the refutation of the Greek and Jewish religions (2.1–4.6) and a presentation of Christian religion and life (5.1–6.10); (b) Chapters 7–10 deal with God, the divine plan and the role of God's Son in this plan. Three of the selected passages, 5.11–16; 6.7–10; 7.7–9, describe aspects of the relationship between Christians and the world and contain several motifs that are prominent in martyr texts: persecution, death and vindication (5.11–12, 16–17; 6.8), contempt for death (1.1), joy during suffering (5.16) and military images applied to martyrdom (6.10; 7.7). *Writing to Diognetus* 5.11–16 offers a brief collection of antitheses about the undeserved treatment of Christians by others and their unselfish response to this treatment. *Diogn.* 6.7–10 rounds off a section about the Christians in the world as compared with the soul in the body. *Diogn.* 7.7–9, finally, forms a small section about the Christians in connection with a description of the mission of Jesus as God's Son.

Translation[230]

(1.1) I see, most excellent Diognetus, that you work very hard to learn about the religion of the Christians[231] and inquire very clearly and carefully about them: what God they believe in, how they venerate him, how all of them take no notice of the world and despise death, why they do not take those as gods who are considered gods by the Greeks nor observe the superstition[232] of the Jews, what affection they feel for one another,[233] and, finally, why this new people came into the world now and not earlier.

---

230 Translation based on Bihlmeyer (1956).
231 About the name 'Christians' (*Diogn.* 1.1; 2.6, 10; 4.6; 5.1; 6.1–9), see n. 99.
232 *Deisidaimonia* can mean 'religion', 'veneration of gods' in a neutral sense, but can also have a negative nuance, like here. Cf. *Diogn.* 4.1, Justin, *Apol.* 1.2.3; Tatian, *Or.* 22.1.
233 The affection towards one another is a *topos* in passages about family life, e.g.

(5.11) They show love to all, yet they are persecuted by all.[234]
(5.12) They are unknown, yet they are being convicted.
They are being killed, yet they are being made alive again.[235]
(5.13) They are poor, yet they make many rich.
They lack everything, yet they abound in everything.[236]
(5.14) They suffer indignities, yet they are glorified through these indignities.[237]
They are being slandered, yet they are being justified.
(5.15) They are being reviled, yet they bless.[238]
They are being maltreated, yet they praise.
(5.16) They do good, yet they are being punished as evildoers.
When they are punished, they are glad[239] as if being made alive again.
5.17) They are fought against by Jews as foreigners and persecuted by the Greeks.
Yet, those who hate them are not able to tell the reason for their hostility.

(6.7) The soul is locked up in the body,[240] but it holds the body together.[241] And the Christians are being kept in the world as in prison, but they hold the world together.[242] (6.8) The immortal soul

---

Epictetus 1.11; Plutarch, *Mor.* 493a-497e; 4 Macc. 15:6, 9. Here, it concerns all Christians as a family or a people.
234 This line echoes several NT passages, among others Jesus' command to love your neighbour (Mark 12:31 and parallels), which is based on Lev. 19:18. Cf. 2 Tim. 3:12.
235 *Diogn.* 5.12 echoes the antithetic Pauline passage of 2 Cor. 6:9.
236 Cf. 2 Cor. 6:10.
237 Cf. 1 Cor. 4:10; 2 Cor. 6:8.
238 This line may allude to 1 Cor. 4:12 and 1 Pet. 3:9.
239 Cf. the motif of joy during experiences of suffering, which occurs already in NT passages: 2 Cor. 6:10 (taken up in *Diogn.* 5.13); 1 Thes. 1:6; Luke 6:22–3; Col. 1:24; 1 Pet. 3:13–5; 4:13. Cf. Ignatius, *Rom.* 6.1; Justin, *Dial.* 46.7; *Mart. Pol.* 12; Tertullian, *Apol.* 41.5; 49.6; Selwyn (1947), 439–58; Schneider (1954), 162–6; 471; Nauck (1955). See also p. 66 and n. 88.
240 The comparison of the Christians with the soul (Chapter 6) reflects popular philosophical motifs about the function of the soul in the body. Cf. Cicero, *Tusc. disp.* 1.30(72–3); already Plato, *Tim.* 34b.
241 That the soul holds the body together is a well-known philosophical concept; Plato, *Phaedo* 79c-80a; Philo, *Spec. leg.* 1.289.
242 The author does not specify the Christians' function in the world. Marrou (1951), 143–6, suggests that they ensured that God remained merciful to humankind, that their intercessory prayers prevented disasters, and that their self-sacrifice through suffering and violent death was beneficial to others.

lives in a mortal housing and Christians live as strangers in a transitory situation,[243] awaiting their everlasting fate in heaven.[244] (6.9) Maltreated by (lack of) food and drinks the soul becomes better and, being punished the Christians become more numerous every day.[245] (6.10) God has placed them at such an important post that they are not allowed to desert it.[246]

(7.7)[247] (Don't you see) that they are thrown to the wild beasts to make them deny their Lord[248] and that they are not being defeated?[249] (7.8) Don't you see that the more of them are punished, the larger the number of the others grows? (7.9) These things do not seem to be the work of humans. They are the mighty work of God. They are evidence of His presence.

243 The vocabulary of *paroikos* of 5.5 is taken up again. A *paroikos* was a stranger living permanently in a city without the rights of the citizens but with a certain protection from the community. Cf. Eph. 2:19 and 1 Pet. 2:11.
244 The author does not elaborate his view of afterlife.
245 The soul is probably an image for the Christians as in 6.7. The first part of 6.9 may imply that the Christians could improve their spiritual life by fasting as training. It may also be a metaphor explained in the second part of the verse.
246 The military imagery suggests that the Christians should keep their position at all costs. The military metaphor also occurs in 4 Macc. 9:23–4; 11:22–3; 13:16; 16:14.
247 The manuscript had a lacuna before 7.7 of about two lines.
248 Denying probably in the double sense of not venerating the emperor and not cursing Christ, cf. *Mart. Pol.* 9.3.
249 Cf. 4 Macc. (see pp. 48 and 73); Rev. 2:10–11, 17; 3:10–12, 21.

4

MARTYRDOM AND NOBLE DEATH IN THE RABBINIC TRADITION

General Introduction

In comparison with the numerous martyrs in the ancient Christian Acts and Passions, there are strikingly few martyrs mentioned in rabbinic sources. This is the case even if one adopts a more general definition which views martyrdom as death caused by religious persecution[1] rather than allowing oneself to be guided by the rabbinic employment of the technical term of *qiddush ha-Shem* ('sanctification of the Name'),[2] which, in fact, occurs only once in the present anthology.[3] A medieval composition[4] dealing with the persecution under Hadrian, which rabbinic tradition recalls as the most dreadful religious oppression in post-biblical times, presents a series of no more than ten persons who suffer martyrdom (the 'Ten Slain by the Kingdom').[5] And only a handful of these ten cases is attested in the ancient rabbinic tradition,[6] i.e., in the Talmuds[7] and in the early Midrashim.[8]

---

1 See Introduction, pp. 3–5.
2 See Introduction, p. 3. For the development of the technical use of this term in the sense of 'death in religious persecution', cf. Safrai (1983).
3 See below, n. 56.
4 *Ma'aseh Asarah Haruge Malkhut* ('Story of the Ten Slain by the Kingdom'); a synoptic edition of the various versions of this composition is given by Reeg (1985).
5 According to versions IV and IX (section 10.31), these are Rabban Shim'on ben Gamli'el, the High Priest R. Yishma'el ben Elisha, R. Aqiva, R. Yehudah ben Bava, R. Hananiah (= Hanina) ben Teradion, R. Yeshevav ha-Sofer, R. El'azar ben Dama, R. Hanina ben Hakhinai, R. Hutspit ha-Meturgeman, R. El'azar ben Shamua; cf. Reeg (1985), § 10.32.
6 The martyrdoms of Rabban Shim'on ben Gamli'el, R. Yishma'el, R. Aqiva and R. Hananiah (= Hanina) ben Teradion are dealt with at some length. Those of R. Yehudah ben Bava and R. Hutspit ha-Meturgeman are mentioned in passing (cf. *T.B. Sanhedrin* 14a and *T.B. Qiddushin* 39b, at variance with *T.Y. Hagigah*

This low occurrence, however, neither indicates that death in persecution was a marginal phenomenon in ancient Judaism, nor does it mean that rabbinic tradition attached only little importance to it.[9] What it reveals is rather that the rabbinic concern for martyrdom was not so much with individual cases and with historical details as it was with theology and ethics. A handful of cases was enough to provide the necessary examples of what was really at stake: theodicy and human guilt, as in the cases of Yose ben Yo'ezer, Pappus and Lulianus,

2.1/77b). The others are not mentioned at all in the early rabbinic literature. The death of R. El'azar ben Dama as reported in *Tos. Hullin* 2.22–3 can hardly be regarded as a martyrdom.

7 These are the *Talmud Yerushalmi* (or *Palestinian Talmud*), which was probably composed in the first third of the fifth century CE, and the *Talmud Bavli* (or *Babylonian Talmud*), the redaction ('sealing') of which took place, according to rabbinic tradition, in the year 500 CE, but in reality was apparently a rather complicated process; cf. Stemberger (1992), 173–4 and 193–8. See also n. 96 below.

8 The term 'Midrash' can denote either an exegetical commentary on a biblical book or on parts of a biblical book, or a single piece of scriptural interpretation, which can be contained in such a commentary or in any other kind of rabbinic literature. Among the earliest 'Midrashic' commentaries (of the former kind) are the *Mekhilta* (*de-Rabbi Yishma'el*) on Exodus, the *Sifra* on Leviticus, and the *Sifre* on Numbers and Deuteronomy, all of them containing both halakhic (i.e. legal) and haggadic (i.e. non-legal) matters and originating from the third or early fourth century CE. *Genesis Rabbah* and *Lamentations Rabbah* are of later origin; they are purely haggadic commentaries on the books of Genesis and Lamentations, dating roughly from the same time as the *Talmud Yerushalmi*. See Stemberger (1992), 245–83.

9 Apart from stories about individual martyrs, the rabbinic literature mentions also smaller or larger groups of martyrs without specifying names (*T.B. Gittin* 57b, e.g., tells of 400 boys and girls committing suicide in order to escape prostitution), and contains many abstract reflections about the reasons, the duty, the value, and the consequences, of martyrdom. The oldest rabbinic texts specifying under which circumstances one must sacrifice one's life are passages in the *Tosefta* and the *Sifra*. *Tosefta Shabbat* 15(16).17 (ed. Lieberman, vol. II, p. 75) states as a general rule that in order to save life any commandment may be transgressed except the prohibitions of idolatry, incest and bloodshed, but adds that 'in a situation of persecution, a man must give his life even for the slightest commandment'. *Sifra Ahare-mot, pereq* 13.14 (ed. Weiss, fol. 86b) relates as a teaching of R. Yishma'el that a person, if in private forced to transgress a commandment, may do so in order to escape death, but that one is bound to 'sanctify God's Name', i.e. to sacrifice one's life, if such a coercion happens in public. Common to both texts is the idea that the only thing worth accepting martyrdom is the Torah, and that transgressing a commandment for the sake of lifesaving is sanctioned by the Torah itself, namely by Lev. 18:5, 'And keep My statutes and My ordinances, which a man shall do and live by them.'

R. Shim'on and R. Yishma'el, and R. Hanina ben Teradion; love of God, as in the tradition about R. Aqiva; the monotheistic confession and the rejection of idolatry, as in the story of the seven sons of Miriam bat Tanhum; the challenge posed by fellow Jews who successfully avoided a violent death either through complying with the oppressor's demands or through tricks and lies, as in the accounts of R. Hanina ben Teradion and R. Aqiva; repentance and conversion in face of the martyr's death, as in the cases of R. Hanina ben Teradion and Yose ben Yo'ezer; the bond of suffering which unifies Israel from the time of Abraham onwards, as illustrated in expositions of the Binding of Isaac and in the story of the mother of the seven sons; and, last but not least, the divine vindication and remuneration of the victims, which are present in almost every rabbinic martyrdom story.[10]

Yose ben Yo'ezer

Following the chronological order of the traditions, the earliest post-biblical case of martyrdom documented in rabbinic literature is that of Yose ben Yo'ezer, a sage who figures in *M. Avot* 1.4 as an early link in the chain of tradition that runs from Moses and the prophets down to the rabbinic present. The name of Yose ben Yo'ezer's nephew and antagonist, Yaqim of Tserorot, may echo that of Alcimus (variant spelling: Iacimus),[11] who had been appointed high priest by the Seleucid ruler Demetrius II during the Maccabaean uprising.[12] But the rabbinic story as such does not lend itself to reconstructing any historical roots. Its concern is not with history, but with theodicy, repentance and post-mortal salvation. The nephew first mocks his ill-fated uncle but then, deeply agitated by his reproof, kills himself, whereupon his uncle has a vision that assures him of the nephew's portion in the world to come. This conclusion shows that suicide was not

---

10 Among the following examples, cf. *Genesis Rabbah* 65.22; *Sifra Emor, pereq* 9.5; *Lamentations Rabbah* 1.16 (see n. 26); *T.B. Berakhot* 61b (section G of the translation below); *Sifre Deuteronomy* 307; *T.B. Avodah Zarah* 17b-18a (section J of the translation below). The exception is *T.Y. Berakhot* 9.7. For the general ancient Jewish and Christian background, cf. 2 Macc. 7; 14:16; Josephus, *War* 1.653; *As. Mos.* 9:7; *1 Clem.* 5.7; 6.2; *Diogn.* 5.12; *Acts of Justin* 5.1–2; Eusebius, *Hist. eccl.* 5.1.36 (*Mart. Lugd.*); Kellermann (1979), 94–109.

11 Cf. Graetz (1876), 369; Hengel (1976), 262, n. 4; 1 Macc. 7:16.

12 Cf. Josephus, *Ant.* 12.385; Schürer (1973–87), vol. I, 168–70.

per se considered as morally dubious. In fact, noble suicide is a recurrent motif in rabbinic martyr stories.[13]

Pappus and Lulianus

The next martyrdom is that of Pappus and Lulianus, whose trial is said to have taken place under Trajan in Syrian Laodicaea. Various independent references to their martyrdom in comparatively early rabbinic sources suggest the historicity of the core of the tradition. The event may indeed have taken place in Laodicaea, since it is difficult to imagine a reason for a fictional association with this Syrian city. The charge on which Pappus and Lulianus were condemned could have been their support of the revolts which broke out during Trajan's rule in various regions of the Jewish diaspora, such as Egypt, Cyrene, Cyprus, and parts of Mesopotamia.[14] The account in *Sifra Emor*, however, focuses mainly on the comparison of the present martyrs with those mentioned in the Bible, and on the problem of theodicy as well as on the eventual punishment of the enemy.

The mother and her seven sons

The martyrdom of Miriam bat Tanhum and her seven sons is likewise located in a Roman setting. In one of the versions, the emperor who conducts the interrogation and orders the execution bears the name Hadrian.[15] The underlying tradition is, however, much older. The motif of the proud resistance of seven brothers and their mother occurs already in 2 Macc. 7,[16] and in 4 Macc. 8–18 it is developed into a lengthy lesson on the persevering strength of moral reason. Although the rabbinic versions differ considerably from these older stories in their central religious concern, there are several points of contact.[17] The most conspicuous feature common to *Lamentations Rabbah* and 4 Maccabees is the comparison of the mother and her sons with Abraham and Isaac.[18] The ruse which the emperor proposes to

---

13 Cf. the cases of Miriam bat Tanhum (see p. 151) and of the executioner of R. Hanina ben Teradion (see p. 166); see also above n. 9 and Chapter 2, section 11, pp. 83ff.

14 Cf. Horbury (1999), 291–3; for the Jewish revolts under Trajan see Schürer (1973–87), vol. I, 529–34.

15 See below n. 75.

16 Cf. above, Chapter 2, pp. 66–70.

17 A detailed comparison is provided by Doran (1980).

18 Cf. 4 Macc. 9:21; 13:12; 14:20; 15:25–9; 16:20, 25; 17:6; 18:23.

the seventh son resembles the manoeuvre of simulating the consumption of pork suggested to the old Eleazar in 2 Macc. 6:21–2 and 4 Macc. 7:12–15.[19] Further common features are the martyrs' belief that they die because of their own transgressions,[20] the advice which the mother gives to her youngest son,[21] the emphasis on the emotional bond between mother and child by the motif of nursing,[22] and, curiously, the employment of 'frying pans' as instruments of torture.[23] The claim of monotheism, however, which in the rabbinic versions appears as the backbone of Jewish resistance, is almost completely absent from the Maccabaean accounts,[24] and conversely, the themes of the tyrant's future divine punishment and the victims' vindication and reward, which figure prominently in 2 and 4 Maccabees,[25] are of marginal importance in the rabbinic tradition.[26] The rabbinic accounts cannot, therefore, be regarded as mere rewritings of the reports in 2 and 4 Maccabees, although a certain dependence is obvious.

One of the striking characteristics of the rabbinic versions is the stereotypical form of the interrogations of the first six brothers. This

---

19 Cf. p. 65 and 4 Macc. 6:15: 'We shall bring you some cooked meat, and you, by pretending to eat of the pork, shall be saved.'

20 Cf. 2 Macc. 7:18, 32, 38.

21 In the version of *Pesiqta Rabbati* 43 (see below n. 69), the seventh son asks his mother whether or not he should prostrate himself before the image. She assures him that his brothers have been transferred to the bosom of Abraham for the world to come, and, therefore, this last son, too, refuses the prostration. Cf. the dialogues in 2 Macc. 7:26–29 and 4 Macc. 12:7; see, however, Doran (1980), 196–7.

22 Cf. 2 Macc. 7:27; 4 Macc. 13:19–21; 16:7 (and the whole of 4 Macc. 15).

23 The version of *Pesiqta Rabbati* 43 uses the Greek loan-words tigano[n] and tiggenu (emended), which are reminiscent of *tēgana* and *tēganizein* in 2 Macc. 7:3, 5 and 4 Macc. 8:13; 12:10, 20; cf. Doran (1980), 196.

24 In 2 Macc. 7:37, the mother, facing Antiochus, calls 'upon God that . . . you will confess because of trials and tortures that He alone is God'. In passing, a monotheistic confession also occurs in 4 Macc. 5:24.

25 For Antiochus' punishment, see 2 Macc. 7:14, 17, 19, 31, 35–7; 4 Macc. 9:9, 24; 10:11, 21; 11:3; 12:12, 18; 18:5; for the martyrs' expectation of vindication, reward and restitution cf. 2 Macc. 7:6, 9, 11, 14, 23, 29, 36; 14:46; 4 Macc. 9:8; 13:17; 16:13, 25; 17:4, 12, 18; 18:3, 23; for the martyrs' avoidance of divine punishment cf. 2 Macc. 6:26; 4 Macc. 13:15. Cf. Chapter 2, sections 5, 6 and 7.

26 The expectation of the punishment of the oppressor is explicit only in *Lamentations Rabbah* (section K of the translation below). The vindication of the victims is mentioned in *Lamentations Rabbah* (sections K, N and Q), *T.B. Gittin* and *Pesiqta Rabbati*, but it is mentioned only at the end of these texts.

makes the focus shift to the seventh brother, whom the emperor engages in a lengthy dialogue (which is in fact a Midrash on Ps. 115:5–7). An equally prominent position is assigned to the mother, whose distress is the central theme of a series of loosely connected narrative units that make up the conclusion of the story. The fact that a woman plays the central role is exceptional, since the heroes of rabbinic martyr traditions are normally men. There are only two other women of whom a conviction and punishment is reported, namely the wife and the daughter of R. Hanina ben Teradion. But these are anonymous characters who are subordinate to the leading role of their husband and father.

R. Aqiva and R. Hanina ben Teradion

If the story of Miriam bat Tanhum is essentially a product of fiction, two other traditions relating to the persecution under Hadrian are presumably based on historical events. R. Aqiva, the most famous rabbinic martyr, is reported to have hailed Bar Kokhba, the leader of the second great Jewish uprising against the Roman occupiers of Palestine (132–135 CE), as Israel's Messiah.[27] As such a piece of information is quite unlikely to have been invented,[28] this may suggest that the tradition about his violent end is basically credible as well. The name of the Roman official mentioned in one of the texts, 'Turnus Rufus', corresponds to that of the Roman governor of Judaea at the time of the Bar Kokhba rebellion, (Quintus) Tineius Rufus. As this detail seems to be rather superfluous considering the mainly religious interest of the text, it may also preserve a historical reminiscence.[29] In the second case, that of R. Hanina ben Teradion and his family, historicity is suggested by the fact that the hero of this story, unlike R. Aqiva, figures quite marginally in other rabbinic traditions.[30] He hardly is a character to whom an entirely fictitious

27 Cf. *T.Y. Ta'anit* 4.8/68d: 'R. Shim'on ben Yohai has taught: Aqiva, my rabbi, expounded: "*A star* [Hebrew *kokhav*] *goes forth from Jacob* (Num. 24:17), (meaning) Kozba goes forth from Jacob." When R. Aqiva saw Bar Kozba [literally, "son of falsehood", a pun on "Bar Kokhba"] he said· This is the king messiah!' Cf. also *Lamentations Rabbah* 2.4. On the historical problem see Schäfer (1978), 86–90.
28 The sobriquet 'son of falsehood' (see above n. 27) clearly shows what kind of reputation Bar Kokhba had in the rabbinic tradition.
29 For a contrary view, see Schäfer (1978), 115–16 and 121.
30 In the *Mishnah*, he is quoted in *Ta'anit* 2.5 and *Avot* 3.2, and in the *Tosefta*, in *Ta'anit* 1.14, *Kelim Bava Qamma* 4.17, and *Miqva'ot* 6.3.

martyrdom would have been attached. Moreover, the traditions gathered in *T.B. Avodah Zarah* 17b–18a are remarkably diversified and independent of each other, which points to an early origin of their common base. Part of this common base is that R. Hanina was burnt together with his Torah scroll, while his wife was beheaded and his daughter sentenced to prostitution. These motifs, therefore, may also be based on historical reminiscences.[31]

In two of these traditions, R. Hanina's conviction is preceded by encounters with colleagues, who, contrary to R. Hanina, succeed in evading martyrdom. The first of these colleagues is a certain R. El'azar ben Perata. Unlike R. Hanina, who frankly admits the charge of having studied the Torah, this R. El'azar outwits his interrogators with cunning answers. A series of burlesque miracles supporting his tricks shows that his shrinking back from martyrdom is met with divine approval. The other colleague, R. Yose ben Qisma, typifies submission to the Roman oppression. He cautions R. Hanina against teaching the Torah, foresees his execution, is doubtful about R. Hanina's trust in God's mercy, and is himself paid every honour by the Roman authorities when he eventually dies a natural death. Nevertheless, he exclaims, 'May your fate be my fate!', when he hears that the only transgression R. Hanina is aware of having committed is a confusion of different types of charity money,[32] a transgression which is so light that it definitely cannot endanger his portion in the world to come. As the portrayal of these colleagues is by no means entirely negative, the stance which the tradition adopts towards martyrdom seems, to say the least, ambiguous. On the other hand, the various transgressions which are considered as the possible deeper reasons for R. Hanina's violent death, not of course from a Roman, but

---

31 For dying at the stake see Eusebius, *De mart. Palaest.* 2.2; 8.8; 9.8 etc. (cf. below nn. 182 and 185, and p. 122, n. 191). Fire as a means of torture and execution figures also prominently in 2 Macc. 6–7; 4 Macc. 5–18; *Mart. Pol.* 13–15; cf. p. 52, n. 30. For the burning of the rabbi together with his Torah, see the description of the eschatological anti-christ king, who will 'enwrap righteous men with the books of the prophets and thus burn them', in Lactantius, *Divinae institutiones* 7.17.8 (*CSEL* 19, 639). For the condemnation of women to prostitution cf. *T.B. Gittin* 57b; *Acta ss. Didymi et Theodorae*: 'The maidservant of God was then brought into a brothel' (*Acta Sanctorum Aprilis*, vol. III, p. 580); Ambrose, *De virginibus* 2.4.23: 'So the sentence was that she should either sacrifice, or be sent to a house of ill-fame' (*PL* 16, 225a). On these and related topics see Lieberman (1939–44), 418–20.

32 Cf. below n. 160.

from a divine perspective, are so trivial that they do not cast the slightest doubt on his moral integrity. The oldest literary version of his martyrdom, which is preserved in *Sifre Deuteronomy*, praises R. Hanina and his family for accepting their grim fate as a divine punishment without even asking which transgression they might have committed. Their exemplary pious behaviour is termed *tsidduq ha-din*, i.e., the 'justification of (God's) judgement', an expression which is in a certain way an early equivalent of the modern notion of 'theodicy'.

R. Aqiva's martyrdom is strikingly different. The only feature it has in common with that of R. Hanina is that R. Aqiva, too, is convicted on the charge of having studied and taught the Torah. But the question of a possible transgression of R. Aqiva, which might account for his violent death, is entirely absent from the tradition. The problem of theodicy is touched on only in an appendix, when God's angels protest against the cruel end of this pious man.[33] The central religious view is rather the idea that the victim fulfils through martyrdom one of the most fundamental commandments, namely that of loving God. Horribly tortured, R. Aqiva only confesses to have troubled himself all his life for lacking the opportunity to love God 'with all his soul', as prescribed in Deut. 6:5. His death turns out to be this long-desired opportunity and thus puts an end to his troubles. The version of *T.Y. Berakhot* 9.7 presents him laughing while he expires reciting the *Shema Yisra'el*.[34] The idea of martyrdom as the culmination of devotion and the fulfilment of one's deepest longing seems to correspond to the very nature of the commandment to love God. Daniel Boyarin even speaks of an 'eroticism'[35] which inspires this story: R. Aqiva suffers because he is 'passionately in love with God'.[36]

---

33 See pp. 156–7 and n. 135.
34 I.e., 'Hear, O Israel' (Deut. 6:4), a prayer which every male Israelite is bound to recite twice a day (cf. *M. Berakhot* 1) and which consists of the text of Deut. 6:4–9 (hence the title), 11:13–21, and Num. 15:27–41, framed by various additional blessings.
35 Boyarin (1999), 107 (and his index, s.v. 'eroticism').
36 Boyarin (1999), 96, paralleling R. Aqiva with several ancient Christian martyrs and contrasting them with the martyrs of 2 and 4 Maccabees, who suffer 'because they fear [God's] punishment or demonstrate their stoic fortitude or apathy.' For Boyarin (1999), 95, the idea of death as fulfilment of 'a religious mandate per se' (i.e., in R. Aqiva's case, the fulfilment of the commandment to love God) is one of the essential novelties 'of late antique martyrdom as a practice of both rabbinic Jews and Christians', over against their Maccabaean predecessors.

R. Shim'on and R. Yishma'el

Along with R. Aqiva and R. Hanina ben Teradion, their contemporaries Rabban Shim'on ben Gamli'el and R. Yishma'el are also counted among the 'Ten Slain by the Kingdom'. But the tradition which relates the martyrdom of these two rabbis cannot be traced back as easily to a historical event. It seems that the decisive impulse for the formation of the tradition came from a gloomy oracle attributed to Shemu'el ha-Qatan, a sage who lived some time before the Hadrianic persecution: 'Shim'on and Yishma'el (are destined) for the sword, and their fellows for slaughter, and the rest of the people for pillage.'[37] Although Shim'on and Yishma'el are not addressed here as rabbis, the mention of their 'fellows' in distinction from the 'rest of the people' may have easily prompted the association with prominent rabbis who bore these names. More important, however, is the fact that 'Shim'on' and 'Yishma'el' are singled out for a particular kind of death, namely, death by the sword. This must have evoked the question concerning the reason of this specification, and it is exactly here that the story in the *Mekhilta* takes off: R. Shim'on wonders for which transgression he is going to be decapitated, for as in other rabbinic martyrdom stories it is the heavenly judgement rather than the Roman government which is thought to determine the martyr's fate. There is, however, only one biblical injunction which is reinforced by the explicit threat that God will punish the offender by the sword, namely Exod. 22:21–3: 'You shall not oppress any widow or orphan. If you oppress them (Hebrew *im anneh te'anneh*), and if they cry out to Me, I will surely heed their cry; and My wrath will be kindled, and I will kill you with the sword, and your wives shall become widows and your children orphans.' Since the verb *innah* not only means 'to oppress' but also 'to detain',[38] and since Exod. 22:22 employs the verb in the emphatic doubling *anneh te'anneh*, rabbinic exegesis infers that the commandment in fact covers both meanings of the verb: widows and orphans must neither be oppressed nor detained. Hence R. Yishma'el only needs to remind his colleague that it must have occurred to him that he kept somebody waiting who had asked him

---

37 *Tos. Sotah* 13.4, ms. Erfurt (Lieberman, 1955–88, vol. III.2, 231); ms. Vienna has 'sword' and 'slaughter' in the reverse order (ibid., p. 232). Cf. also *T.Y. Sotah* 9.13–14/24b (ed. Schäfer and Becker, 1991–2001: 9,13.14/5); *T.B. Sotah* 48b; *T.B. Sanhedrin* 11a; *Semahot* 8.7–8 (Higger, 1970b, 152–4).

38 Cf., e.g., *M. Sanhedrin* 11.4. For *M. Avot* 5.8, see below n. 192.

for a decision or some advice. R. Shim'on gladly accepts this solution, and thus their martyrdom turns into a case of theodicy as well as into a demonstration of the high morality of these rabbis, who cannot be accused of any graver transgression.

The Binding of Isaac

In addition to this range of post-biblical martyr traditions, the present selection includes a sample of interpretations of the 'Binding of Isaac',[39] i.e. the story of Gen. 22:1–19. Of course, neither the story itself nor its various rabbinic amplifications deal in a strict sense with martyrdom. Abraham is not a persecutor like Antiochus or Hadrian, nor does Isaac actually die. Even if the expression 'the blood of the Binding of Isaac' in the *Mekhilta*[40] implies that Isaac had at least been injured, the oldest rabbinic text which explicitly says that 'when the blade touched his neck, Isaac's soul flushed and departed' (and immediately returned upon divine intervention) is of medieval origin.[41] Nevertheless, the Binding of Isaac is included here for two reasons. First, Isaac serves as a perfect model of self-sacrifice in ancient Jewish martyr texts. In 4 Macc. 13:12, one of the seven boys exhorts his brothers as follows: 'Remember where you came from and at what father's hand Isaac gave himself to be sacrificed for the sake of piety.' And in 16:20, their mother reminds them of that other son who, 'seeing the father's blade-wielding hand descending upon him, did not duck'. Isaac's willingness is, in fact, one of the most typical traits which ancient Jewish elaborations of Gen. 22 emphasise,[42] deviating

---

39 'Binding of Isaac' renders the Hebrew *Aqedat Yitshaq*, which is a current rabbinic designation for the story of Gen. 22:1–19. Cf. Davies and Chilton (1978), 514–15.

40 *Mekhilta Pisha* 7 and 11 (ed. Horovitz and Rabin, 1970, 24, 39). For a shedding of 'a fourth' of Isaac's blood, see *Mekhilta de-Rabbi Shim'on ben Yohai* on Exod. 6:2 (ed. Epstein and Melamed, 1979, p. 4). Cf. Rose (1993), 239–43. The mention of Isaac's being 'offered' in Heb. 11:17 seems, however, not as unequivocal, as it does not necessarily imply the completion of the sacrifice; cf. Davies and Chilton (1978), 529. On Ps.-Philo, *Biblical Antiquities* 18.5, see below nn. 244 and 245.

41 *Pirqe de-Rabbi Eli'ezer* 31. According to Stemberger (1992), 322, *Pirqe de-Rabbi Eli'ezer* was composed in the eighth or ninth century. The same tradition is resumed in the still later *Yalqut Shim'oni*, part I, § 101. For other late texts describing a dying and immediate revivification of Isaac, see Rose (1993), 241–2.

42 Cf. Josephus, *Ant.* 1.232 (Isaac received his father's words 'with joy'); on Ps.-Philo see below n. 242. *Genesis Rabbah* 87.5 transfers this readiness to Isaac's

from the biblical account, which accords Isaac a rather passive role. Second, the rabbinic treatments of Gen. 22 have themselves adopted features and motifs which are otherwise characteristic of martyr stories. Apart from the victim's willingness to accept his death, these include, for example, his vision on the verge of death,[43] and his ultimate vindication and reward.[44] Also the emphatic employment of sacrificial imagery is a widespread common feature.[45] Finally, it is worth noting that the central theological importance of Gen. 22 for ancient Judaism is documented not only by these variegated literary elaborations of the matter, but also by the pictorial representation of the story in antique synagogue art, such as in the paintings of Dura-Europos (mid-third century CE) or in the mosaic floor of Bet Alfa (early sixth century CE).

1 *Genesis Rabbah* 65.22: Yose ben Yo'ezer and Yaqim of Tserorot

In the context of *Genesis Rabbah*, the story of the martyrdom of Yose ben Yo'ezer is embedded in a Midrash[46] on Gen. 27:27, 'And he smelled the smell of his garments'. By a pun on *begadaw*, 'garments', the verse is taken to refer to *bogedaw*, i.e., 'his apostates'. Even apostates may, under certain circumstances, end up as martyrs, whose death is (as the Midrash seems to imply) received by God as if it were the pleasing odour of a sacrifice. Two examples of such 'apostates' are given. The first is Yose Meshitah, who collaborated with the enemies, entered the temple, and stole a golden lamp. But then he refused to enter a second time ('Enough that I angered my God once, so should I anger

---

grandson Joseph, who resists the passion of Potiphar's wife by arguing, 'perhaps I have been chosen to be a burnt offering . . .'. However, the motif of Isaac's willingness is absent from *Jub.* 18:1–13 and only marginal in Philo, *De Abrahamo* 169–204; cf. Hayward (1981), 135. Both texts focus on the obedience of Abraham, just as the shorter reference to Gen. 22 in Heb. 11:17–19 and Jas. 2:21.

43 Cf. *Asc. Is.* 5:7, 14; Acts 7:55; *T.B. Avodah Zarah* 18a; *T.B. Berakhot* 61b; *Genesis Rabbah* 65.22; *Mart. Pol.* 2.2; 5.2; 9.1; for further examples, see p. 113, n. 124, and Kellermann (1979), 38, n. 31.

44 Particularly noteworthy is the association of Isaac's Binding with the expectation of a resurrection; cf. Heb. 11:19; *Pesiqta de-Rav Kahana* 31 (Buber, 1868, fol. 200b); *Pirqe de-Rabbi Eli'ezer* 31 (see n. 41).

45 Cf. *Tos. Sanhedrin* 13.11; *Prayer of Azariah* 40; Ignatius, *Rom.* 2.2; 4.2; *Mart. Pol.* 14.1–2; Eusebius, *Hist. eccl.* 5.1.40 (*Mart. Lugd.*).

46 See above n. 8.

Him a second time?') and, therefore, was sawed asunder.[47] The second example is Yaqim of Tserorot. *Genesis Rabbah* provides the earliest version of the story. Later versions are found only in medieval writings.

Translation[48]

Yaqim of Tserorot[49] was the son of the sister of (Yose ben)[50] Yo'ezer of Tseredah. And he was riding on his horse and came before the beam (upon which his uncle)[51] was going to be crucified.[52] He (Yaqim) said to him: 'See the horse on which my master makes me ride, and see the horse on which your master makes you ride!' He (Yose ben Yo'ezer) said to him: 'If (He deals in this way) with those who anger Him, how much more (will He deal so) with him who does His will!' He (Yaqim) said to him: 'Has then (any) man done His will more than you?' He (Yose ben Yo'ezer) said to him: 'And if (He deals in this way) with him who does His will, how much more (will He deal so) with those who anger Him!' This word pierced him like the venom of a snake. He went and applied to himself the four death penalties: stoning, burning, slaying and strangulation. What did he do? He fetched a beam and rammed it into the earth and tied a rope to it, and he surrounded it with a wall and made a pile of wood in front of it and fixed a sword in the middle. He hanged himself (on) the beam, the cord was split, and (after) he had been strangled,[53] the sword caught him and the wall collapsed over him and he was burnt. Yose ben Yo'ezer of

---

47 Like the prophet Isaiah, see Chapter 3, pp. 92–4 and 111–14.
48 According to ms. Vatican 60, with emendations by Theodor and Albeck (1996), 742–4.
49 Variant spelling: 'Tserodot', which closer resembles 'Tsereda', the home town of his uncle.
50 The bracketed words are lacking from the Vatican ms., probably due to a copying error. The full name is given below in the story.
51 Bracketed text here and henceforth (including subdivisions by letters) does not have a literal equivalent in the source but is added in the translation to facilitate comprehension.
52 For Jews in rabbinic times, the mention of a crucifixion implied that Yose ben Yo'ezer was executed by non-Jews, for crucifixion (or 'hanging alive', in line with the broader meaning of the Aramaic term) was not reckoned among the four death penalties provided by the Torah (see below and *M. Sanhedrin* 7.1, notwithstanding the possibility of a divergent pre-rabbinic tradition preserved in *Targum Ruth* 1:17).
53 Emended according to Theodor and Albeck (1996): *nehnaq*; ms. Vatican reads *nehlaq* ('he was divided'), presumably due to a copying error.

Tseredah (who was close to dying) went into a trance and saw his (Yaqim's) bier flying in the air. He said: 'Indeed, by a little while this one preceded me into the Garden of Eden.'[54]

2 *Sifra Emor, pereq*[55] 9.5: Pappus and Lulianus

The context in which the martyrdom of Pappus and Lulianus is related in *Sifra* (division *Emor*) is determined by an exegesis of Lev. 22:32, 'You shall not profane My holy name, that I may be sanctified among the children of Israel.' The segment 'that I may be sanctified' is here explained to mean: 'yield yourself to sanctify My name'.[56] The theme of martyrdom, thus introduced, provides the opportunity for a short digression which includes, among others, the story of Pappus and Lulianus. This is the earliest explicit mention of their martyrdom in rabbinic literature,[57] but the comparison of martyrdom in rabbinic times with that of Hananiah, Mishael and Azariah is found in other early Midrashim, too.[58]

Translation[59]

(A)[60] Hence[61] they said: Everybody who yields himself with the purpose that a miracle will be wrought for him – for him no miracle will be wrought.[62] But (everybody who yields himself with the purpose) that no miracle will be wrought for him – for him a miracle will be wrought.

---

54 For an equally swift attainment of eternal life, cf. *T.B. Avodah Zarah* 18a (see below n. 189).
55 I.e., 'section' (a subdivision within *Sifra*).
56 *Pereq* 9.4, translation according to ms. Assemani 66 (Finkelstein, 1956), 442, cf. Weiss (1862), fol. 99d.
57 An allusion is given also in *Sifra Behuqqotai, pereq* 5.2 (Weiss, 1862, fol. 111d); for later references, see Horbury (1999), 294–5. Parallels to the version of *Sifra Emor* (section C of our translation) are found in *T.B. Ta'anit* 18b; *Semahot* 8.15 (Higger, 1970b, 164–5); *Ecclesiastes Zuta, parashah* 3 (Buber, 1894, fol. 62a).
58 Cf. *Lamentations Rabbah* 1.16 (see below); *Sifra Ahare, pereq* 13.14 (Weiss, 1862, fol. 86b).
59 According to ms. Assemani 66 (Finkelstein, 1956), 442, cf. Weiss (1862), fol. 99d.
60 Cf. above n. 51.
61 I.e., with respect to the foregoing exegesis of Lev. 22:32.
62 The Hebrew has a verb in the plural without specifying the grammatical subject. This functions as a circumlocution for God being the agent.

(B)   For thus we find concerning Hananiah, Mishael and Azariah:
that they said to Nebuchadnezzar: '*We have no need to give you an
answer in this matter. If our God whom we serve is able to save us
from the furnace of blazing fire, He will also save us from your
hands, O king. But if not, be it known to you, O king, that we will
not worship your god nor prostrate ourselves before the golden statue
that you erected*' (Dan. 3:16–18).

(C)   And when Trugianus[63] killed Pappus and his brother Lulianus
in Laodicaea, he said to them: 'Are you not of the people of
Hananiah, Mishael, and Azariah? May your god come and
deliver you from my hand!' They said to him: 'Hananiah,
Mishael and Azariah were (of) clean (character), and
Nebuchadnezzar was worthy of a miracle being wrought at his
hands. But you, you are a wicked king, and you are not worthy
of a miracle being wrought at your hands. And (as for) us, (we)
are liable to death before Heaven.[64] If you will not kill us,
(there are) many destructive beings[65] before the Omnipresent,
many bears, many lions, many leopards, many snakes, many
serpents, many scorpions, which can strike us! But in the end,
the Omnipresent will demand our blood from your hands.' It
was said that he had not yet departed from there when a
letter[66] came against him from Rome, and they knocked his
brain out with clubs.

3 *Lamentations Rabbah* 1.16: Miriam bat Tanhum and her seven sons

The earliest rabbinic account of the martyrdom of the mother and her
seven sons,[67] which is at the same time the most elaborate one, is
found in *Lamentations Rabbah*.[68] It concludes with the Holy Spirit

---

63 A misspelling for 'Traianus'.
64 The confession of guilt is a current motif in rabbinic martyrdom stories; cf. pp.
    156–7 and n. 135.
65 Or perhaps more precisely: 'demons', cf. Horbury (1999), 294.
66 Hebrew *tipli*, either from Latin *tabella* (cf. Jastrow, 1903, 297), or from Greek
    diploi = *duumviri*, a deputation of two officials (cf. Krauss, 1899, 201). The sin-
    gular feminine of the verb seems to favour the first possibility.
67 On the earlier versions contained in 2 and 4 Maccabees see the introduction to
    this chapter.
68 It is available in two printed versions, a longer one in the traditional editions
    (such as Vilna, 1887), and a more concise one in the edition by S. Buber. On the

commenting on the events with a quotation from Lam. 1:16 ('For these I weep'), which accounts for the incorporation of the story into the present section of *Lamentations Rabbah*. The slightly younger version in *T.B. Gittin* 57b is analogous in design and structure, but it is crafted somewhat more concisely. Its contextual embedding is based on a quotation of Ps. 44:23 ('For Your sake we are slain all day long'). Still shorter is the version of *Pesiqta Rabbati* 43.[69] The scriptural proofs which underscore the monotheistic claim of the seven brothers in *Lamentations Rabbah* and *T.B. Gittin* are absent from *Pesiqta Rabbati*. Also, the seventh son does not engage here in debate with the emperor but takes counsel with his mother as to whether he should perhaps prostrate himself before the image, which the mother, of course, discourages.[70] When in the end the mother commits suicide, God gives her the promise of bliss in the future world[71] and cites Ps. 113:9, the beginning of which links the story to the further context of chapter 43 ('He gives the barren woman a home').[72]

Translation[73]

(A)[74] The story of Miriam bat Tanhum,[75] who was arrested together with her seven sons. What did the ruler do? He imprisoned each of them separately.[76]

(B) He brought out the first and said to him: 'Prostrate yourself before the image as your brothers did!' He said to him: 'Heaven forbid! My brothers did not prostrate themselves, so

---

date of *Lamentations Rabbah*, see n. 8. The text of *Yalqut Shim'oni, Tavo*, § 938, is almost identical with that of Buber (1899). Another version which seems to be largely dependent on *Lamentations Rabbah* is found in *Seder Eliahu Rabbah* 30 (ed. Friedmann, 1880, 151–3).

69 Ed. Friedmann, 1880, fol. 180b.
70 See above n. 21.
71 See below n. 94.
72 For a more detailed comparison of *Lamentations Rabbah* 1.16, *Pesiqta Rabbati* 43, *T.B. Gittin* 57b, and 2 Macc. 7, see Doran (1980).
73 According to Buber (1899), fol. 42b-43a, with selected variants from ed. Vilna, fol. 17d–18b.
74 See above n. 51.
75 Ed. Vilna: 'Miriam bat Nahtom', i.e., 'Miriam the daughter of the baker'. *Pesiqta Rabbati*: 'Miriam bat Tanhum'. *Seder Eliahu Rabbah*: 'Adrianus Caesar came and arrested a widowed woman, whose name was Miriam bat Tanhum, and her seven sons.' *T.B. Gittin* 57b does not give any name.
76 Ed. Vilna: 'Caesar took them and put them inside seven cells.'

I shall not prostrate myself before it, either.' He said to him:
'Why?' 'Because it is written in the Torah:[77] *I am the Lord your
God* (Exod. 20:2).' He gave the order to slay him.

(C)   He brought out the second. He said to him: 'Prostrate yourself
before the image as your brothers did!' He said to him:
'Heaven forbid! My brothers did not prostrate themselves, so
I shall not prostrate myself before it, either.' He said to him:
'Why?' 'Because it is written in the Torah: *You shall not have
other gods before Me* (Exod. 20:3).' Immediately he gave the
order to slay him.

(D)   He brought out the third. He said to him: 'Prostrate yourself
before the image as your brothers did!' He said to him:
'Heaven forbid! My brothers did not prostrate themselves, so
I shall not prostrate myself before it, either.' He said to him:
'Why?' 'Because it is written in the Torah: *Whoever sacrifices to
any god (except to the Lord alone) shall be cut off* (Exod. 22:19).' He
gave the order to slay him.

(E)   He brought out the fourth. He said to him: 'Prostrate yourself
before the image as your brothers did!' He said to him:
'Heaven forbid! My brothers did not prostrate themselves, so
I shall not prostrate myself before it, either.' He said to him:
'Why?' 'Because it is written in the Torah: *You shall not pros-
trate yourself before them, and you shall not serve them* (Exod. 20:5).'
He gave the order to slay him.

(F)   He brought out the fifth. He said to him: 'Prostrate yourself
before the image as your brothers did!' He said to him:
'Heaven forbid! My brothers did not prostrate themselves, so
I shall not prostrate myself, either.' He said to him: 'Why?'
'Because it is written in the Torah: *So acknowledge today and take
to your heart that the Lord is God in heaven above and on the earth
below; there is no other* (Deut. 4:39).' He gave the order to slay
him.

---

77 The series of the following proof-texts varies in the different versions. In ed.
Buber, the order is: (i) Exod. 20:2, (ii) Exod. 20:3, (iii) Exod. 22:19, (iv) Exod.
20:5, (v) Deut. 4:39, (vi) Deut. 6:4, (vii) Deut. 26:17–18. The Vilna edition has:
(i) Exod. 20:2, (ii) Exod. 20:3, (iii) Exod. 34:14, (iv) Exod. 22:19, (v) Deut. 6:4,
(vi) Deut. 7:21, (vii) Deut. 4:39 and 26:17–18. *T.B. Gittin*: (i) Exod. 20:2, (ii)
Exod. 20:3, (iii) Exod. 22:19, (iv) Exod. 34:14, (v) Deut. 6:4, (vi) Deut. 4:39,
(vii) Deut. 26:17–18. *Seder Eliahu Rabbah*: (i) Deut. 4:39, (ii) Deut. 10:17, (iii)
Exod. 20:3, (iv) Exod. 34:14, (v) Exod. 22:19, (vi) Exod. 15:18, (vii) Deut.
26:17–18.

(G)   He brought out the sixth and said to him: 'Prostrate yourself before the image as your brothers did!' He said to him: 'Heaven forbid! My brothers did not prostrate themselves, so I shall not prostrate myself, either.' He said to him: 'Why?' 'Because it is written in the Torah: *Hear, O Israel, the Lord our God, the Lord is one* (Deut. 6:4).[78]

(H)   He brought out the seventh, who was the youngest of them. He said to him: 'Prostrate yourself before the image as (your brothers) did!' He said to him: 'Heaven forbid! My brothers did not prostrate themselves before the image, so I shall not prostrate myself, either.' He said to him: 'Why?' 'Because we have sworn to our God that we do not exchange Him out of fear, as it is said: *Today you have accepted*[79] *the Lord (to be God for you)* (Deut. 26:17). And as we have sworn to Him, so He has sworn to us not to exchange us for any other people, as it is said: *And the Lord has accepted you today (to be for Him a chosen people)* (Deut. 26:18).'[80]

(I)   He said to him: 'If this is so, I shall throw my signet ring in front of the image, and you shall go and fetch it, so that they see (it) and say: He has fulfilled Caesar's commandment!' He said to him: 'Woe to you, Caesar! Should I be afraid of you, who are flesh and blood, and not of the King of the kings of kings, the Holy one blessed be He, who is the God of the world?'

---

78   Unlike ed. Vilna ('He pronounced sentence on him and they slew him'), ed. Buber (1899) lacks the concluding phrase 'He gave the order to slay him.' However, the execution of this son, too, is clearly implied.

79   The rabbinic understanding of the somewhat difficult Hebrew of this verse can be guessed from its present context. It converges with both the Septuagint and the Vulgate translations, which take these words to mean, 'Today you have chosen the Lord . . .'.

80   Ed. Vilna continues: 'Caesar said to him: "Your brothers were satiated with days and satiated with life and experienced well-being. But you are an infant, you are not satiated with days and not satiated with life and you did not experience well-being in the world. Prostrate yourself before the image, and I shall bestow favours upon you!" He said to him: "It is written in our Torah: *The Lord will be King for ever and ever* (Exod. 15:18), and it says: *The Lord is King for ever and ever, the nations shall perish from His land* (Ps. 10:16). And you are void, and His enemies are void. Flesh and blood is alive today and tomorrow dead, rich today and tomorrow poor. But the Holy one, blessed be He, lives and endures for ever and ever." Caesar said to him: "Look, your brothers have been killed in front of you, but here I throw my signet ring on the ground in front of the image",' etc.

(J)   He said to him: 'But is there a god in the world?' He said to him: 'Woe to you, Caesar! Have you ever seen a world void of dominion?' He said to him: 'But does your god have a mouth?' He said to him: 'Concerning your idolatry, it is written: *They have a mouth but do not speak* (Ps. 115:5). But concerning our God, it is written: *By the word of the Lord the heavens were made* (Ps. 33:6).' He said to him: 'But does your god have eyes?' He said to him: 'Concerning your idolatry, it is written: *They have eyes but do not see* (Ps. 115:5). But concerning our God, it is written: *The eyes of the Lord your God are always on it* (Deut. 11:12).'[81] He said to him: 'But does your god have ears?' He said to him: 'Concerning your idolatry, it is written: *They have ears but do not hear* (Ps. 115:6). But concerning our God, it is written: *And the Lord listened and heard* (Mal. 3:16).' He said to him: 'But does your god have a nose?' He said to him: 'Concerning your idolatry, it is written: *They have a nose but do not smell* (Ps. 115:6). But concerning our God, it is written: *And the Lord smelled the pleasing odour* (Gen. 8:21).' He said to him: 'But does your god have hands?' He said to him: 'Concerning your idolatry, it is written: *They have hands but do not feel* (Ps. 115:7). But concerning our God, it is written: *And My hand has founded the earth* (Is. 48:13).' He said to him: 'But does your god have feet?' He said to him: 'Concerning your idolatry, it is written: *They have feet but do not walk* (Ps. 115:7). But concerning our God, it is written: *And on that day His feet shall stand (on the Mount of Olives)* (Zech. 14:4), *and He will stand and tread upon the high places of the earth* (Micah 1:3).' He said to him: 'But does your god have a throat?' He said to him: 'Concerning your idolatry, it is written: *They do not sound with their throat* (Ps. 115:7). But concerning our God, it is written: *His palate is most sweet, and He is altogether desirable* (Cant. 5:16).'[82]

(K)   He said to him: 'If He has all these qualities, why did He not deliver you from my hand as He delivered Hananiah, Mishael and Azariah?'[83] He said to him: 'Hananiah, Mishael and

---

81 Ed. Vilna: 'But concerning our God it is written: *These are the eyes of the Lord, which range through the whole earth* (Zech. 4:10).'

82 Ed. Vilna: 'But concerning our God it is written: *And the rumble that comes from His mouth* (Job 37:2).'

83 For Hananiah, Mishael and Azariah as models of Jewish martyrs, see 4 Macc. 13:9, 16:3, 21, 18:12. A close parallel to the present section exists in *Sifra*, see

Azariah were righteous and fell into the hands of a righteous king, but we are guilty[84] and fell into the hands of a guilty and cruel king, so that our blood shall be exacted. For the Holy one, blessed be He, has many bears and many leopards which can attack us. But the Holy one, blessed be He, has given us into your hand with the sole purpose that He will exact our blood from your hand.'[85] Immediately he gave the order to slay him.

(L)   His mother said to him: 'By your life, Caesar, give me my son so that I can kiss him and hug him.' And he gave her son to her, and she took out her breasts and nursed him with milk.[86] (This happened) to fulfil what has been said: *Honey and milk are under your tongue* (Cant. 4:11).

(M)   She said to him: 'By the life of your head, Caesar, let the sword come upon my neck and upon his neck together.'[87] He said to her: 'Heaven forbid! I shall not do such a thing, as it is written in your Torah: *You shall not slaughter it with its young on the same day* (Lev. 22:28).' The child said to him: 'Wicked one,[88] have you perhaps fulfilled the whole Torah except this verse alone?' Immediately they snatched him away from her in order to kill him.

(N)   His mother said to him: 'My son, may your heart not faint, and may you not despair. You are going to your brothers, and you will be seated in the bosom of our father Abraham.[89] And tell him in my name: You built one altar and did not sacrifice your son, but I built seven altars and sacrificed my sons on them. And for that matter, yours was (merely) a trial, but mine was a fact.'[90]

(O)   And when he had been slain,[91] the sages calculated the age of

---

p. 145. The wording of ed. Vilna resembles this passage of the *Sifra* even closer than that of Buber (1899).

84 See p. 136 and n. 20.

85 See above nn. 25 and 26.

86 For the motif of nursing within a martyrdom account, cf. 4 Macc. 13:21 and *Pas. Perp.* 6.7–8 (see pp. 101–2 and 126–7).

87 Ed. Vilna: 'By the life of your head, Caesar, slay me first and then slay him!'

88 Ed. Vilna: 'They said to him: (O greatest) fool of the world', etc.

89 Ed. Vilna: 'His mother fell on him and hugged him and kissed him and said to him: Go to Abraham your father', etc. For the reception of the deceased in Abraham's bosom cf. Luke 16:22–3; 4 Macc. 13:17.

90 See p. 135 and n. 18.

91 Ed. Vilna: 'When she still kissed and hugged him, he pronounced sentence on him and they slew him over her. And when he had been slain', etc.

this child, and it was found to be six and a half years and two hours[92] old.

(P) At this hour all the nations of the world cried out and said: 'Why does the god of these do such things to them? They are slain for his sake at every hour!'

(Q) They said: After some days, that woman went mad. And she went to the top of a roof and flung herself down and died.[93] And they said concerning her: '*A joyful mother of sons* (Ps. 113:9).'[94] And the Holy Spirit says: '*For these I weep* (Lam. 1:16).'

4 *Talmud Yerushalmi, Berakhot* 9.7: R. Aqiva

The earliest accounts of R. Aqiva's martyrdom are those of *Talmud Yerushalmi Berakhot* 9.7 and *Sotah* 5.7.[95] The two versions are almost identical, except that *T.Y. Sotah* (by careless copying?) lacks the words from 'and troubled myself' to 'all three of them' as well as the very last sentence. In *T.Y. Sotah*, the story is presented simply as one example among others of pious love towards God. *T.Y. Berakhot* 9.7, however, is a section which depends as a whole on a teaching of the *Mishnah*[96] which already contains the pivotal idea of R. Aqiva's martyrdom, namely, the idea of dying out of love for God. This teaching (*M. Berakhot* 9.5) opens with the words: 'A man is bound to say a blessing

---

92 Ed. Vilna: 'two years and six months and six and a half hours'.

93 In 4 Macc. 17:1 the mother commits suicide by throwing herself into the fire. 2 Macc. 7:41, too, mentions the death of the mother but does not specify the way she dies.

94 Ed. Vilna: 'and died, so as to fulfil what had been said: *She who bore seven has lan-guished* (Jer. 15:9). And a heavenly voice (literally, 'a daughter of a voice', i.e. an echo) goes forth and says: *A joyful mother of sons*', etc. *T.B. Gittin* and *Seder Eliahu Rabbah*, too, have this verse proclaimed by a heavenly voice, which is certainly not only to intimate that death brings relief, but also, and foremost, that the future of the woman will be eternal bliss, since the usual function of heavenly voices at death scenes is to assure the deceased of a portion in the world to come (see below n. 137). In *Pesiqta Rabbati* 43, Ps. 113:9 is even adduced by God, who introduces the citation by the words, 'I gladden her for the time that is to come . . .'.

95 On the dating of the *Talmud Yerushalmi*, see above n. 7.

96 The *Mishnah* is the fundamental rabbinic compendium of legal matters ('halakhah'). It was edited at about 200 CE on the basis of older traditions and constitutes the textual substratum of both Talmuds (see above n. 7), which are basically commentaries on the *Mishnah*.

on account of a bad thing as much as he says a blessing on account of a good thing. For it is said: *And you shall love the Lord, your God, with all your heart and with all your soul and with all your might* (Deut. 6:5).' As the mere quotation of Deut. 6:5 does not yet explain why one should say blessings on unpleasant occasions as much as on pleasant ones, the *Mishnah* adds some exegetical clarification:[97] '*With all your heart* (this means) with both of your inclinations, with the good inclination and with the evil inclination.[98] *And with all your soul* (this means) even if He[99] takes your soul. *And with all your might* (this means) with all your wealth. Another interpretation: *With all your might* (this means) for whichever measure He measures out to you, you should give thanks to Him very much, very much.'[100] If saying a blessing is an expression of love for God, it is now clear why blessings are due even for bad things. For to love God means to love Him even if one's wealth, indeed, even if one's life is at stake. And this precisely is the thematic link with the story of R. Aqiva. Unlike later versions of the story, those of the *Talmud Yerushalmi* are striking because of their brilliant concentration on the fundamental contrast between suffering and love, death and fulfilment, even to the point of leaving out the customary final proclamation of the martyr's portion in the world to come.

Translation[101]

R. Aqiva was brought on trial before the wicked Turnus Rufus,[102] and it was time for the recital of the *Shema*.[103] He began to recite the *Shema* and laughed. He (Turnus Rufus) said to him: 'Old man, either you are a sorcerer[104] or you despise suffering!' He said to

---

97 Technically speaking, this clarification is a Midrash (see above n. 8). A more elaborate version of this Midrash is found in *Sifre Deuteronomy* 32 (ed. Finkelstein, 1993, 55–9; see below n. 113). It includes various comments by R. Aqiva, but no hint at his martyrdom.

98 The duality is probably inferred from the spelling of Hebrew *levav* ('heart') with a double *Bet*.

99 I.e. God, who is the grammatical object of Deut. 6:5.

100 This 'other interpretation' consists of a series of puns on Hebrew *me'od* ('might'), *middah* ('measure'), *modeh* ('say thanks'), and *me'od* ('very much').

101 According to ms. Leiden (ed. Schäfer and Becker, 1991–2001, vol. I/1–2, 250); cf. mss. Paris and London (ibid.).

102 'Turnus Rufus' as in mss. Paris and London; ms. Leiden has 'Tunustrufus'.

103 See above n. 34.

104 Which would explain why R. Aqiva does not react to pain.

him: 'May the spirit of this man (Turnus Rufus) evaporate! I am neither a sorcerer, nor do I despise suffering. But all my days I recited this verse and troubled myself and said: When will I have the opportunity (to fulfil) all three of them,[105] *And you shall love the Lord, your God, with all your heart and with all your soul and with all your might?* I loved Him with all my heart, and I loved Him with all my wealth, but (loving Him) with all my soul was unknown to me. And now (the occasion) has arrived (for me to love Him) with all my soul, and the time has come for the recital of the *Shema*, and my mind has not been distracted. Therefore I am reciting (the *Shema*) and laughing.' He had not yet finished saying (this) when his soul departed.

5 *Talmud Bavli, Berakhot* 61b: R. Aqiva

In *T.B. Berakhot* 61b, the contextual embedding of R. Aqiva's martyrdom is the same as in *T.Y. Berakhot* 9.7. Its starting point is the exegesis of Deut. 6:5 given in *M. Berakhot* 9.5 in order to substantiate the duty to say a blessing even in cases of misfortune.[106] The story itself, however, is in the *Talmud Bavli*'s version far more elaborate than in the earlier version in the *Talmud Yerushalmi*. The most salient amplifications are, first, an encounter by R. Aqiva with a fellow Jew which precedes his trial and explains his refusal to comply with the Roman decrees; second, a dialogue with his disciples which takes place while he is being tortured and which sets forth his interpretation of Deut. 6:5; and third, a heavenly epilogue which serves as a contrast to his violent end by affirming his eternal salvation. This broader form of *T.B. Berakhot* 61b became the basis for many later treatments of the matter.[107]

---

105 I.e., the three specifications made in Deut. 6:5.
106 See the introductory remarks on *T.Y. Berakhot* 9.7 on pp. 151–2.
107 Cf. *Midrash Tanhuma, Tavo* 2; *Midrash Tanhuma,* version B, *Tavo* 4 (ed. Buber, 1885, fol. 23b–24b); *Yalqut Shim'oni,* part I, § 837; *Ma'aseh Asarah Haruge Malkhut* (ed. Reeg, 1985, §§ 29–32). For a survey of the various versions see Goldberg (1997), 355–60.

Translation[108]

(A)[109] *And you shall love the Lord your God* (Deut. 6:5).

(B) It has been taught:[110] Rabbi Eli'ezer[111] says: If it has been said, *with all your soul* (Deut. 6:5), why has it been said, *with all your might* (ibid.), and if it has been said, *with all your might*, why has it been said, *with all your soul*? If there is a man whose body[112] is dearer to him than his possessions, for him it has been said, *with all your soul*, and if there is a man whose possessions are dearer to him than his body, for him it has been said, *with all your might*.[113]

(C) Rabbi Aqiva says: *With all your soul* (this means) even if He takes your soul.[114]

(D) Our rabbis taught:[115] Once the Wicked Kingdom[116] issued a decree[117] forbidding Israel to occupy herself with the Torah. Pappus ben Yehudah[118] came and found Rabbi Aqiva who was calling assemblies in public and occupying himself with

---

108 According to ed. Vilna, with selected amendments from ms. Munich (ed. Strack, 1912), fol. 156b.

109 See above n. 51.

110 A formula indicating that the following text is a 'baraita', i.e. a teaching going back to Tannaitic (= Mishnaic) times, hence from before 200 CE.

111 R. Eli'ezer ben Hyrcanus, who flourished around 100 CE.

112 I.e., his physical existence, his this-worldly life. For a detailed analysis of R. Eli'ezer's exegesis of Deut. 6:5, see Goldberg (1997), 371–2.

113 This Midrash is also contained in *Sifre Deuteronomy* 32 (ed. Finkelstein, 1993, 55); *T.B. Pesahim* 25a; *T.B. Yoma* 82a; *T.B. Sanhedrin* 74a.

114 In *M. Berakhot* 9.5 and in *Sifre Deuteronomy* 32 this exposition lacks the attribution to R. Aqiva.

115 Another formula introducing a baraita (cf. n. 110).

116 A current sobriquet for the Roman empire. One of the later version reads 'the kingdom of Greece' (cf. *Midrash Tanhuma, Tavo* 4, ed. Buber, 1885, fol. 23b-24a, n. 18), which may result from a confusion of R. Aqiva with the Maccabaean martyrs. This testifies to the little interest the Midrashists took in questions of historicity; Goldberg (1997), 356.

117 Ms. Munich: 'Once the Wicked Kingdom decreed a persecution upon Israel'.

118 A person bearing this name is mentioned elsewhere as an example of a husband's bad conduct towards his wife, cf. *Tos. Sotah* 5.9; *T.Y. Sotah* 1.7/17a (ed. Schäfer and Becker, 1991–2001: 1,7/4), *T.Y. Qiddushin* 4.4/66a (ed. Schäfer/Becker, 1991–2001: 4,4/3), *T.B. Gittin* 90a. More important, however, is *T.B. Shabbat* 104b, where a variant reading in ms. Munich puts Pappus ben Yehudah alternatively in the place of 'Pandera', whereby he is indirectly identified as the father of Jesus of Nazareth (cf. Rabbinowicz, 1959–1960, vol. II ad loc.). Boyarin (1999), 103, concludes from this that in *T.B. Berakhot* 61b

the Torah.[119] He said to him: 'Aqiva, are you not afraid of the Kingdom?' He said to him: 'I shall tell you a parable:[120]

Like what is the matter? Like a fox who was walking alongside of a river[121] and saw the fish who were going in crowds from one place to another. He said to them: "Why are you fleeing?" They said to him: "Because of the nets which men cast for us." He said to them: "(May it be) your will that you come up to the dry land, and we shall live (together), I and you, in the way my ancestors lived together with your ancestors!" They said to him: "You, who are said to be the smartest of animals, you are not smart but you are a fool. If at the place of our life we are afraid, how much more so at the place of our death!"

We, too: (If) now, as we are sitting and occupying ourselves with the Torah, concerning which it is written: *For this is your life and the length of your days* (Deut. 30:20),[122] (our fate is) thus, how much more will it be so if we go and desist from it!'[123]

(E) They said: It was not even a few days (later) when they arrested R. Aqiva and threw him in prison. And they arrested Pappus ben Yehudah and imprisoned him together with him. He said

Pappus 'is a figure for a Christian'. This suggestion seems to be supported by the allegation that Pappus is arrested for 'idle things', a term which in *T.B. Avodah Zarah* 16b refers to the heresy of Christianity; cf. Boyarin (1999), 104. At any rate, the following parable suggests considering the fox as the personification of a third party distinct from both Israel and Rome, who are personified by the fish and the men. The Church, herself persecuted in early Talmudic times by the Roman empire, would certainly make a match. However, the possibility cannot be ruled out that Pappus simply represents those Jews who submitted to the Roman oppression, such as R. Yose ben Qisma in *T.B. Avodah Zarah* 18a.

119 I.e., he studied and taught the Torah.
120 Ms. Munich: 'are you not afraid of this nation?' He said to him: 'Are you Pappus ben Yehudah, who is said to be a sage? But you are nothing but a fool. I shall tell you a parable . . .'.
121 Ms. Munich: 'on the shore of the sea'.
122 Implicitly, this quotation raises the question of theodicy. However, an answer will be given only at the end by the second heavenly voice (see below).
123 Ms. Munich lacks the whole sentence from 'We, too' onwards.

to him: 'Pappus, who brought you here?'[124] He said to him: 'Happy are you, Rabbi Aqiva, that you have been arrested on account of the study[125] of the Torah. Alas for Pappus, for he has been arrested on account of idle things.'

(F)   They said:[126] When they brought R. Aqiva out for execution it was the time for the recital of the *Shema*.[127] And they were combing his flesh with combs of iron,[128] and he took upon himself the yoke of the Kingdom of Heaven.[129] His disciples said to him: 'Our rabbi, even to this point?'[130] He said to them: 'All my days I have been troubling myself about this verse[131]: *With all your soul* (this means) even if He takes your soul. I said, When shall I have the opportunity to fulfil this? And now that I have the opportunity, should I not fulfil it?' He prolonged (the word) *one*[132] until his soul departed at (the word) *one*. A heavenly voice[133] went forth and said: 'Happy are you, R. Aqiva, that your soul departed at (the word) *one*.'

(G)   The ministering angels[134] said before the Holy one, blessed be He, 'This is the Torah, and this is its reward?!'[135] *From the dead*

---

124   Ms. Munich: 'Pappus, on account of what did they bring you here?'
125   Literally, 'things'.
126   This introductory formula occurs in ms. Munich but not in ed. Vilna. A caesura, however, seems appropriate here, as the focus shifts from prison to execution and Pappus is no more mentioned.
127   See above n. 34.
128   R. Aqiva's flesh was torn from his body while he was alive; cf. Schäfer (1978), 116; cf. 4 Macc. 9:28; see Chapter 1, p. 28 and n. 70.
129   The expression 'to take upon oneself the Kingdom of Heaven' designates the act of submitting to the God of Israel by reciting the first section of the *Shema*, i.e. Deut. 6:4–9. Cf. *M. Berakhot* 2.2: 'Why does (the section) *Hear, O Israel* (Deut. 6:4–9) precede (the section) *And it shall come to pass if you hear* (Deut. 11:13–21)? In order that one first takes upon himself the yoke of the Kingdom of Heaven and afterwards takes upon himself the yoke of the commandments.'
130   The question apparently expresses amazement at R. Aqiva's self-control at this moment of greatest pain. Although a dialogue seems rather unrealistic in such a situation, conversations of this kind are found in other martyrdom accounts as well; cf. *T.B. Avodah Zarah* 18a; *Semahot* 8.11; 2 Macc. 7; John 19:25–7.
131   Strictly speaking, the verse *as interpreted* by the following Midrash (which, by the way, is superscribed as a motto to the whole story).
132   The last word of Deut. 6:4: *Hear, O Israel, the Lord our God, the Lord is one*.
133   Literally, 'a daughter of a voice', i.e. an echo.
134   Members of God's heavenly retinue, whose presence permits an intra-celestial dialogue.
135   An expression of protest: such a devote person cannot have deserved such an

ones, your hand, oh Lord, from the dead ones, (from the pit)[136] (Ps. 17:14)?!' He said to them: *'Their portion is in the life* (ibid.).' A heavenly voice went forth and said: 'Happy are you, Rabbi Aqiva, for you are summoned for the life of the world to come!'[137]

6 *Sifre Deuteronomy* 307: R. Hanina ben Teradion

A central motif of the martyrdom tradition concerning R. Hanina[138] ben Teradion is the readiness of the rabbi and his family to accept their fate as a deserved punishment at the hands of God. This 'justification of the judgement' (*tsidduq ha-din*) is expressed by a series of

atrocious end. If other martyr stories contain a confession of guilt by which the martyr justifies his end as due to God's just judgement (cf., e.g., *Prayer of Azariah* 29–31; 2 Macc. 7:18, 32, 38; *Mekhilta Mishpatim* 18; *Sifra Emor, pereq* 9.5; *T.B. Avodah Zarah* 17b–18a), this feature is conspicuously absent from the story of R. Aqiva, which makes the angels' protest appear all the more justified.

136 Instead of the bracketed words, ed. Vilna has the abbreviation 'etc.'. But obviously the quotation is not meant to cover all of verse 14, as the last words make up the answer of God. For a likely rabbinic understanding of the difficult Hebrew, cf. Aquila's Greek translation, *'apo tethnēkotōn . . . ek katadyseōs'* ('from the deceased . . . out of the pit'); thus, the anterior part of the verse might ask, as part of the angels' protest, whether God's hand has forsaken R. Aqiva. An alternative paraphrase is suggested by the *Tosafot* (i.e. mediaeval explanations given in the current editions of the *Talmud Bavli* on the outer margin of the page): 'From *Your* hand he should have died, not from the hands of flesh and blood!' Further suggestions: 'Your hand kills them', or: 'They let themselves be killed for Your sake', see Goldberg (1997), 357. The version of *Midrash Tanhuma*, version B, *Tavo* 4 (ed. Buber, 1885, fol. 24a) introduces a Midrashic change in the wording of the verse and adds an explicit interpretation: 'Do not read *mimtim* (literally, "men"), but read *memitim* (i.e. "they kill"), for they kill themselves for the sake of the Torah, which was given for this purpose. For people who see them say to each other, "There are sins in their hands, therefore they are killed." But they do not know that their portion is in the life of the world to come . . .'

137 The proclamation of a deceased person's eternal bliss is quite a common function of heavenly voices; cf. *T.B. Ketubbot* 104a (Rabbi Yehudah the Prince); *T.B. Gittin* 57b (the mother of the seven sons; for parallels, see above n. 94); *T.B. Avodah Zarah* 10b (Qetia bar Shalom); *T.B. Avodah Zarah* 17a (R. El'azar ben Durdeia); *T.B. Avodah Zarah* 18a (R. Hanina ben Teradion and his executioner). Cf. also the index in Kuhn (1989), 369–76 (esp. nos. 10, 14, 32, 48, 54, 58, 65, 71, 72, 111, 112).

138 *Sifre Deuteronomy* actually employs the variant spelling 'Haninah'. Another spelling attested in the sources is 'Hananiah' (see above n. 5).

biblical quotations, the first of which is the beginning of Deut. 32:4: 'The Rock, His work is perfect.' Thus, *Sifre Deuteronomy*, which is a third-century Midrash on the last book of the Pentateuch,[139] includes an account of R. Hanina's martyrdom in its exposition of Deut. 32:4. As this account focuses almost exclusively on the theme of *tsidduq ha-din*, it is a comparatively short text, much shorter than *T.B. Avodah Zarah* 17b–18a.[140] Only in the end is there a deviation from the central theme: A 'philosopher' appears, who points out the futility of the attempt to suppress the Torah and is, therefore, threatened with the same sentence of death. He welcomes this, however, as good tidings which assure him of a portion in the world to come. Such a final perspective of salvation is quite common in rabbinic martyr stories.[141]

Translation[142]

(A)[143]   Another interpretation: *The Rock, His work is perfect* (Deut. 32:4).

(B)   When they arrested R. Hanina ben Teradion, a decree was imposed upon him to be burnt together with his scroll. They said to him: 'A decree has been imposed upon you to be burnt together with your scroll.' He recited the verse, '*The Rock, His work is perfect.*' They said to his wife: 'A decree has been imposed upon your husband to be burnt, and on you to be slain.' She recited the verse: '*A God of faithfulness and without deceit* (ibid.).' They said to his daughter: 'A decree has been imposed upon your father to be burnt, and on your mother to be slain, and on you to do work.'[144] She recited the verse: '*Great in counsel and mighty in deed, Your eyes are watching (over all the ways of the children of men, giving to each according to his ways and according to the fruit of his deed)* (Jer. 32:19).'

(C)   Rabbi[145] said: How great were these righteous ones! For in the hour of their distress they thought of three verses of justifica-

---

139   See above n. 8.
140   The narrative of the triple *tsidduq ha-din*, however, is neatly paralleled in *T.B. Avodah Zarah* (see sections E, G, and H of our translation).
141   See above n. 10.
142   According to ed. Finkelstein (1993), 346.
143   See above n. 51.
144   Doing work is presumably a euphemism for prostitution; see n. 168.
145   Short for 'Rabbi Yehudah the Prince', the leader of Palestinian Jewry in the late second century CE.

tion of the judgement (*tsidduq ha-din*) which have no equal in all the Scriptures.

(D)   The three of them straightened their heart and declared their judgement to be just.

(E)   A philosopher stood up before his government.[146] He said to him:[147] 'My lord, your mind should not boast that you have burnt the Torah. For it has returned to the place from which it came, to the house of its Father.' He said to him: 'Tomorrow your sentence (will be) the same as theirs!' He said to him: 'You have brought me good tidings, for tomorrow my portion will be with them in the world to come.'

7 *Talmud Bavli, Avodah Zarah* 17b–18a: R. Hanina ben Teradion

The cluster of stories about R. Hanina ben Teradion in *T.B. Avodah Zarah* 17b–18b constitutes by far the most extensive martyrdom narrative in ancient rabbinic literature. Doublets and inconsistencies as well as digressions from the narrative order strongly suggest that this complex was indeed made up of a variety of more or less independent traditions. R. Hanina's conviction is reported twice (sections E and J of the following translation); in one case it is preceded by a stay in prison (section A), while in the other it immediately follows his arrest (J). Dialogues with rabbinic colleagues dealing with the impending martyrdom are also reported twice. One of them takes place in prison (A) and is followed by the tricky and miraculous release of the colleague (D). The other one precedes R. Hanina's apprehension and is followed by the colleague's natural death (I, J). Questions concerning a possible transgression by R. Hanina which may account for his martyrdom from a divine perspective occur in three places (A–C, F, I), and, most revealing, two of the offences taken into consideration are, as is explicitly observed in (C), mutually exclusive: In one instance, R. Hanina says that, after a confusion of charity money entrusted to him, he had solved the problem by a donation of his own (I), and in the other instance, he reproaches himself for not having practised charity at all (A). The most likely explanation is that the two respective passages, which also contain the encounters with R. Hanina's colleagues, derive from different traditions, and that the discussion of their contradiction (C) was possible only in the wake of their editorial fusing. The third reflection about R. Hanina's guilt (F) relates to a further tradition which, as it also considers the faults of his wife and his daughter, has apparently left untouched the two aforementioned ones (A and I). It is the tradition of the triple conviction of the whole family, including their *tsidduq ha-din* (end of E, G, H).[148] A further inconsistency lies in the appearance of R. Hanina's daughter along with his disciples in the execution scene after she had been sentenced to prostitution (J), whereas his wife, who had likewise been condemned, is not mentioned at all in the execution scene. In this connection it is particularly striking that the final heavenly voice declares the salvation of his executioner who commits suicide, but not that of the wife. Of course, there is no technical impossibility in all this, but it may imply that there were still more independent traditions of which the narrative was made up. Furthermore, the narrative continues even after the climax of the execution scene, the sequel being the tricky rescue of Hanina's daughter from the brothel (not included in the following translation). Later accounts of R. Hanina's martyrdom are on the whole much shorter than that of *T.B. Avodah Zarah*,[149] but generally dwell on the same basic motifs and ideas.[150]

Translation[151]

(A)[152] Our rabbis taught:[153] When R. El'azar ben Perata and R. Hanina ben Teradion were arrested,[154] R. El'azar ben Perata

---

148 Conversely, the parallel to this triple conviction extant in *Sifre Deuteronomy* 307 (see above) lacks any reference to conversations of R. Hanina with colleagues.

149 The exception is the large elaboration in the *Ma'aseh Asarah Haruge Malkhut* (Reeg, 1985, §§ 38–41), which not only amplifies the matter by further narrative motifs, but also presents the whole in a clearly better chronological order than *T.B. Avodah Zarah*.

150 They contain, however, also various individual traits, such as the conviction of R. Hanina 'on account of heresy' (*minut*) and the consolation of his daughter who weeps at his imminent death in *Semahot* 8.11 (47b = Higger, 1970b, 8.12, 159); as well as the interpretation of his confusion of charity money as the immediate occasion of his martyrdom in *Kallah* 23 (51b, cf. Higger, 1970a, 161–3).

151 According to ed. Vilna, with selected amendments from ms. Munich (ed. Strack, 1912), fol. 376b–7a.

152 See above n. 51.

153 See above n. 115.

154 Ms. Munich: 'When there were arrested R. El'azar ben Perata on account

said to R. Hanina ben Teradion: 'Happy are you, for you were arrested on one charge; woe is me, for I was arrested on five charges.' R. Hanina said to him: 'Happy are you, for you were arrested on five charges and you will be rescued; woe is me, for I was arrested on one charge and I will not be rescued. For you have occupied yourself with the Torah and with works of loving kindness, and I have occupied myself only with the Torah.'

(B)   This accords with Rav Huna,[155] for Rav Huna said: Everybody who occupies himself only with the Torah is like one who has no God, for it is said: *For a long time Israel was without the true God* (2 Chron. 15:3). What is meant by *without the true God?* That everyone who occupies himself only with the Torah is like one who has no God.

(C)   'But[156] did he not occupy himself with works of loving kindness? For it has been taught:[157] "R. Eli'ezer ben Ya'aqov says: One should not put his small coins in a charity bag unless a scholar like R. Hanina ben Teradion is entrusted with it."' 'He was trustworthy, but he did not practise it.' 'But it has been taught:[158] "He said to him: I confused Purim money with charity money, so I distributed it from my own (resources)[159] to the poor."[160] (So) he did practise (works of loving kindness).' '(But) he did not practise (works of loving kindness) as much as is necessary.'

of heresy (*minut*) and R. Hanina ben Teradion'. See n. 150 on *Semahot* 8.11.

155   There are various rabbinic teachers bearing this name, the earliest of whom flourished around 200 CE.

156   Single quotation marks in this section are not to indicate direct speech but to make transparent the dialogical structure of the Talmudic discussion.

157   See above n. 110.

158   Another formulation introducing a baraita (see above n. 110). The text from 'He said to him' to 'to the poor' is a quotation from R. Hanina's conversation with R. Yose ben Qisma, which is related below (see section I).

159   Ed. Vilna lacks 'from my own (resources)', which, however, appears in ms. Munich.

160   Charity money designated as Purim money may be spent only for a Purim banquet (cf. *T.B. Bava Metsi'a* 78b and Esther 9:19), whereas ordinary charity money may be used for any purpose. This is why R. Hanina, when having mistaken Purim money for ordinary charity money, compensated for the Purim money from his own means. See *Rashi* (a mediaeval commentator, whose explanations are given in the current editions of the *Talmud Bavli* on the inner margin of the page) on *T.B. Avodah Zarah* 17b.

(D)   They brought up R. El'azar ben Perata. They said: 'For what reason did you teach, and for what reason did you steal?' He said to them: 'If one is a swordsman, one is not a scholar, and if one is a scholar, one is not a swordsman,[161] and since I am not the one, I am not the other, either.' 'And for what reason did they call you *rabbi*?' 'I am a master (= *rabbi*) of weavers.' They brought him two coils (and) said to him: 'Which is that of the warp, and which is that of the woof?' A miracle happened for him: a female bee came and sat on that of the warp, and a male bee came and sat on that of the woof.[162] He said to them: 'This is the one of the warp, and that is the one of the woof.' They said to him: 'And for what reason did you not go to the house of *Avidan*?'[163] He said to them: 'I am an old man, and I was afraid that you might trample me under your feet.' They said: 'And how many old people have (actually) been trampled (there) until now?' A miracle happened: On this day, an old man was trampled. (They said to R. El'azar:) 'And for what reason did you release your slave to freedom?'[164] He said to them: 'Such things never happened.' One of them stood up in order to testify against him. Elijah[165] came (and) pretended to be one of the dignitaries of the kingdom. He said to them: 'Since a miracle has happened for him (R. El'azar) in all those

---

161 This means that the two charges are mutually exclusive.

162 One may wonder for what reason the Talmud credits R. El'azar with greater expertise in apiculture than in weaving. But perhaps this simply belongs to the irony of this story. Anyway, ancient scientists were almost (though erroneously) unanimous as to the sexes of bees, as they took the biggest of bees to be the 'king' (Pliny, *Naturalis historia* 11.46; Aristotle, *Historia animalium* 553a–b; Vergil, *Georgica* 4.68, 95, 106; Columella, *De re rustica* 9.10–11; Aelian, *De natura animalium* 5.10–11). Only Aristotle mentions, among others, one opinion according to which the drones were male and the bees female.

163 Literally, the 'house of ruin', a derogatory expression apparently designating a non-Jewish institution or place that Jews avoided for religious reasons, perhaps a place of, or connected with, idolatry.

164 Cf. Exod. 21:2, Deut. 15:12. The fulfilment of the commandment of releasing a Hebrew slave was, according to the story, regarded as an offence by the Roman authorities. Cf. Herr (1972), 97, n. 49*.

165 Ms. Munich: 'Elijah, of blessed memory'. Since 2 Kings 2 says nothing about Elijah's death, rabbinic tradition assumes that he is still alive, so that he miraculously can appear even in stories that take place in rabbinic times. In the following episode, the wording of ms. Munich differs considerably from that of ed. Vilna, but this does not seem to affect the substance of the narrative.

(other) matters, a miracle will happen for him also in this one, and it will show the wickedness of this man (the witness).' But (the latter) did not pay attention to him. He stood up in order to speak to them. (But) there was a letter which was written by the dignitaries of the kingdom to be sent to the house of Caesar, and they had it sent by that man. (When he had gone,) Elijah came (and) flung him 400 parasangs[166] away. He[167] went and did not come back.

(E) They brought up R. Hanina ben Teradion. They said to him: 'Why did you occupy yourself with the Torah?' He said to them: '*As the Lord, my God, commanded me* (Deut. 4:5).' Immediately they sentenced him to be burnt, and his wife to be slain, and his daughter to sit in a vault of whores.[168]

(F) (They sentenced) him to be burnt, because he pronounced the (divine) Name by its letters. But how could he do so, since we learn:[169] 'These are they who have no portion in the world to come: he who says that the Torah is not from Heaven, and (he who says that) the resurrection of the dead is not (inferable) from the Torah. Abba Sha'ul says: Also he who pronounces the (divine) Name by its letters'? He did it (only) for the purpose of teaching,[170] as it has been taught:[171] '*You shall not learn in order to do* (Deut. 18:9), but you (may) learn in order to understand and to enlighten.'[172] But for what reason (then) was he punished? Because he pronounced the (divine) Name in public. And (they sentenced) his wife to be slain, because she did not prevent him (from pronouncing the divine Name in public). With regard to this, they said: 'Everyone who is able to prevent (someone from transgressing) and does not prevent (him) is punished on account of him.'[173] And (they sentenced) his daughter to sit in a vault of whores, because, (as) R.

---

166 A parasang is a Persian 'mile', roughly equivalent to 5.55 km.
167 This could refer either to the witness (regarding the context, this seems most likely) or to Elijah or to R. El'azar.
168 I.e., a brothel. Cf. above n. 31.
169 A formula referring to the *Mishnah*; cf. *M. Sanhedrin* 10.1 (from which, however, the present quotation slightly differs).
170 It is presupposed that in this case *M. Sanhedrin* 10.1 does not apply.
171 See above n. 110.
172 A fuller version of this exegesis of Deut. 18:9 is found in *Sifre Deuteronomy* 170.
173 Ms. Munich lacks this sentence from 'In regard of this' onwards. Similar sayings occur in *T.Y. Ketubbot* 13.1/35c; *T.B. Shabbat* 54b and 55a; *Leviticus Rabbah* 25.1.

Yohanan said, 'Once his daughter was walking before the great ones of Rome.[174] They said: "How beautiful are the steps of this maiden!" Immediately she began to take care of her steps.' And this is what R. Shim'on ben Laqish said: 'What is the meaning of the following verse: *The sin of my heel surrounds me* (Ps. 49:6)? The sins which a man in this world treads with his heels surround him for the Day of Judgement.'[175]

(G) At the hour when the three of them went out (from the trial), they declared their judgement to be just. He said: '*The Rock, His work is perfect* (Deut. 32:4).' And his wife said: '*A God of faithfulness and without deceit* (ibid.).' His daughter said: '*Great in counsel and mighty in deed; Your eyes are watching over all the ways (of the children of men, giving to each according to his ways and according to the fruit of his deed)* (Jer. 32:19).'

(H) Rabbi[176] said: How great are these righteous ones that three verses of justification of the judgement (*tsidduq ha-din*) occurred to them at the hour of (their) judgement.[177]

(I) Our rabbis taught:[178] When R. Yose ben Qisma was ill, R. Hanina ben Teradion went to pay him a visit. He said to him: 'Hanina, my brother, do you not know that from Heaven they made this nation[179] reign? For it destroyed His house and burnt His temple and slew His pious ones and exterminated His noble ones, and still it persists. Yet I heard of you that you sit and occupy yourself with the Torah and gather assemblies in public, and a Torah[180] scroll lies in your bosom.' He said to him: 'From Heaven they will have mercy.' He said to him: 'I am telling you words of reason, and you tell me, "From Heaven they will have mercy"! I wonder whether they will not burn you and the Torah scroll with fire!' He said to him: 'Am I (destined) for the life in the world to come?' He said to him:

174 Ms. Munich: 'Once I was sitting with the great ones of Rome, and she was passing in front of us.' This, however, results in an anachronism, as R. Yohanan lived about a century later than R. Hanina.
175 Instead of 'Day of Judgement', ms. Munich reads 'world to come'.
176 See above n. 145.
177 Translation following ms. Munich; ed. Vilna reads: 'at the hour of the justification of the judgement.'
178 See above n. 115.
179 I.e., the Roman people.
180 According to ms. Munich; from ed. Vilna 'Torah' is absent here.

'Has any (sinful) deed come about at your hand?' He said to him: 'I confused Purim money with charity money, so I distributed it (from my own resources)[181] to the poor.' He said to him: 'If it is so, then may your portion be my portion, and may your fate be my fate!'

(J) They said that it was only a few days later that R. Yose ben Qisma passed away, and all the great ones of Rome came to bury him, and they held a great mourning. And when they returned, they found R. Hanina ben Teradion sitting and occupying himself with the Torah and gathering assemblies in public, and a Torah scroll was lying in his bosom. They brought him and wrapped him in the Torah scroll and placed fagots of rods around him and kindled the fire with them. And they brought tufts of wool and soaked them in water and placed them over his heart, so that his soul should not expire quickly.[182] His daughter said to him: 'My father, should I see you in such circumstances!' He said to her: 'If I[183] alone would be burnt, the matter would be hard for me. (But) now, since I am burnt and the Torah scroll together with me, He who resents the insult offered to the Torah scroll will resent the insult offered to me.' His disciples said to him: 'Rabbi, what do you see?' He said to them: 'The parchment is burning but the letters are flying off.' They said:[184] 'You should open your mouth so that the fire can enter!'[185] He said to them: 'It is better that He who gave (the soul) should take it away; and one should not harm oneself.' The executioner[186] said to him: 'Rabbi, if I raise the flame and remove the tufts of wool from your heart, will you bring me to the life of the world to come?' He said to him: 'Yes.' He said to him: 'Swear to me!' He swore to him. Immediately, (the executioner) raised the flame and

---

181 Cf. above n. 159.

182 Cf. Eusebius, *De mart. Palaest.* 3.1: 'was subjected to a slow and moderate fire' (*GCS* 9.2, 910), 4.12: 'covered his feet with linen cloths soaked in oil and set them on fire' (*GCS* 9.2, 916).

183 Ms. Munich refers to R. Hanina throughout his answer by the third rather than the first person singular.

184 Translation following ms. Munich; ed. Vilna lacks 'They said'.

185 Cf. Eusebius, *De mart. Palaest.* 11.19: 'But when the fire was kindled at some distance around him in a circle, he inhaled the flame into his mouth and continued most nobly in silence from that time till his death' (*GCS* 9.2, 941–2).

186 The Hebrew text has here the Latin loan word *quaestionarius*.

removed the tufts of wool from his heart, (and) quickly his soul expired. He (the executioner) leaped and fell into the fire, too. A heavenly voice[187] went forth and said: 'R. Hanina ben Teradion and the executioner are summoned to the life of the world to come.'

(K)   Rabbi[188] wept and said: 'There is he who acquires his (portion in the future) world in one instant,[189] and there is he who acquires his (portion in the future) world in many years.'

8 *Mekhilta Mishpatim* 18: R. Shim'on and R. Yishma'el

The starting point of the account of R. Shim'on's and R. Yishma'el's martyrdom, which also explains its embedding in a Midrash on Exodus,[190] is an exegesis of Exod. 22:21–3: 'You shall not oppress any widow or orphan. If you oppress them, and if they cry out to Me, I will . . . kill you with the sword . . .'. The Midrash takes the double employment of the Hebrew verb *innah* at the beginning of v. 22 (*im anneh te'anneh*, i.e. literally, 'if you oppress, oppress') to imply a reference to two types of 'oppression', a 'major' and a 'minor' one, the 'minor' one being the detainment of counsel, decision and judgement. Since the two rabbis are to be executed by the sword, and since the only biblical commandment which explicitly includes the threat of a sword is Exod. 22:21–3, and since it can be safely assumed that neither rabbi ever has 'oppressed' a widow or an orphan, it is the reference to detainment which leads to the solution: It must have occurred to the rabbis that they kept people waiting who had been seeking their counsel or judgement.[191] Due to the concise formulation of the story most of this reasoning is implicit rather than explicit.

Further early versions of this martyrdom exist in *Semahot* 8 and in the two versions of *Avot de-Rabbi Natan*.[192] In comparison with the

---

187 Literally, 'a daughter of a voice', i.e. an echo. See above n. 137.

188 See above n. 145.

189 Literally, 'in one hour'. For a similarly rapid attainment of eternal salvation, see *Genesis Rabbah* 65.22 (p. 144 above).

190 On the *Mekhilta (de-Rabbi Yishma'el)*, see above n. 8.

191 Cf. the General Introduction to the present chapter.

192 *Semahot* 8.8 (Higger, 1970b, 153); *Avot de-Rabbi Natan,* version A 38 and version B 41 (both ed. Schechter, 1887, 114). *Semahot* 8.8 reverses the roles of R. Shim'on and R. Yishma'el, and *Avot de-Rabbi Natan* in both versions adduces the tradition as an illustration of *M. Avot* 5.8: 'The sword comes into the

Mekhilta, they seem to reflect a more developed stage of tradition, as they identify R. Shim'on more precisely as 'Rabban Shim'on ben Gamli'el'[193] and lay greater emphasis on the pettiness of the rabbis' offence.[194]

Translation[195]

(A)[196] *If you oppress, oppress* (Exod. 22:22): one is a major oppression, and one is a minor oppression. Another interpretation: *If you oppress, oppress*: this means that one is not liable until one has done (it) and repeated (it).[197]

(B)   When R. Yishma'el and R. Shim'on came out to be beheaded, R. Shim'on said to R. Yishma'el: 'Rabbi, it breaks my heart, for I do not know for what reason I am (to be) beheaded.' R. Yishma'el said to R. Shim'on: 'Did it never happen in your life that a man came to you for a judgement or for a question, and you detained him until you had sipped your cup or until you had tied your sandal or until you had put on your *tallit*?[198] For the Torah says: *If you oppress, oppress*: one is a major oppression, and one is a minor oppression.' And upon these words, he said to him: 'You have comforted me, rabbi.'

(C)   When R. Shim'on and R. Yishma'el had been killed, R. Aqiva

---

world because of the delay of justice and because of the perversion of justice.' The mediaeval *Ma'aseh Asarah Haruge Malkhut* (ed. Reeg, 1985, § 22) dramatizes above all the execution scene.

193 A leading figure in rabbinic Judaism who flourished from 90 CE onwards.

194 Cf. *Avot de-Rabbi Natan,* version B 41: R. Yishma'el asks his colleague: 'Did never in your life a woman come to ask you concerning her menstrual impurity, or a man (to ask you) concerning his vow, and you were sleeping or dining, or there was no spare time, or (your) servant did not let them come in?' Whereupon R. Shim'on replies: 'Whether I was sleeping or dining, the servant was instructed not to withhold anybody from coming in.' Yet when R. Yishma'el insists that their death will not be without reason, R. Shim'on all of a sudden recalls that once when he was teaching and people were listening, his heart was filled with pride. Feeling deeply sorry for this pride, he can now accept his death. Thus, R. Shim'on is here not even guilty of that 'minor affliction' which the *Mekhilta* exegetically infers from Exod. 22:21–3.

195 According to Horovitz and Rabin (1970), 313.

196 See above n. 51.

197 This exegetical alternative also draws on the repetition of the verb. It is, however, irrelevant with regard to the following martyrdom story.

198 A cloak or shawl which is part of the traditional attire of male Jews (cf. Num. 15:38).

said to his disciples: Prepare yourselves for punishment,[199] for if good fortune had been about to come in our generation, the first to receive it would have been no one but R. Shim'on and R. Yishma'el. But it was open and known before Him who spoke so that the world came into being that a great punishment is destined to come about in our generation, and (therefore) He removed these from among us, as it is said: *The righteous one perishes, but no one takes it to heart; the pious men are taken away, and no one understands* (Is. 57:1), and it says: *May peace come, may they rest in their sleeping-places,*[200] *those who walk uprightly* (Is. 57:2), and in the end: *But as for you, come here, you children of a sorceress, you seed of an adulterer and a whore* (Is. 57:3).

9 *Targum Neofiti*, Gen. 22:1–19: The Binding of Isaac

The various Aramaic translations of the Pentateuch which are commonly subsumed under the label of the 'Palestinian Targums'[201] are distinguished by a multitude of shorter or longer insertions into the Bible text. They range from simple explications of what could be already implied (such as the 'perfect heart' in Gen. 22:6 and 8) and other brief clarifications (e.g., 'Mount' before 'Moriah' in v. 2) to verbose circumlocutions which eliminate the idea that God is materially involved in earthly events ('from before . . .', 'the Name of the Word of . . .', 'the Glory of the Shekhinah of . . .'), and lengthy digressions which greatly elaborate the contents of the story. In the paraphrase of Gen. 22:1–19 in *Targum Neofiti*, these larger embellishments are confined mainly to vv. 10 and 14.[202] They introduce a series of motifs which are quite typical of the general ancient Jewish reception of

---

199 A similar interpretation (attributed to R. Yehudah ben Bava and R. Hanina ben Teradion) of R. Aqiva's own martyrdom as an omen of bloodshed is preserved in *Semahot* 8.9 (ed. Higger, 1970b, 154–5). Herr (1972), 113, inferred from this that R. Aqiva's 'execution must have taken place before the [i.e., Bar Kokhba's] rebellion was finally crushed'. Considering *Mekhilta Mishpatim* 18, the same should then *a fortiori* hold for the death of R. Yishma'el and R. Shim'on. It is possible, however, that the tradition of *Semahot* 8.9 is merely a secondary variant of that of *Mekhilta Mishpatim* 18, which would thwart Herr's deduction; cf. Schäfer (1978), 117.
200 Which in the present context are presumably taken to be graves rather then beds.
201 Cf. Glessmer (1995), 95–6.
202 Cf., however, nn. 213 and 215.

Gen. 22: Abraham's obedience,[203] Isaac's willingness,[204] the emphasis of the sacrificial aspect,[205] and the expectation that God in remembrance of this act of obedience will help Isaac's offspring in future distress.[206] All these motifs occur likewise in the parallel version of *Targum Pseudo-Jonathan*.[207] The latter, however, additionally contains a variety of allusions to other pieces of ancient Jewish folklore: Abraham's temptation was caused by a rivalry between Isaac and Ishmael (v. 1), the wood which Abraham cut would have been appropriate for the Temple service (v. 3), the altar was the one that Noah had erected (v. 9), and the like.

The dating of these Targums is highly controversial,[208] but in the present instance the phraseology is so close to the Midrashic idiom[209] that the assumption that this paraphrase of Gen. 22 has an early rabbinic setting cannot be too far off the mark.

Translation[210]

(22:1) *And*[211] *it came to pass after these things that* YYY[212] *tested Abraham* with the tenth[213] trial. *And He said to him: 'Abraham!'* Abraham

---

203 'I carried out Your word with joy' (v. 14), cf. above n. 42 and below n. 242.
204 'Tie me well' (v. 10), see above n. 42.
205 'Lest your sacrifice be rendered unfit' (v. 10), see below n. 254 and above n. 40. Cf. also Davies and Chilton (1978), 537–45; Hayward (1981), 134–42.
206 'Remember the binding of their father Isaac and hear the voice of their prayer' (v. 14), cf. *T.Y. Ta'anit* 2.4 (section B in the translation below).
207 For the text, see *Biblia Polyglotta Matritensia* (1977), series IV, vol. I, pp. 139–45. The various Palestinian Fragment-Targums (ibid.) cover only vv. 1, 2, 8, 10, 11 and 14.
208 Cf. the discussion of the dating of *Targum Pseudo-Jonathan* in Glessmer (1995), 185–93, who reviews suggestions ranging from the second century BCE to the seventh century CE and in the end leaves the question open. Regarding the Binding of Isaac, cf. also the controversy between Davies and Chilton (1978) and Hayward (1981).
209 Cf. 'open and known before (You)' in v. 14, *Mekhilta Mishpatim* 18 (section C in our translation), and *T.Y. Ta'anit* 2.4 (section B in our translation); 'a daughter of a voice' in v. 10, *T.B. Berakhot* 61b (sections F and G in our translation), and elsewhere (see nn. 94 and 137); furthermore, the victim's fear of being rendered unfit for sacrifice in v. 10, in *Genesis Rabbah* 56.5 and 87.5 (Theodor and Albeck, 1996, 600 and 1066).
210 According to *Biblia Polyglotta Matritensia* (1977) series IV, vol. I, pp. 138–44.
211 Italics indicate literal correspondence between *Targum Neofiti* and the Hebrew original.
212 A current abbreviation for the biblical tetragrammaton in the Targums and in rabbinic manuscripts.
213 For the ten trials of Abraham, see *Jub.* 19:8; *M. Avot* 5.3; *Avot de-Rabbi Natan*, version A 33 and version B 36.

answered in the language of the sanctuary[214] *and said to Him: 'Here I am.' (22:2) And He said: 'Take now your son, your only one, whom you love, Isaac, and go to the land of* Mount *Moriah and offer him there as a burnt offering on one of the mountains which I shall tell you.' (22:3) And Abraham rose early in the morning and* took care of *his ass and took his two servants with him and his son Isaac and split pieces of wood for the burnt offering. And he set out and went to the place which* YYY *had told him. (22:4) On the third day Abraham raised his eyes and saw the place from afar. (22:5) (And) Abraham (said) to his servants: Stay here with the ass, and I and the lad shall go over there and pray and return to you. (22:6) And Abraham took the pieces of wood for the burnt offering and loaded* (them) *on his son Isaac and took the fire and the knife in his hand. And both of them went together* with a perfect heart. *(22:7) And Isaac spoke to his father Abraham and said: 'My father!' And he said: 'Here I am, my son.' And he said: 'Here is the fire and the pieces of wood, but where is the lamb for the burnt offering? (22:8) And Abraham said*: 'From before YYY there will be provided *a lamb for the burnt offering.*[215] And if not, you are the lamb for the burnt offering.' *And the two of them went together* with a perfect heart. *(22:9) And they came to the place which* YYY *had told him, and there Abraham built the altar and put the pieces of wood on it and bound his son Isaac and laid him on top of the pieces of wood. (22:10) And Abraham stretched out his hand and took the knife in order to slaughter his son* Isaac. Isaac answered and said to his father Abraham: 'My father, tie me well, lest I kick you and your sacrifice be rendered unfit and I be thrust into the pit in the world to come.'[216] Abraham's eyes were looking at the eyes of Isaac, and Isaac's eyes were looking at the angels on high.[217] Abraham did not see them. At this hour an echo[218] went forth from heaven and said: 'You see the two unique ones in My world. One slaughters and one is slaughtered. The one who slaughters does not hesitate, and the one who is slaughtered stretches out his neck.'[219] *(22:11) And the angel of* YYY *called him from heaven and said: 'Abraham, Abraham!' And he said:*

---

214 I.e. Hebrew. In fact, the Targum does not translate the expression denoting 'Here I am' into Aramaic.

215 After 'for the burnt offering', the Hebrew original reads: 'my son'. The Targum seems to interpret this not as an address but as the specification of the preceding general statement: God will 'provide a lamb for the burnt offering, (namely) my son'. This would explain the subsequent Targumic addition to the text.

216 Cf. above n. 209.

217 Cf. above n. 43.

218 Literally, 'a daughter of a voice'; cf. above n. 209.

219 Cf. Ps.-Philo, *Biblical Antiquities* 40.2 (see n. 242 below).

'Here I am.' (22:12) And he said: 'Do not stretch out your hand against the lad and do not do anything to him, for now I know that you are respectful before YYY and (that) you did not withhold your only son from Me.' (22:13) And Abraham raised his eyes and looked, and behold, a ram had been (entangled) with its horns in the tree. And Abraham went and took the ram and offered it as a burnt offering instead of his son. (22:14) And Abraham worshipped and prayed to the Name of the Word of YYY and said in prayer: 'By the mercy from before You, YYY, it is entirely open and known before You that there was no discord in my heart when You told me to offer my son Isaac (and) to turn him into dust and ashes before You, but I immediately rose in the early morning and set out and carried out Your word with joy and fulfilled Your decree. And now, when my descendants are in a period[220] of distress,[221] remember the binding of their father Isaac and hear the voice of their prayer and answer them and deliver them from all distress. For the generations that will come after him *will say*: On the mountain of the sanctuary[222] of YYY, where Abraham offered his son Isaac, *on this mountain* the Glory of the Indwelling[223] of *YYY revealed itself.*' (22:15) And the angel of YYY called Abraham once more from heaven. (22:16) And he said: "'By the Name of My[224] Word I swore", said YYY, "that because you carried out this order and did not withhold your son, your only one, (22:17) behold, I shall surely bless you, and I shall surely multiply your children as the stars of heaven and as the sand which is on the shore of the sea, and your children will inherit the towns of their accusers. (22:18) And all nations of the earth will be blessed by your seed because you gave heed to the voice of My[225] Word."' (22:19) And Abraham returned to his servants, and they stood up and went together to Beer-sheba, and Abraham dwelt in Beer-sheba.

10 *Talmud Yerushalmi, Ta'anit* 2.4: The Binding of Isaac

Within the broader context of a chapter describing the liturgical order to be observed on days of fasting, *Mishnah Ta'aniot* 2.4 gives the

---

220 Literally, 'hour'.
221 A pun on *aqta* ('distress') and *aqedah* ('binding').
222 For the identification of Mount Moriah with the Temple Mount of Jerusalem, cf. 2 Chron. 3:1.
223 *Shekhinteh*, i.e., God's *shekhinah*, His divine presence.
224 Literally, 'His'.
225 Literally, 'His'.

wording of various additional blessings that must be recited on such days. The first of these reads: 'He who answered to our father Abraham on Mount Moriah may answer to you, and He may hear the voice of your supplication today. Blessed are You, O Lord, the redeemer of Israel.' The pertinent discussion of this blessing in the *Talmud Yerushalmi* begins with the question of why the *Mishnah* does not mention Isaac rather than Abraham. This becomes the starting point for a series of short haggadic texts which illuminate the ever-lasting salvific power of Isaac's Binding for the whole nation of Israel.[226] With different degrees of variation, these pieces also occur elsewhere in early rabbinic literature.[227]

Translation[228]

(A)[229]   But was (it) not Isaac (who was) redeemed? (The *Mishnah* does not mention him, however,) because when Isaac was redeemed it was as if all Israel had been redeemed.

(B)   R. Bevai (bar[230]) Abba[231] (said) in the name of R. Yohanan: Abraham said before the Holy one, blessed be He, 'Master of the worlds, it is open and known before You that when You told me to offer my son Isaac I could have raised an objection, saying before You: "Yesterday You told me, *For it is through Isaac that offspring shall be named after you* (Gen. 21:12), and now You say, Offer him there as a burnt offering!" Heaven forbid, I did not do so (i.e., argue in this way) but I vanquished my inclination and carried out Your will. So may it be Your will,[232] Lord my God, that when the children of my son Isaac

---

226   For the benefit of the individual's self-sacrifice for the whole nation, cf. also *Targum Neofiti* Gen. 22:14 and Chapter 2, sections 5, 6, 7, and p. 16, n. 19.

227   Cf. *Genesis Rabbah* 56.10 (Theodor and Albeck, 1996, 607); *Leviticus Rabbah* 29.9–10 (ed. Margulies, 1993, 682–84); *Midrash Tanhuma*, version B, Wayyera 46 (Buber, 1885, fol. 58a); for further references, see Margulies on *Leviticus Rabbah* 29.9 (footnote p. 682).

228   Translation according to ms. Leiden (Schäfer and Becker, 1991–2001, vol. II/5–12, p. 240).

229   See above n. 51.

230   Emended according to *Leviticus Rabbah* 29.9; ms. Leiden lacks the word.

231   The rabbis mentioned in sections B and C are teachers of the 'Amoraic' period, i.e., the time between the redaction of the *Mishnah* and that of the *Talmud Bavli* (about 200–500 CE). See above nn. 7 and 96.

232   Literally, 'a will from before You'.

get into troubles and there is no one who speaks in their defence, You shall speak in their defence.[233] *The Lord will see* (Gen. 22:14), (this means) You remember on their behalf the binding of their father Isaac and will be filled with mercy for them.'

(C) What is written after this? *Abraham raised his eyes and looked, and behold, a ram at the back* etc. (Gen. 22:13). What is (the meaning of) *at the back*? R. Yudah the son of R. Simon said: After[234] all generations your children will be caught in sins[235] and entangled in distress, and in the end they will be redeemed by the horns of this ram, as it is said: *And the Lord God will sound the shofar*[236] *and march forth in the whirlwinds of the south* (Zech. 9:14).

(D) R. Hunah (said) in the name of R. Hinenah bar Yitshaq: All that day long Abraham saw the ram, (who) got caught in this tree and got out and went forth, got caught in that thicket and got out and went forth, got caught in that tangle and got out and went forth. The Holy one, blessed be He, said to Abraham: 'Thus will your children be caught in sins[237] and entangled in (foreign) kingdoms: from Babel to Media, from Media to Greece, from Greece to Edom.'[238] He said before Him: 'Master of the worlds, will it be so forever?' He said to him: 'And in the end they will be redeemed by the horns of this ram, (as it is said:) *And the Lord God will sound the shofar and march forth in the whirlwinds of the south* (Zech. 9:14).

11 Pseudo-Philo, *Biblical Antiquities* 32.1–4: The Binding of Isaac

The Pseudo-Philonic *Liber antiquitatum biblicarum*, an adaptation of the biblical history from Adam to David, is certainly not a rabbinic

---

233 *Leviticus Rabbah* 29.9: 'when the children of Isaac fall into transgressions and bad deeds, remember on their behalf the binding of their father Isaac and atone for them.'

234 The exegesis plays on the identical consonantal spelling of *ahar* ('at the back') and *aher* ('after').

235 *Avonot* ('sins') or *onot* ('troubles'); the consonant text permits either reading.

236 A trumpet made of a ram's horn.

237 See n. 235.

238 Rabbinic literature often employs 'Edom' as a symbolic name for Rome.

text. It has come down to us through the Christian tradition, and since it was composed some time in the first century,[239] it is older than any extant rabbinic writing. But for many haggadic motifs of the later Jewish tradition, including the story of the Binding of Isaac, it is 'the earliest witness'.[240] Therefore, there is good reason to include this document in the present chapter.

Ps.-Philo does not relate the event of Isaac's Binding within the chronological order of the history of the patriarchs (Chapters 6–8) but presents it by way of various retrospectives: in a revelation imparted to Balaam (18.5; cf. Num. 22–4), in the hymn of Deborah and Barak (32.2–4; cf. Judg. 5), and in the speech of Jephthah's daughter who declares her submission to her father's fatal vow (40.2; cf. Judg. 11:30–40). Deviations from the biblical account are plenty: Isaac is told in advance that he will be sacrificed (30.2)[241] and, although he points out that human beings are normally destined for a fate other than that of animals (30.3), he readily consents, and Abraham rejoices (40.2).[242] Isaac considers his sacrifice to be a model for other human self-sacrifice (30.3, end). His feet are tied, as is otherwise done to sacrificial animals (30.4).[243] Although God gave Isaac back to his father, He accepted the 'sacrifice' (18.5). And 'for the sake of his blood', which is not said to have been shed,[244] but which, as it seems, is accounted as if it had been shed,[245] God chooses Abraham and his offspring (ibid.).

Translation[246]

1   Then Deborah and Barak the son of Abino and the whole people unanimously sang a hymn to the Lord on this day (cf. Judg. 5:5), saying: Behold, from above the Lord has revealed to

239   A more precise dating is difficult, Harrington (1985), 299.
240   Harrington (1985), 300.
241   Cf. *Targum Neofiti* Gen. 22:8.
242   'Or do you not remember what happened in the days of our fathers when a father made (his) son a burnt offering, and he did not contradict him, but appreciatively he gave him consent, and he who was offered was ready and he who offered was rejoicing?' (40.2); cf. *Targum Neofiti* Gen. 22:14.
243   See below n. 254.
244   Cf. Harrington (1985), 325, note g; Davies and Chilton (1978), 528. But cf. above, n. 40.
245   As far as it is the *shedding* from which the sacrificial blood derives its salvific potency. Cf. Heb. 9:22; *Sifra Nedavah, pereq* 4.10 (Weiss, 1862, fol. 6a); *T.B. Menahot* 93b; *T.Y. Yoma* 5.7/43a.11–20.
246   According to Harrington (1976), 224–6.

us His glory, as He did in the higher places when He sent forth His voice in order to confuse the tongues of men. And He chose our nation, and He took Abraham our father out of the fire,[247] and He preferred him to all his brothers, and He preserved him from the fire and delivered him from the bricks[248] of the construction of the tower. And He gave him a son in his old age and drew him (i.e., the son) out from a barren womb. And all the angels were jealous of him, and the (heavenly) hosts' adorers[249] were envious of him.

2   And as they were jealous of him, God said to him: 'Kill the fruit of your body for Me, and offer to Me as a sacrifice what you were given from Me.' And Abraham did not contradict but set out immediately. And when he had set out, he said to his son: 'Behold now, my son, I shall offer you up as a burnt offering, and I shall render you to the hands that gave you to me.'

3   The son, however, said to the father: 'Listen to me, father. If a lamb from the flocks is accepted as an offering to the Lord with pleasing odour, and if for the iniquities of men flocks are provided for slaughter, whereas man is appointed for inheriting the world, how can you now say to me: "Come and inherit secure life and immeasurable time?"[250] What, if I had not been born in the world in order to be offered as a sacrifice for Him who made me? However, (now) my blessedness will be upon all men,[251] for there will not be another thing (like this),[252] and (future) generations will be informed concerning me, and through me nations will understand that the Lord deemed the soul of a man worthy to be a sacrifice.'

4   And when the father had placed[253] the son upon the altar and

---

247 I.e. the fiery furnace into which the builders of the tower of Babel had thrown him; cf. *Biblical Antiquities* 6.

248 These bricks had been thrown into the furnace together with Abraham.

249 I.e. the heavenly hosts who adore God.

250 The eternal life is what Isaac expects to gain in recompense for his self-sacrifice.

251 Or perhaps, 'my blessedness will be beyond (that of) all men'?

252 The meaning is not evident, but cf. Harrington (1985), 345: 'there will be nothing like this'; Hayward (1981), 144: 'there shall be none other'. The more precise rendering of Davies and Chilton (1978), 524: 'there will not be another [sacrifice]', seems, however, at variance with the following general statement of the aptness of 'the soul of a man' for sacrifice.

253 Literally, 'had offered', which is meant here in the sense of the very first step of the sacrificial procedure.

had tied his feet[254] in order to kill him, the Most Powerful one hastened to send His voice from on high, saying: 'Do not slay your son nor destroy the fruit of your body! For now I have revealed Myself so that you will be known to those who ignore you, and I have shut the mouth of those who always reviled you. For your memory will be eternally before Me, and your name and his will remain from generation to generation.'

254 The motif of the Binding of Isaac's feet is probably inspired by the cultic rule of tying the foreleg to the hindleg of the sacrificial animal (cf. *M. Tamid* 3.1). This would explain why neither the hands nor any other of Isaac's limbs are bound.

BIBLIOGRAPHY

Acerbi, A. (1983) *L'Ascensione di Isaia: Cristologia e profetismo in Siria nei primi decenni del II secolo*, Studia patristica mediolanensia 17, Milan: Pubblicazioni della Università Cattolica del Sacro Cuore, 2nd edn, 1989.

Adinolfi, M. (1969) *Questioni bibliche di storia e storiografia*, Esegesi biblica 5, Brescia: Paideia.

Ariès, P. (1978) *L'histoire de la mort*, Paris: Editions du Seuil.

Attridge, H.W. (1984) 'Historiography', in M.E. Stone (ed.), *Jewish Writings of the Second Temple Period: Apocrypha, Pseudepigrapha, Qumran Sectarian Writings, Philo, Josephus*, CRINT II.2, Assen–Philadelphia: Van Gorcum/Fortress Press.

Austin, C. (1968) *Nova fragmenta Euripidea in papyris reperta*, Berlin: De Gruyter.

Barnard, L.W. (1967) *Justin Martyr: His Life and Thought*, Cambridge: Cambridge University Press.

Barnes, T.D. (1968) 'Pre-Decian Acta Martyrum', *JTS* 19: 509–31.

Bartelink, G.J.M. (1961) 'Sur les allusions aux noms propres chez les auteurs grecs chrétiens', *Vig Chr* 15: 32–9.

Bastiaensen, A.A.R., Hilhorst, A., Kortekaas, G.A.A., Orban, A.P. and van Assendelft, M.M. (1987) *Atti e Passioni dei martiri*, Milan: Fondazione Lorenzo Valla/Arnoldo Mondadori.

Bauer, A. (1901) 'Heidnische Märtyrerakten', *Archiv* 1: 29–47.

Bauer, W., Aland, B. and Aland, K. (1988) *Griechisch-deutsches Wörterbuch zu den Schriften des Neuen Testaments und der frühchristlichen Literatur*, Berlin: De Gruyter.

Baumeister, T. (1980) *Die Anfänge der Theologie des Martyriums*, Münsterische Beiträge zur Theologie 45, Münster: Aschendorff.

—— (1983) '"Anytos und Meletos können mich zwar töten, schaden jedoch können sie mir nicht"', in H.-D. Blume and F. Mann (eds) *Platonismus und Christentum*, FS H. Dörrie, JAC Ergänzungsband 10, Münster: Aschendorff.

—— (1988) 'Zur Datierung der Schrift an Diognet', *Vig Chr* 42: 105–11.

Bentzen, A. (1950) 'Daniel 6. Ein Versuch zur Vorgeschichte der Märtyrerlegende', in W. Baumgartner, O. Eissfeldt, K. Elliger and L.

Rost (eds) *Festschrift A. Bertholet zum 80. Geburtstag gewidmet von Kollegen und Freunden*, Tübingen: Mohr, 58–64.

Ben-Yehuda, N. (1995) *The Masada Myth: Collective Memory and Mythmaking in Israel*, Madison, WI: The University of Wisconsin Press.

Berger, K. (1984) 'Hellenistische Gattungen im Neuen Testament', *ANRW* II.25.2: 1031–432; 1831–85.

Berve, H. (1967) *Die Tyrannis bei den Griechen*, 2 vols, Munich: Beck.

Beyschlag, K. (1966) *Clemens Romanus und der Frühkatholizismus. Untersuchungen zu I Clemens 1–7*, Beiträge zur historischen Theologie 35, Tübingen: Mohr (Siebeck).

Biblia Polyglotta Matritensia (1977) Series IV, *Targum Palestinense in Pentateuchum*, vol. I, Madrid: CSIC.

Bickerman(n), E. (1933) 'Ein jüdischer Festbrief vom Jahre 124 v. Chr. (II Macc 1:1–9)' *ZNW* 32: 233–54.

Bihlmeyer, K. (1956) *Die apostolischen Väter*, Neubearbeitung der Funkschen Ausgabe, Tübingen: Mohr.

Bilde, P. (1988) *Flavius Josephus between Jerusalem and Rome: His Life, His Works and Their Importance*, Journal for the Study of the Pseudepigrapha Supplement Series 2, Sheffield: Sheffield Academic Press.

Bisbee, G.A. (1988) *Pre-Decian Acts of Martyrs and Commentarii*, Harvard Dissertations in Religion 22, Philadelphia: Fortress Press.

Blass, F. (1927) *Demosthenis Orationes*, vol. 3, 4th edn, Leipzig: Teubner.

Boeft, J. den and Bremmer, J. (1981) 'Notiunculae Martyrologicae', *Vig Chr* 35: 43–56.

—— (1991) 'Notiunculae Martyrologicae IV', *Vig Chr* 45: 105–22.

Bommes, K. (1970) *Weizen Gottes: Untersuchungen zur Theologie des Martyriums bei Ignatius von Antiochien*, Cologne and Bonn: Hanstein.

Borgen, P. (1984) 'Philo of Alexandria: A Critical and Synthetical Survey of Research since World War II', *ANRW* II.21.1: 98–154.

Boyarin, D. (1999) *Dying for God: Martyrdom and the Making of Christianity and Judaism*, Stanford, CA: Stanford University Press.

Brändle, R. (1975) *Die Ethik der "Schrift an Diognet": Eine Wiederaufnahme paulinischer und johanneischer Theologie am Ausgang des zweiten Jahrhunderts*, Zürich: Theologischer Verlag.

Breitenstein, U. (1976) *Beobachtungen zu Sprache, Stil und Gedankengut des Vierten Makkabäerbuchs*, Basel-Stuttgart: Schwabe & Co.

Brekelmans, A.J. (1965) *Märtyrerkranz: Eine symbolgeschichtliche Untersuchung im frühchristlichen Schrifttum*, Analecta Gregoriana 150, Rome: Libreria dell'Università Gregoriana.

Bremmer, J.N. (1991) 'Christianus sum. The Early Christian Martyrs and Christ', in G. Bartelink, A. Hilhorst *et al.* (eds), *Eulogia: Mélanges offerts à Antoon A. R. Bastiaensen à l'occasion de son soixante-cinquième anniversaire*, Steenbrugge: In abbatia S. Petri, The Hague: Nijhoff International, 11–20.

Brennecke, H.C. (1977) 'Danaiden und Dirken. Zu 1 Cl 6,2', *Zeitschrift für Kirchengeschichte* 88: 302–8.

Buber, S. (ed.) (1868) *Pesikta, die älteste Hagada, redigirt in Palästina von Rab Kahana*, Lyck: Mekize Nirdamim.

—— (ed.) (1885) *Midrasch Tanchuma: Ein agadischer Commentar zum Pentateuch von Rabbi Tanchuma ben Rabbi Abba*, Vilna: Romm.

—— (ed.) (1894) *Midrasch suta. Hagadische Abhandlungen über Schir ha-Schirim, Ruth, Echah und Koheleth, nebst Jalkut zum Buche Echah*, Berlin.

—— (1899) *Midrasch Echa Rabbati: Sammlung agadischer Auslegungen der Klagelieder*, Vilna: Romm.

Buchheit, V. (1960) *Untersuchungen zur Theorie des Genos Epideiktikon von Gorgias bis Aristoteles*. Munich: Hueber.

Buschmann, G. (1994) *Martyrium Polycarpi – Eine formkritische Studie: Ein Beitrag zur Frage nach der Entstehung der Gattung Märtyrerakte*, BZNW 70, Berlin and New York: De Gruyter.

—— (1998) *Das Martyrium des Polykarp übersetzt und erklärt*. Kommentar zu den Apostolischen Vätern 6, Göttingen: Vandenhoeck & Ruprecht.

Campbell, D.A. (1992) *The Rhetoric of Righteousness in Romans 3.21–26*, JSNT Sup 65, Sheffield: Sheffield Academic Press.

Campenhausen, H. von (1936) *Die Idee des Martyriums in der alten Kirche*, Göttingen: Vandenhoeck & Ruprecht.

Carlson, D.C. (1982) 'Vengeance and Angelic Mediation in Testament of Moses 9 and 10', *JBL* 101: 85–98.

Cassin, E. (1951) 'Daniel dans la "fosse" aux lions', *RHR* 139: 129–61.

Cavander, K. (1973) *Iphigeneia at Aulis by Euripides*, Englewood Cliffs, NJ: Prentice-Hall Inc.

Chevallier, R. (1975) 'Gallia Lugdunensis: Bilan de 25 ans de recherches historiques et archéologiques', *ANRW* II.3: 860–1060.

Cohen, S.J.D. (1979) *Josephus in Galilee and Rome: His Vita and Development as a Historian*, Columbia Studies in the Classical Tradition 8, Leiden: Brill.

—— (1982) 'Masada: Literary Tradition, Archaeological Remains and the Credibility of Josephus', *JJS* 28 [= G. Vermes and J. Neusner (eds), *Essays in Honour of Yigael Yadin*]: 385–405.

Cohn, L. and Reiter, S. (1915) *Philonis Alexandrini Opera quae supersunt*, vol. 6, Berlin: G. Reimerus.

Collins, J.J. (1975) 'The Court-Tales of Daniel and the Development of Apocalyptic', *JBL* 94: 218–34.

—— (1993) *Daniel: A Commentary on the Book of Daniel*, Hermeneia, Minneapolis: Fortress Press.

Conybeare, F., Rendel Harris, J. and Smith Lewis, A. (1913) *The Story of Ahiqar from the Aramaic, Syriac, Arabic, Armenian, Ethiopic, Greek and Slavonic Versions*, 2nd edn, Cambridge: Cambridge University Press.

Cotton, H.M. (1989) 'The Date of the Fall of Masada: the Evidence of the Masada Papyri', *ZPE* 78, 157–62.

Cotton, H.M. and Geiger, J. (1989) *Masada II*, see Y. Yadin *et al.* (1989–99).

Cowley, A. (1923) *Aramaic Papyri of the Fifth Century B.C., Edited, with Translation and Notes*, Oxford: Clarendon Press.

Davies, P.R. and Chilton, B.D. (1978) 'The Aqedah: A Revised Tradition History', *Catholic Biblical Quarterly* 40: 514–46.

Dehandschutter, B.A.G.M. (1979) *Martyrium Polycarpi: Een literair-kritische studie*, BETL 52; Leuven: Peeters.

—— (1989) 'Some Notes on *1 Clement* 5, 4–7', in A.A.R. Bastiaensen, A. Hilhorst and C.H. Kneepkens (eds), *Fructus centesimus: Mélanges offerts à Gerard J. M. Bartelink*, Instrumenta Patristica 19, Dordrecht: Kluwer, 83–9.

—— (1993) 'The Martyrium Polycarpi: A Century of Research', *ANRW* II. 27.1: 485–522.

Dehandschutter, B.A.G.M. and Henten, J.W. van (1989) 'Einleitung', in J.W. van Henten *et al.* (eds), *Die Entstehung der jüdischen Martyrologie*, Studia Post-Biblica 38; Leiden: Brill, 1–19.

Delatte, A. (1953) 'Le sage-témoin dans la philosophie stoïco-cynique', *Bulletin de l'Académie Royale de Belgique*, Classe des Lettres 39: 166–86.

DeSilva, A. (1998) *4 Maccabees*, Guides to the Apocrypha and Pseudepigrapha 7, Sheffield: Sheffield Academic Press.

Deubner, L. (1905) 'Die Devotion der Decier', *ARW* 8: 66–81 [= *Beiheft gewidmet H. Usener zum siebzigsten Geburtstage*].

Diels, H. (1951–56) *Die Fragmente der Vorsokratiker Griechisch und Deutsch*, Berlin: Weidmann, 3 vols.

Diggle, J. (1994) *Euripidis Fabulae*, vol. 3, Oxford: Clarendon Press.

Dölger, F.J. (1933) 'Das Martyrium als Kampf mit dem Teufel', *AC* 3: 177–88.

Doran, R. (1980) 'The Martyr: A Synoptic View of the Mother and Her Seven Sons', in J.J. Collins and G.W.E. Nickelsburg (eds), *Ideal Figures in Ancient Judaism: Profiles and Paradigms*, SBL Septuagint and Cognate Studies, vol. 12, Chico: Scholars Press, pp. 189–221.

Döring, K. (1979) *Exemplum Socratis: Studien zur Sokratesnachwirkung in der kynisch-stoischen Popularphilosophie der frühen Kaiserzeit und im frühen Christentum*, Hermes Einzelschriften 42. Wiesbaden: Franz Steiner Verlag.

Droge, A.J. and Tabor, J.D. (1992) *A Noble Death: Suicide and Martyrdom among Christians and Jews in Antiquity*, San Francisco: HarperCollins.

Dronke, P. (1984) *Women Writers of the Middle Ages: A Critical Study of Texts from Perpetua to Marguerite Porete*, Cambridge: Cambridge University Press.

Duke, E.A., Hicken, W.F., Nicoll, W.S.M., Robinson, D.B. and Strachan, J.C.G. (1995) *Platonis Opera*, vol. 1, Oxford: Clarendon Press.

Dupont-Sommer, A. (1939) *Le quatrième livre des Maccabées: Introduction, traduction et notes*, Bibliothèque de l'École des Hautes Études 274, Paris: Champion.

Eck, W. (1970) *Senatoren von Vespasian bis Hadrian: prosopographische Untersuchungen mit Einschluss der Jahres- und Provinzialfasten der Statthalter*, Munich: Beck.

Elliger, K. and Rudolph, W. (1977) *Biblia Hebraica Stuttgartensia*, Stuttgart: Württembergische Bibelanstalt.

Emonds, H. (1938) 'Geistlicher Kriegsdienst: Der Topos der militia spiritualis in der antiken Philosophie', in O. Casel (ed.), *Heilige Überlieferung* 1, Beiträge zur Geschichte des Alten Mönchtums und des Benediktiner Ordens, Supplementband, Münster: Aschendorff, 21–50; reprinted in: A. von Harnack (ed.), *Militia Christi*, Darmstadt: Mohr, 1963, 133–62.

Engel, H. (1985) *Die Susanna-Erzählung. Einleitung, Übersetzung und Kommentar zum Septuaginta-Text und zur Theodotion-Bearbeitung*, OBO 61, Freiburg and Göttingen: Universitätsverlag-Neukirchener.

Epstein, J.N. and Melamed, E.Z. (eds) (1979) *Mekhilta d'Rabbi Šim'on b. Jochai*, 2nd edn, Jerusalem: Hillel Press.

Farkasfalvy, D. (1992) 'Christological Content and its Biblical Basis in the Letter of the Martyrs of Gaul', *The Second Century* 9: 5–25.

Finkelstein, L. (1956) *Sifra or Torat Kohanim According to Codex Assemani LXVI* (facsimile edition), New York: Jewish Theological Seminary.

—— (ed.) (1993), *Siphre ad Deuteronomium*, Corpus Tannaiticum III.III.II, Berlin: Jüdischer Kulturbund, 1939, reprinted New York: Jerusalem: Jewish Theological Seminary.

Finley, M.I. and Pleket, H.W. (1976) *The Olympic Games: The First Thousand Years*, London: Chatto and Windus.

Fishwick, D. (1987–92) *The Imperial Cult in the Latin West. Studies in the Ruler Cult of the Western Provinces of the Roman Empire*, 4 vols, EPRO 108, Leiden: Brill.

Frend, W.H.C. (1965) *Martyrdom and Persecution in the Early Church: A Study of a Conflict from the Maccabees to Donatus*, Oxford: Blackwell.

Freudenberger, R. (1968) 'Die Acta Justini als historisches Dokument', in K. Beyschlag *et al.* (eds), *Humanitas – Christianitas: Walter von Loewenich zum 65. Geburtstag*, Witten: Luther, 24–31.

Friedmann, M. (ed.) (1880) *Pesikta Rabbati. Midrasch für den Fest-Cyclus und die ausgezeichneten Sabbathe*, Vienna: J. Kaiser.

—— (ed.) (1902) *Seder Eliahu rabba und Seder Eliahu zuta (Tanna d'be Eliahu)*, Vienna and Warsaw: Achiasaf.

Fritz, K. von (1972) 'Zenon (1–5)', *PW* 2. Reihe 19: 53–138.

Gera, D. (1998) *Judea and Mediterranean Politics: 219 to 161 BCE*, Brill's Series in Jewish Studies 8, Leiden: Brill.

Ginzberg, L. (1967–8) *The Legends of the Jews I–VII*, Philadelphia: The Jewish Publication Society of America.

Glessmer, U. (1995) *Einleitung in die Targume zum Pentateuch*, Texte und Studien zum Antiken Judentum 48, Tübingen: Mohr Siebeck.

Goldberg, A. (1997) 'Das Martyrium des Rabbi Aqiva', in A. Goldberg, *Mystik und Theologie des rabbinischen Judentums: Gesammelte Studien* I, Texte und Studien zum Antiken Judentum 61, Tübingen: Mohr Siebeck, 351–412.

Goldstein, J.A. (1983) *II Maccabees: A New Translation with Introduction and Commentary*, AB 41a, New York: Doubleday.

Graetz, H. (1876) *Geschichte der Juden von den ältesten Zeiten bis auf die Gegenwart,* vol. II, Leipzig: Oskar Leiner.

Grenfell, B.P. and Hunt, A.S. (1898) *The Oxyrynchus Papyri*, vol. I, London: The Egypt Exploration Society.

Guillaumin, M.-L. (1972) 'Une jeune fille qui s'appelait Blandine', in J. Fontaine and C. Kannengiesser (eds), *Epektasis: Mélanges patristiques offerts au Cardinal J. Daniélou*, Paris: Beauchesne, 93–8.

Gutman, J. (1949) 'The Story of the Mother and her Seven Sons in the Aggadah and in II and IV Maccabees', in *Commentationes Iudaico-Hellenisticae in Memoriam I. Lewy*. Jerusalem (in Hebrew).

Haag, E. (1983) *Die Errettung Daniels aus der Löwengrube: Untersuchungen zum Ursprung der biblischen Danieltradition*, SBS 110, Stuttgart: Verlag Katholisches Bibelwerk.

Habermehl, P. (1992) *Perpetua und der Ägypter oder Bilder des Bösen im frühen afrikanischen Christentum: Ein Versuch zur Passio Sanctarum Perpetuae et Felicitatis*, Texte und Untersuchungen 140, Berlin: Akademie Verlag.

Hadas, M. (1953) *The Third and Fourth Books of Maccabees*: New York: Harper & Brothers.

Hall, R.G. (1990) 'The Ascension of Isaiah: Community Situation, Date, and Place in Early Christianity', *JBL* 109: 289–306.

Hamman, A. (1975) 'Valeur et signification des renseignements liturgiques de Justin', *Studia Patristica* 13, Texte und Untersuchungen 116, Berlin: Akademie-Verlag, 364–74.

Harrington, D.J. (ed.) (1976) *Pseudo-Philon, Les antiquités bibliques, vol. I. Introduction et texte critiques*, Paris: Cerf.

—— (1985) 'Pseudo-Philo (First Century A.D.): A New Translation and Introduction', in J. H. Charlesworth (ed.), *The Old Testament Pseudepigrapha*, Garden City, NJ: Doubleday, vol. 2, 297–377.

Harrison, P.N. (1936) *Polycarp's Two Epistles to the Philippians*, Cambridge: Cambridge University Press.

Harnack, A. von (1924) *Die Mission und Ausbreitung des Christentums in den ersten drei Jahrhunderten*, 4th edn, Leipzig: J.C. Hinrich.

Hayward, R. (1981) 'The Present State of Research into the Targumic Account of the Sacrifice of Isaac', *JJS* 32: 127–50.

Hengel, M. (1976) *Die Zeloten. Untersuchungen zur jüdischen Freiheitsbewegung in der Zeit von Herodes I. bis 70 n. Chr.*, Arbeiten zur Geschichte des antiken Judentums und des Urchristentums 1, 2nd edn, Leiden and Cologne: Brill.

Hennig, D. (1974) 'Zu der alexandrinischen Märtyrerakte P. Oxy. 1089', *Chiron* 4: 425–40.

Henten, J.W. van (1986) 'Datierung und Herkunft des Vierten Makkabäerbuches', in J.W. van Henten, H.J. de Jonge *et al.* (eds) *Tradition and Re-interpretation in Jewish and Early Christian Literature: Essays in Honour of Jürgen C.H. Lebram*, SPB 36, Leiden: Brill, 136–49.

—— (1990) 'The Story of Susanna as a Pre-Rabbinic Midrash to Dan. 1:1–2', in A. Kuyt, E.G.L. Schrijver and N.A. van Uchelen (eds), *Variety of Forms: Dutch Studies in Midrash*, Amsterdam: Publications of the Juda Palache Institute, 1–14.

Henten, J.W. van (1993) 'Zum Einfluß jüdischer Martyrien auf die Literatur des frühen Christentums, II. Die Apostolischen Väter', *ANRW* II.27.1: 700–23.

—— (1997) *The Maccabean Martyrs as Saviours of the Jewish People: A Study of 2 and 4 Maccabees*, JSJ Sup 57, Leiden: Brill.

—— (1999) 'The Ancestral Language of the Jews' in W. Horbury (ed.) *Hebrew Study from Ezra to Ben-Yehuda*, Edinburgh: T & T Clark, 53–68.

—— (2001) 'Daniel 3 and 6 in Early Christian Literature', in J.J Collins and P.W. Flint (eds) *The Book of Daniel: Composition and Reception* I, Leiden: Brill, 149–69.

Henten, J.W. van and Abusch, R.S. (1996) 'The Depiction of the Jews as Typhonians and Josephus' Strategy of Refutation in "Contra Apionem"', in L.H. Feldman and J.R. Levison (eds), *Josephus' 'Contra Apionem': Studies in its Character and Context with a Latin Concordance to the Portion Missing in Greek*, Leiden: Brill, 271–309.

Herr, M.D. (1972) 'Persecution and Martyrdom in Hadrian's Days', in D. Asheri and I. Shatzman (eds), *Studies in History 1972*, Scripta Hierosolymitana 23, Jerusalem: Magnes, 85–125.

Higger, M. (ed.) (1970a) *Massekhtot Kallah Rabbati*, New York, 1936, reprinted Jerusalem: Makor.

—— (ed.) (1970b) *Treatise Semahot and Treatise Samahot of R. Hiyya . . .*, New York, 1931, reprinted Jerusalem: Makor.

Holl, K. (1914) 'Die Vorstellung vom Märtyrer und die Märtyrerakte in ihrer geschichtlichen Entwicklung', *Neue Jahrbücher für das klassische Altertum* 33 (1914) 521–56; reprinted in *Gesammelte Aufsätze zur Kirchengeschichte*, Tübingen: Mohr, 3 vols, 1921–28, 2.68–102.

Holladay, C.R. (1983) *Fragments from Hellenistic Jewish Authors* I, Chico, CA: Scholars Press.

Holleman, J. (1996) *Resurrection and Parousia: A Traditio-Historical Study of Paul's Eschatology in 1 Corinthians 15*, NovT Sup 84, Leiden: Brill.

Hooff, A.J.L. van (1990) *From Autothanasia to Suicide: Self-killing in Classical Antiquity*, London and New York: Routledge.

Horbury, W. (1999) 'Pappus and Lulianus in Jewish Resistance to Rome', in J. Targarona Borrás and A. Sáenz-Badillos (eds), *Jewish Studies at the Turn of the Twentieth Century. Proceedings of the 6th EAJS Congress, Toledo, July 1998*, vol. I: Biblical, Rabbinical, and Medieval Studies, Leiden, Boston and Cologne: Brill, 289–95.

Horovitz, H.S. and Rabin, I.A. (1970) *Mechilta d'Rabbi Ismael*, Corpus Tannaiticum III.I.I, Frankfurt: J. Kauffmann, 1931.

Horst, P.W. van der (1991) *Ancient Jewish Epitaphs: An Introductory Survey of a Millennium of Jewish Funerary Epigraphy (300 BCE–700 CE)*, Contributions to Biblical Exegesis and Theology 2, Kampen: Kok Pharos.

—— (1994) '"The Elements will be Dissolved with Fire." The Idea of Cosmic Conflagration in Hellenism, Ancient Judaism, and Early

Christianity', in *Hellenism-Judaism-Christianity: Essays on their Interaction*, Contributions to Biblical Exegesis and Theology, Kampen: Kok Pharos, 1994, 227–51.

Jastrow, M. (1903) *A Dictionary of the Targumim, the Talmud Babli and Yerushalmi, and the Midrashic Literature* I–II, London: Luzac & Co.; New York: G.P. Putnam's & Sons.

Jeremias, J. (1965) *Theophanie: Die Geschichte einer alttestamentlichen Gattung*, WMANT 10, Neukirchen-Vluyn: Neukirchener Verlag des Erziehungsvereins.

Jones, A.H.M. (1940) *The Greek City from Alexander to Justinian*, Oxford: Clarendon.

Kellermann, U. (1979) *Auferstanden in den Himmel: 2 Makkabäer 7 und die Auferstehung der Märtyrer*, SBS 95, Stuttgart: Verlag Katholisches Bibelwerk.

Klauck, H.-J. (1989) '4. Makkabäerbuch', *JSHRZ* 3.6: 645–763.

Knibb, M.A. (1985) 'Martyrdom and Ascension of Isaiah (Second Century B.C.-Fourth Century A.D.), in J.H. Charlesworth (ed.), *The Old Testament Pseudepigrapha*, Garden City, NJ: Doubleday, vol. 2, 143–76.

Koch, K. (1987) *Deuterokanonische Zusätze zum Danielbuch. Entstehung und Textgeschichte*, AOAT 38, 2 vols, Kevelaer-Neukirchen-Vluyn: Butzon & Bercker-Neukirchener.

Koch, K., Niewisch, T. and Tubach, J. (1980) *Das Buch Daniel*, Erträge der Forschung 144, Darmstadt: Wissenschaftliche Buchgesellschaft.

Kottsieper, I. (1990) *Die Sprache der Ahiqarsprüche*, BZAW 194, Berlin and New York: Walter de Gruyter.

Kratz, R.G. (1991) *Translatio imperii: Untersuchungen zu den aramäischen Danielerzählungen und ihrem theologiegeschichtlichen Umfeld*, WMANT 63, Neukirchen-Vluyn: Neukirchener Verlag.

Krauss, S. (1899) *Griechische und lateinische Lehnwörter im Talmud, Midrasch und Targum* II, Berlin: S. Calvary.

Kuhl, C. (1930) *Die drei Männer im Feuer: Daniel Kapitel 3 und seine Zusätze*, BZAW 55, Giessen: Töpelmann.

Kuhn, P. (1989) *Offenbarungsstimmen im Antiken Judentum: Untersuchungen zur Bat Qol und verwandten Phänomenen*, Texte und Studien zum Antiken Judentum 20, Tübingen: Mohr Siebeck.

Ladouceur, D.J. (1980) 'Masada: Consideration of the Literary Evidence', *GRBS* 21: 245–60.

—— (1987) 'Josephus and Masada', in L.H. Feldman and G. Hata (eds), *Josephus, Judaism and Christianity*, Detroit: Wayne State University Press, 95–113.

Lampe, G.W.H. (1961) *A Patristic Greek Lexicon*, Oxford: Clarendon Press.

Lampe, P. (1987) *Die stadtrömischen Christen in den ersten beiden Jahrhunderten: Untersuchungen zur Sozialgeschichte*, WUNT 2nd series 18, Tübingen: Mohr Siebeck.

Lanata, G. (1973) *Gli atti dei martiri come documenti processuali*, Studi e testi per un Corpus judiciorum 1, Milan: Giuffrè.

Levinger, J. (1977) 'Daniel in the Lions' Den: A Model of National Literature of Struggle', *Beth Mikra* 70: 329–33; 394–5 (in Hebrew).

Licht, J. (1961) 'Taxo, or the Apocalyptic Doctrine of Vengenace', *JJS* 12: 95–103.

Lichtheim, M. (1980) *Ancient Egyptian Literature: A Book of Readings*, Berkeley, CA: University of California Press.

Lieberman, S. (1939–44) 'The Martyrs of Caesarea', *Annuaire de l'Institut de Philologie et d'Histoire Orientales et Slaves* 7: 395–446.

—— (ed.) (1955–88) *The Tosefta According to Codex Vienna, with variants from Codex Erfurt, Genizah mss. and editio princeps*, 4 vols, New York: Jewish Theological Seminary.

Lieu, J. (1996) *Image and Reality: The Jews in the World of the Christians in the Second Century*, Edinburgh: T & T Clark.

Lindblom, J. (1961) 'Theophanies in Holy Places in Hebrew Religion', *HUCA* 32: 91–106.

Lindenberger, J.M. (1983) *The Aramaic Proverbs of Ahiqar*, Baltimore and London: The John Hopkins University Press.

—— (1985) 'Ahiqar', in J.H. Charlesworth (ed.), *The Old Testament Pseudepigrapha*, Garden City, NJ: Doubleday, vol. 2, 479–507.

Loewenclau, I. von (1961) *Der Platonische Menexenos*, Tübinger Beiträge zur Altertumswissenschaft 41, Stuttgart: Kohlhammer.

Löhr, W.A. (1989) 'Der Brief der Gemeinden von Lyon und Vienne (Eusebius, h.e. V1–2(4))' in D. Papandreou (ed.), *Oecumenica et Patristica: Festschrift W. Schneemelcher*, Chambéry–Genève: Kohlhammer, 135–49.

Long, H.S. (1964) *Diogenis Laertii Vitae Philosophorum*, vol. 2, Oxford: Clarendon Press.

Loraux, N. (1986) *The Invention of Athens: The Funeral Oration in the Classical City*, Cambridge, MA: Harvard University Press.

MacDonald, D.R. (1994) *Christianizing Homer, the Odyssey, Plato, and the Acts of Andrew*, New York: Oxford University Press.

Mach, M. (1996) 'Philo von Alexandrien', *TRE* 26: 523–31.

Margulies, M. (ed.) (1993) *Midrash Wayyikra Rabbah: A Critical Edition Based on Manuscripts and Genizah Fragments with Variants and Notes*, 3rd printing, New York and Jerusalem: Jewish Theological Seminary.

Marrou, H.I. (1951) *À Diognète: Introduction, Édition critique, traduction et commentaire*, Sources Chrétiennes 33, Paris: Éditions du Cerf.

Martola, N. (1984) *Capture and Liberation: A Study in the Composition of the First Book of Maccabees,* Acta Academiae Aboensis Ser. A 63:1, Åbo: Åbo Akademi.

Mason, S. (1991) *Flavius Josephus on the Pharisees: A Composition-Critical Study*, SPB 39, Leiden: Brill.

Mellink, A.O. (2000) *Death as Eschaton: A Study of Ignatius of Antioch's Desire for Death*, Diss. Amsterdam.

Merkelbach, R. (1975) 'Der griechische Wortschatz und die Christen', *Zeitschrift für Papyrologie und Epigraphik* 18: 101–48.

Michel, O. and Bauernfeind, O. (1959–69), *Flavius Josephus De Bello Judaico*.

Der jüdische Krieg: Griechisch und Deutsch, 3 vols, Munich and Darmstadt: Kösel-Wissenschaftliche Buchgesellschaft.

Midrash Bereshit Rabba (1972) *Codex Vatican 60 (ms. Vat. Ebr. 60): A Previously Unknown Manuscript Recently Established as the Earliest and Most Important Version of Bereshit Rabba*, a limited facsimile edition, Jerusalem: Makor.

Midrash Rabbah al Hamishah Humshe Torah we-Hamesh Megillot (1887), 2 vols, Vilna: Romm, reprinted Jerusalem.

Modrzejewski, J.M. (1997), *Les juifs d'Égypte de Ramses II à Hadrien*, 2nd edn, Paris: Quadrige–PUF.

Moore, C.A. (1977) *Daniel, Esther and Jeremiah: The Additions. A New Translation with Introduction and Commentary*, The Anchor Bible 44, Garden City, NJ: Doubleday.

Moore, S.D. and Anderson, J.C. (1998) 'Taking It Like a Man: Masculinity in 4 Maccabees', *JBL* 117: 249–73.

Morris, J. (1986) 'The Jewish Philosopher Philo', in E. Schürer, *The History of the Jewish People in the Age of Jesus Christ (175 B.C.–A.D. 135): A New English Version*, rev. and ed. by G. Vermes, F. Millar and M. Goodman; 3 vols, Edinburgh: T & T Clark, 1973–87, 3.2, 809–89.

Müller, H.-P. (1977) 'Die weisheitliche Lehrerzählung im Alten Testament und seiner Umwelt', *Welt des Orients* 9: 77–98

Musurillo, H.A. (1954) *The Acts of the Pagan Martyrs: Acta Alexandrinorum*, Oxford: Clarendon Press.

—— (1961) *Acta Alexandrinorum: De mortibus Alexandriae nobilium fragmenta papyracea graeca*, Leipzig: Teubner.

Nauck, W. (1955) 'Freude im Leiden. Zum Problem einer urchristlichen Verfolgungstradition', *ZNW* 46: 68–80.

Netzer, E. (1991) *Masada IV*, see Y. Yadin *et al.* (1989–99).

Nickelsburg, G.W.E. (1972) *Resurrection, Immortality, and Eternal Life in Intertestamental Judaism*, HTS 26, Cambridge, MA: Harvard University Press.

Nikiprowetzky, V. (1971) 'La mort d'Éléazar fils de Jaïre et les courants apologétiques dans le *De bello judaico* de Flavius Josèphe', in *Hommages à André Dupont-Sommer*, Paris: Librairie d'Amérique et d'Orient Adrien-Maisonneuve, 461–90.

Norelli, E. (1993) *Ascension du Prophète Isaïe*, Apocryphes, Turnhout: Brepols.

—— (1994) *L'Ascensione di Isaia: Studi su un apocrifo al crocevia dei cristeanisimi*, Origini, Nuove serie 1, Bologna: EDB.

—— (1995) *Ascensio Isaiae*, Corpus Christianorum Series Apocryphorum 7–8, 2 vols, Turnhout: Brepols.

Oakley, S.P. (1997–98) *A Commentary on Livy Books VI–X*, 2 vols, Oxford: Clarendon Press.

O'Connor-Visser, E.A.M.E (1987) *Aspects of Human Sacrifice in the Tragedies of Euripides*, Amsterdam: Gruener.

Oepke, A. (1950) *Das neue Gottesvolk*, Gütersloh: Bertelsmann Verlag.

Oltramare, A. (1926) *Les origines de la diatribe romaine*, Lausanne.

Pellegrino, M. (1955–56) 'Semen est sanguis christianorum, Tertulliano,

Apologeticum 50,13', *Atti della Academia delle Scienze di Torino* 90: 371–442.

Perkins, J. (1995) *The Suffering Self: Pain and Narrative Representation in the Early Christian Era*, London: Routledge.

Perler, O. (1949) 'Das vierte Makkabäerbuch, Ignatius von Antiochien und die ältesten Martyrerberichte', *Rivista di archeologia cristiana* 25: 47–72.

Pesce, M. (1983) 'Presupposti per l'utilizzazione storica dell' *Ascensio di Isaia*. Formazione e tradizione del testo, genere letterario, cosmologia angelica', in M. Pesce (ed.), *Isaia, il diletto e la Chiesa: Visione ed esegesi profetica cristiano-primitiva nell'Ascensione di Isaia*, Testi e ricerche di Scienze religiose 20, Brescia: Paideia Editrice.

——— (1984) *Il 'Martirio di Isaia' non esiste: L'Ascensione di Isaie e le tradizioni giudaiche sull' uccisione del profeta*, Bologna: Edizioni Dehoniane.

Petit, M. (1974) *Quod omnis probus liber sit. Introduction, texte, traduction et notes*, Les Oeuvres de Philon d'Alexandrie 28, Paris: Éditions du Cerf.

Pfister, F. (1927) 'Soteria (2)' *PW* 2nd series 3.1.1221–31.

Plumpe, J.C. (1943) *Mater ecclesia: An Inquiry into the Concept of the Church as Mother in Early Christianity*, Studies in Christian Antiquity 5, Washington, DC: The Catholic University of America Press.

Porten, B. and Yardeni, A. (1993) *Textbook of Aramaic Documents from Ancient Egypt: Newly Copied, Edited and Translated into Hebrew and English*, vol. 3, Jerusalem: The Hebrew University.

Rabbinovicz, R. (1959–60) *Variae lectiones in Mischnam et in Talmud Babylonicum quum ex aliis libris antiquissimis et scriptis et impressis tum e codice monacensi praestantissimo collectae*, 15 vols, Munich: Huber 1867–97, reprinted New York: Edison Lithographic Corp. (1959–60).

Rahlfs, A. (1935) *Septuaginta: Id est Vetus Testamentum graece iuxta* LXX *interpretes*, Stuttgart: Deutsche Bibelgesellschaft.

Rajak, T. (1983) *Josephus: The Historian and his Society*, London: Duckworth.

——— (1997) 'Dying for the Law: The Martyr's Portrait in Jewish-Greek Literature', in M.J. Edwards & S. Swain (eds), *Portraits: Biographical Representation in the Greek and Latin Literature of the Roman Empire*, Oxford: Clarendon Press.

Rebuffat, R. (1972) 'Le sacrifice du fils de Créon', *REA* 74: 14–31.

Reeg, G. (1985) *Die Geschichte von den zehn Märtyrern. Synoptische Edition mit Übersetzung und Einleitung*, Texte und Studien zum Antiken Judentum 10, Tübingen: Mohr Siebeck.

Renehan, R. (1972) 'The Greek Philosophic Background of Fourth Maccabees', *Rheinisches Museum für Philologie* 115: 223–38.

Risberg, B. (1918) 'Textkritische und exegetische Anmerkungen zu den Makkabäerbüchern', *Beiträge zur Religionswissenschaft* 2: 6–31.

Romilly, J. de (1965) 'Les *Phéniciennes* d'Euripide ou l'actualité dans la tragédie grecque', *Revue Philologique* 39: 28–47.

Rose, M. (1993) *Die Wolke der Zeugen: Eine exegetisch-traditionsgeschichtliche Untersuchung zu Hebräer 10,32–12,3*, Wissenschaftliche Untersuchungen zum Neuen Testament, 2nd series, 60, Tübingen: Mohr Siebeck, 239–43.

Roth, J. (1995) 'The Length of the Siege of Masada', *Scripta Classica Israelica* 14: 87–110.

Rougé, J. and Turcan, R. (1978), *Les Martyrs de Lyon (177)*, Colloques Internationaux du Centre National de la Recherche Scientifique 575, Paris: Éditions CNRS.

Safrai, S. (1983) 'Martyrdom in the Teachings of the Tannaim', in T.C. de Kruijff and H. van der Sandt (eds), *Sjaloom: Ter nagedachtenis van Mgr. Dr. A.C. Ramselaar*, Arnhem, 145–64.

Salisbury, E. (1997) *Perpetua's Passion: The Death and Memory of a Young Roman Woman*, New York and London: Routledge.

Satran, D. (1995) *Biblical Prophets in Byzantine Palestine: Reassessing the Lives of the Prophets*, SVTP 11, Leiden: Brill.

Schäfer, P. (1978) 'R. Aqiva und Bar Kokhba', in P. Schäfer, *Studien zur Geschichte und Theologie des rabbinischen Judentums*, Arbeiten zur Geschichte des antiken Judentums und des Urchristentums 15, Leiden: Brill, 65–121.

Schäfer, P. and Becker, H.-J. (1991–2001) *Synopse zum Talmud Yerushalmi*, 4 vols, Tübingen: Mohr Siebeck.

Schechter, S. (ed.) (1887) *Aboth deRabbi Nathan: Hujus libri recensiones duas . . .*, Vienna: Lippe, London: Nutt, Franfurt: Kauffmann.

Schneider, C. (1954) *Geistesgeschichte des Antiken Christentums*, 2 vols, Munich: Beck.

Schoedel, W.R. (1985) *Ignatius of Antioch: A Commentary on the Letters of Ignatius of Antioch*, Philadelphia: Fortress Press.

Schoeps, H.-J. (1943) 'Die jüdischen Prophetenmorde', *Symbolae Biblicae Upsalienses* 2: 3–22; reprinted in *Aus frühchristlicher Zeit*, Tübingen: Mohr, 1950, 26–143.

Schüpphaus, J. (1971) 'Das Verhältnis von LXX- und Theodotion-Text in den apokryphen Zusätzen zum Danielbuch', *ZAW* 83: 49–72.

Schürer, E. (1973–87) *The History of the Jewish People in the Age of Jesus Christ (175 B.C.–A.D. 135): A New English Version*, rev. and ed. by G. Vermes, F. Millar and M. Goodman; 3 vols, Edinburgh: T & T Clark.

Schwartz, D.R (1990) *Agrippa I: The Last King of Judea*, TSAJ 23, Tübingen: Mohr Siebeck.

—— (1993) *Leben durch Jesus versus Leben durch die Torah: Zur Religionspolemik der ersten Jahrhunderte*, Franz-Delitzsch-Vorlesung 1991, Münster: Institutum Judaicum Delitzschianum.

Schwartz, E. and Mommsen, T. (1903) *Eusebius Kirchengeschichte*, GCS 9.1, Leipzig: J.C. Hinrich.

Schwartz, S. (1986) 'The Composition and Publication of Josephus' Bellum Judaicum Book 7', *HTR* 79: 373–86.

Schwemer, A.M. (1995–96) *Studien zu den frühjüdischen Prophetenlegenden Vitae Prophetarum*, 2 vols, Texte und Studien zum Antiken Judentum 49–50,

Tübingen: Mohr Siebeck.

—— (1999) 'Prophet, Zeuge und Märtyrer: Zur Entstehung des Märtyrerbegriffs im frühesten Christentum', *Zeitschrift für Theologie und Kirche* 96: 320–50.

Selwyn, E.G. (1947) *The First Letter of St. Peter: The Greek Text with Introduction, Notes and Essays*, London, 2nd edn.

Shaw, B. (1993) 'The Passion of Perpetua', *Past and Present* 139: 3–45.

Simon, M. (1955) *Hercule et le christianisme*, Paris: Les Belles Lettres.

Skarsaune, O. (1987) *The Proof from Prophecy: A Study in Justin Martyr's Proof-text Tradition: Text-type, Provenance, Theological Profile*, NT Supplements 56, Leiden: Brill.

Skutsch, O. (1985) *The Annals of Q. Ennius*. Oxford: Clarendon Press.

Smallwood, E.M. (1981) *The Jews under Roman Rule. From Pompey to Diocletian: A Study in Political Relations*, revised edition, Studies in Judaism in Late Antiquity 20, Leiden: Brill.

Soffel, J. (1974) *Die Regeln Menanders für die Leichenrede in ihrer Tradition dargestellt, herausgegeben, übersetzt und kommentiert*, Beiträge zur klassischen Philologie 57, Meisenheim am Glan: Hain.

Solin, H. (1982) *Die griechischen Personennamen in Rom*, 3 vols, Berlin: De Gruyter.

Sperling, S.D. (1995) 'Belial', in B. Becking, P.W. van der Horst and K. van der Toorn (eds), *Dictionary of Deities and Demons*, Leiden: Brill, 322–7.

Steck, O.H. (1967) *Israel und das gewaltsame Geschick der Propheten: Untersuchungen zur Überlieferung des deuteronomistischen Geschichtsbildes im Alten Testament, Spätjudentum und Urchristentum*, WMANT 23, Neukirchen and Vluyn: Neukirchener Verlag.

Stemberger, G. (1992) *Einleitung in Talmud und Midrasch*, 8th edn, Munich: Beck.

Stern, M. (1974–84) *Greek and Latin Authors on Jews and Judaism*, 3 vols, Jerusalem: The Israel Academy of Sciences and Humanities.

—— (1982–83) 'The Suicide of Eleazar Ben Jair and his Men at Masada and the "Fourth Philosophy"', *Zion* 47: 367–98 (in Hebrew).

Stewart, Z. (1984) 'Greek Crowns and Christian Martyrs', in E. Lucchesi and H.D. Saffrey (eds), *Antiquité païenne et chrétienne: Mémorial André-Jean Festugière*, Geneva: Cramer, 119–24.

Stoneman, R. (1995) 'Naked Philosophers', *JHS* 115: 99–114.

Strack, H.L. (1912) *Der Babylonische Talmud nach der einzigen vollständigen Handschrift München Codex Hebraicus 95, mittelst Facsimile-Lichtdruck vervielfältigt*, 2 vols, Leiden: A.W. Sijthoff's Uitgevers Maatschappij.

Strathmann, H. (1942) 'martys etc.', *TWNT* 4: 477–520.

Tajra, H.W. (1994) *The Martyrdom of St. Paul: Historical and Judicial Context, Tradition and Legends*, WUNT 2nd series 67, Tübingen: Mohr Siebeck.

Talmud Bavli (1880–86), *im kol ha-mefareshim ka-asher nidpas mi-qedem, we-im hosafot hadashot ki-mevo'ar ba-sha'ar ha-sheni*, Vilna: Romm, reprinted Jerusalem

Theodor, J., Albeck, C. (1996) *Bereschit Rabba: mit kritischem Apparat und*

Kommentar, 5 vols, Berlin: Itzkowski, 1912–36, 2nd edition (3 vols), Jerusalem: Shalem.

Toki, K. (1981) 'Der literarische Charakter des Bell. Jud. II 151b–153', *Annual of the Japanese Biblical Institute* 7: 53–69.

Thompson, L.L. (1990) *The Book of Revelation: Apocalypse and Empire*, Oxford and New York: Oxford University Press.

Tromp, J. (1990) 'Taxo, the Messenger of the Lord', *JSJ* 21: 200–9.

—— (1993) *The Assumption of Moses: A Critical Edition with Commentary*, Studia Veteris Testamenti Pseudepigrapha 10, Leiden: Brill.

Vellacott, P. (1975) *Ironic Drama: A Study of Euripides' Method and Meaning*, Cambridge: Cambridge University Press.

Vergote, J. (1972) 'Folterwerkzeuge' *RAC* 8: 112–41.

Vermes, G. and Goodman, M. (1989) *The Essenes According to Classical Sources*, Sheffield: JSOT Press.

Versnel, H.S. (1976) 'Two Types of Roman Devotio', *Mnemosyne* 29: 365–410.

—— (1977) 'Polycrates and his Ring: Two Neglected Aspects', *Studi Storico-Religiosi* 1: 17–46.

—— (1980) 'Destruction, *Devotio* and Despair in a Situation of Anomy: The Mourning for Germanicus in Triple Perspective', *Perennitas: Studi in onore di A. Brelich*, Rome, 541–618.

—— (1981) 'Self-Sacrifice, Compensation and the Anonymous Gods', in O. Reverdin and B. Grange (eds), *Le sacrifice dans l'antiquité*, Entretiens sur l'Antiquité classique 27, Vandoeuvres and Geneva: Fondation Hardt.

Vessey, D. (1971) 'Menoeceus in the *Thebaid* of Statius', *CP* 66: 236–43.

Vilna, see *Midrash Rabbah* and *Talmud Bavli*.

Walters, C.F. and Conway, R.S. (1969) *Titi Livi Ab urbe condita*, vol. 2, Oxford: Clarendon Press.

Wanke, G. and Balz, H. (1973) 'phobeō etc.', *TWNT* 9: 186–216.

Weber, R. (1991) 'Eusebeia und Logismos. Zum philosophischen Hintergrund von 4 Makkabäer', *JSJ* 22: 212–34.

Weinreich, W.C. (1981) *Spirit and Martyrdom: A Study of the Work of the Holy Spirit in the Context of Persecution and Martyrdom in the New Testament and Early Christian Literature*, Washington, DC.

Weiss, I.H. (1862) *Sifra de-Be Rav: Hu Sefer Torat Kohanim*, Vienna: Schlossberg.

Wengst, K. (1984) *Didache (Apostellehre), Barnabasbrief, Zweiter Klemensbrief, Schrift an Diognet*, Schriften des Urchristentums II, Darmstadt: Wissenschaftliche Buchgesellschaft.

White, J.L. (1972) *The Form and Function of the Body of the Greek Letter: A Study of the Letter-Body in the Non-Literary Papyri and in Paul the Apostle*, SBLDS 2, Missoula MT: Society of Biblical Literature.

Williams, D.S. (1999) *The Structure of 1 Maccabees*, CBQMS 31, Washington, DC: The Catholic Biblical Association of America.

Wills, L.M. (1990) *The Jew in the Court of the Foreign King: Ancient Jewish Court Legends*, HDR 26; Minneapolis: Fortress Press.

Winkler, K. and Stuiber, A. (1957) 'Devotio', *RAC* 3: 849–62.

Woodward, K.L. (1997) *Making Saints*, New York: Simon & Schuster.

Yadin, Y. (1966) *Masada: Herod's Fortress and the Zealots' Last Stand*, London: Weidenfeld and Nicolson.

Yadin, Y. and Naveh, J. (1989) *Masada I*, see Y. Yadin *et al.* (1989–99).

Yadin, Y., Naveh, J., Cotton, H.M. *et al.* (1989–99) *Masada I–VI: The Yigael Yadin Excavations 1963–1965: Final Reports,* The Israel Exploration Society, Jerusalem: The Hebrew University of Jerusalem.

Zerubavel, Y. (1995) *Recovered Roots: Collective Memory and the Making of Israeli National Tradition*, Chicago and London: The University of Chicago Press.

Zias, J., Segal, D., Carmi, I. (1994) 'Addendum: The Human Skeletal Remains from the Northern Cave at Masada – A Second Look', in D. Barag, A. Sheffer *et al.*, *Masada IV*, see Y. Yadin *et al.* (1989–99): 366–7.

INDEX

DATE DUE

	MAR 0 8 2010	
GAYLORD		PRINTED IN U.S.A.